HOW TO BUILD A
BILLION DOLLAR BUSINESS

HOW TO BUILD A
BILLION DOLLAR BUSINESS

ON PURPOSE FOR PROFIT WITH PASSION

RADEK SALI

ENTREPRENEUR AND FORMER CEO OF SWISSE
WITH BERNADETTE SCHWERDT

WILEY

First published in 2024 by John Wiley & Sons Australia, Ltd
Level 4, 600 Bourke St, Melbourne, Victoria 3000, Australia

Typeset in Kazimir Text 10 pt/14 pt

© John Wiley & Sons Australia, Ltd 2024

The moral rights of the authors have been asserted

ISBN: 978-1-394-21604-8

A catalogue record for this book is available from the National Library of Australia

Cover design by Wiley

Disclaimer

CONTENTS

ABOUT THE AUTHORS

ABOUT RADEK SALI

Radek Sali is the former CEO of Swisse and a brand visionary who revolutionised the vitamin and supplements industry. Under his leadership, Swisse surged from a company worth $15 million with 30 employees to an astounding $2.1 billion enterprise with over 1000 employees in less than a decade. Swisse became Australia's largest global wellness company and the number 1 natural health brand in Australia and China. Swisse was awarded Australia's *Best Private Business* 2012 and *The Best Place to Work in Australia* for 2015 and 2016 and in 2012 Radek won *GQ Australia*'s Entrepreneur of the Year award. Radek is the Founder and Executive Chairman of Light Warrior, the Reinventor and Executive chair of Wanderlust, and a Founder and Director of Conscious Investment Management, Stratosphere and Anthem. He has successfully started/reinvented 8 organisations and returned over 1000x the initial investment with 3 exits. In the not-for-profit space he is chairman of Igniting Change, the founder of Lightfolk foundation, a founding member of the Climate Leaders Coalition, LaTrobe Campaign Cabinet and BTeam Australasia, and serves as a director at the National Institute of Integrative Medicine.

Find Radek on LinkedIn at: linkedin.com/in/radeksali/

ABOUT BERNADETTE SCHWERDT

Bernadette Schwerdt is an award-winning Australian entrepreneur, author, TEDx speaker and copywriter. She was a senior account director at a global advertising agency Wunderman Cato Johnson and in 2004 founded the Australian School of Copywriting. She is the author of two bestselling books *How to Build an Online Business* and *Secrets of Online Entrepreneurs*; the ghost-writer of *Catch of the Decade* and *How to Build a Business Others Want to Buy*, a book coach for *Find Build Sell* and *The Very Good Marketing Guide* and is the host of the popular podcast, *So you want to be a copywriter*. She has worked as a professional actor on popular shows including *Jack Irish, Neighbours, Winners and Losers* and *Round the Twist*, is a qualified yoga teacher and was the inaugural in-house mindfulness coach for the Carlton Football Club. You could say she's had a 'portfolio' career.

Find Bernadette at:

linkedin.com/in/bernadetteschwerdt

www.bernadetteschwerdt.com.au

INTRODUCTION

Not everyone is cut out to build a billion-dollar business. It takes an enormous amount of self-belief, internal drive and ambition. (A bit of madness, too.) I am wired differently to many people. I acknowledge that. I don't say that to be boastful; I say it because this level of unwavering determination, commitment to purpose and relentless passion does not come naturally to most people.

The hard truth is that serious entrepreneurship — the kind that I will detail throughout this book, the kind that creates vast and life-changing wealth for all involved — is not for everyone. Looking back, after everything that happened, I feel lucky to still be standing in one piece. We are told 'everything is possible' — think, dream, believe and all that — but it must be backed up with years of effort, energy and application. There are few, if any, formulas for making fast money. (For the record, it will most likely take a minimum of a decade to turn a fledgling concept into a multimillion-dollar proposition.) It starts with making an extraordinary product, selling it for a profit, and then doing it again, again and again.

Whether you want to build a billion-dollar business, a ten-million-dollar business, or a million-dollar business, this book will be of value. You can apply the lessons to any business, at any level, in any sector. In the case of Swisse, with the help of many extraordinary individuals, we took a $15 million business that employed 30 people and turned it into a $2.1 billion enterprise that resulted in one of biggest private company transactions in Australian history, and we did it all in under ten years.

It has been a roller-coaster journey, and it's now my privilege to share both the highs and lows of this exhilarating time with you so that you can benefit from my experiences and use those lessons to build your own purpose-led, multimillion-dollar business.

Success was never assured

When I joined Swisse, I didn't set out to build a billion-dollar business. I joined it to build a business that I truly believed could be a positive force. I joined it because I believed that our product had the potential to make people healthier and happier. I found a product I loved and an industry I cared about, and I wanted to share them both with the world. Yes, I was ambitious for it to be a global operation, but it was never about making money for the sake of making money. My goal was to make something big, create a lasting legacy and have fun.

I bought into the Swisse business a year after joining, but I was an employee for the entire duration of my time there. I turned up to work, did my job, went home, got paid and did it all again the following week. Yet I always treated the business as if it was my own. I had a home loan, a car loan and $30 000 in credit card debt. I had to budget and balance my finances like everyone else. When I was offered a stake in the Swisse business, I took out loans worth millions of dollars to pay for those shares. If the business didn't do well, neither did I. If it failed, I would have gone bankrupt. You could say I was invested.

I say this because I want you to know that, like many of you reading this book, I started out as an ordinary employee working for a small business. I did not come from a family where wealth was talked about at the dinner table every night. My mum and dad were medical professionals so we mostly talked about health. I won't be disingenuous and pretend I had a 'log cabin' origin story. Yes, both my parents came from refugee families, landed in Australia with nothing, and worked hard to create financially rewarding lives, but as a result of that hard work, they were able to offer me and my younger sister and brother a world of opportunities. I took what they offered (not always gratefully) with both hands, and ran with it. I am deeply indebted to them for the opportunities they provided. They made me who I am.

I have been on both sides of the financial spectrum. I started with very little, and now, having built a business that has rewarded me with an incredible amount of wealth, I can say with some authority that *money will not solve all your problems.* If you think it will, I can assure you that you will be bitterly disappointed. I know many may scoff at this and think, with some justification, 'Well, that's easy for him to say,' but I'm happy to incur that wrath because I can only tell you what I know to be true for me (and for many I know who have generated a similar amount of life-changing wealth.)

While money is of course important, the pursuit of it at the expense of everything you love, and are passionate about, is folly. It will remove a range of problems but it will create a raft of others too. Problems, or challenges as I like to call them, are like aeroplanes on the runway. As soon as one takes off, another arrives to take its place. Yes, it will enable you to live a life *upgraded,* but you will still be the same person you are now. So, choose your business endeavour with care; choose something that you can fully devote yourself to, that doesn't feel like work, that comes easily to you. Choose something that makes a difference in people's lives and has the potential to make a positive impact. Don't sacrifice what you know to be important and valuable in your life for the pursuit of profit.

This doesn't mean you have to choose a wellness business like I did, or a business even remotely connected to health or wellbeing. Whatever business you choose, find the *higher purpose* beyond it, the reason 'why' it will help others be happier, healthier, in whatever context that may be — financial, artistic, cultural, emotional, spiritual — and focus on that. If you follow your principles, maintain the passion and put people first, the profit will follow.

By the way, pursuing purpose-led entrepreneurship won't guarantee you an easy or simple life. If you want that, stay where you are as a valued employee or public servant. But if you want a life filled with challenges, risks, thrills and spills — a life that will ask more of you than you ever thought possible, and maybe deliver you a more satisfying, gratifying and life-affirming adventure than you ever thought imaginable — then you are in the right place. Your journey to building a purpose-led, profitable business begins here.

What you'll learn

Delve into this book to learn how to:

- turn your passion into profit:
  - ☐ align your passion with a purpose-driven, profitable venture
  - ☐ contribute positively to society through your business
  - ☐ infuse your core values into every business decision
- select the ideal business idea:
  - ☐ identify business concepts that match your unique talents
  - ☐ assess market feasibility and demand
  - ☐ uncover a niche trend undetected by others
- diversify and manage risk:
  - ☐ hedge your business bets and mitigate potential risks
  - ☐ discover your distinctive 'flywheel' and challenge industry norms
  - ☐ leverage design thinking principles to identify untapped market opportunities
- systematise creativity:
  - ☐ codify the creative process for consistent innovation
  - ☐ create a repeatable and scalable approach for sales growth
  - ☐ leverage your passion to sell without effort
- craft effective marketing:
  - ☐ devise marketing campaigns and promotions that retailers love
  - ☐ differentiate yourself in the market without relying on price competition

- select the right celebrity ambassadors to authentically represent your brand

■ strategically expand your category:

- grow your product offerings without cannibalising your existing range

- manage competing sales channels effectively

- navigate meetings, negotiations, and secure distribution with major retailers

■ foster a high-performance workplace:

- create a workplace that values honesty and encourages 360-degree feedback

- attract and retain top-tier talent

- become an employer-of-choice

- hire family, friends, and friends of friends, work harmoniously and save on recruitment expenses

■ execute a turnaround:

- conduct a comprehensive company-wide turnaround to cut costs and boost profitability

- skilfully manage an executive team and board of directors

- craft comprehensive business, culture and communications plans

■ expand internationally:

- use your core business to fund international expansion

- leverage data to identify international growth opportunities

- tap into third-party sales channels to optimise global reach

- prepare the business for sale:
  - ☐ attract the right investors and leverage 'smart money'
  - ☐ strategically prepare your business for sale and gauge market value
  - ☐ engage the right investment bank for a successful business sale.

The critical question

The question that kept me up at night throughout my entire career was this: do people enjoy coming to work? As such, I made it my mission to create a workplace that ensured people did. I believe business leaders have a responsibility to give back to their community, and cultivating a positive workplace culture is one way of achieving that. Can you imagine how much happier society would be if everyone enjoyed going to work? If this book can go some way towards helping you create a happy, high-performing and profitable workplace, my purpose will be fulfilled.

Best,

Radek Sali

PART I

CHAPTER 1

BORN THIS WAY

I was an unusual child from an eclectic family. Born in Scotland and raised in Australia, my father was of Albanian extraction while my mother hailed from the Czech Republic. I am a product of them in so many ways. I'm warm, loyal and hard-working like my father, and direct, creative and disciplined like my mother. This confluence of traits paved the way for my journey into entrepreneurship.

I grew up in leafy Hawthorn, a well-heeled, genteel suburb 9 kilometres east of Melbourne. It was a far cry from the farmland of Shepparton, where Dad was raised, and a long way from the soviet-ruled Czech Republic where Mum was born. As one of the only European families in this quintessentially Australian neighbourhood, our distinctive identity set us apart. I felt different. Actually, it wasn't a feeling; it was a fundamental truth. I *was* different.

For a start, there was my name. In a classroom of Craigs and Steves, I was Radek. Once the teachers stumbled their way through my first name, they'd encounter my middle name, Rudolf, the namesake of my beloved grandfather. Well, you can just imagine the reaction that got from my classmates.

My food was different. Most kids had a vegemite sandwich, a coconut doughnut and an apple for lunch; I had frankfurts, a boiled egg and green bananas.

I looked different. I was inordinately tall for my age, lanky and wide jawed in that classic Slavic way. I towered over everybody and compensated by stooping so I could blend in. My hair was different too. I had a flat-top haircut, quite a contrast to the bowl-cut style the other kids had.

Even my shoes were different. Mum, being European, thought that the standard-issue Clark's were orthopaedically inappropriate for growing feet so she made me wear a pair of T-bar girl's sandals that were cartoonishly two sizes too big for me. I can still hear their thwap-thwap-thwap on the hard tiled floor as I made my way down the corridor into class.

We did different activities on the weekend too. Most seven-year-old boys spent their Saturday mornings playing footy or soccer. I spent mine at Mangala Studios, a hippie-inspired sanctuary for free spirits and unconventional thinkers nestled within what was then the vibrant counter-cultural landscape of Carlton in Melbourne's inner north. I spent the day learning the esoteric arts of yoga, Japanese ink brush painting, creative dance and meditation. When we weren't at Mangala, we spent the weekends at our Uncle Bill and Aunty Bev's farm in Shepparton, picking fruit, hoeing the veggie patch and playing with my cousins amongst the land, trees and dams that surrounded the farm.

This early exposure to creativity fundamentally altered my perspective, and enabled me to perceive intricate links between ideas, individuals and procedures that might elude others. Above all, it ingrained in me the profound influence of the mind. My interest in all things esoteric began at this time and moulded me into a young thinker who saw the world not as it was, but as it could be.

Family is everything

Spending time with my large, extended Albanian family in Shepparton shaped me as a person. I didn't realise it was unusual to sit down to a lunch with up to forty of my closest relatives on a weekly basis; to be greeted with a hug and a kiss on both cheeks every time I arrived at every family occasion; to feel unconditionally loved and supported by a huge array of uncles and aunties and cousins and other family members from the wider Albanian community who accepted me for who I was and provided me with the love and mentoring I needed to achieve any goal I set my mind too. I was blessed to grow up in this Mediterranean culture that valued family so dearly and it gave me the inspiration to re-create that same sense of family in the workplaces of my future.

I brought down the Iron Curtain

Both my parents were refugees from Communist-ruled countries. My mother, in particular, talked openly and often about the repressive politics in their respective countries, and what life was like under Communist rule — how restrictive and oppressive it was; how a progressive thought or transgressive action could land you in jail; how trust was elusive; and how even your closest neighbour could betray you. As a soulful child, I grew up with a strong desire for both my parents' countries of origin to be free. It wasn't just a passing wish; it was an obsession. The Iron Curtain symbolised this repression and over time, it became the focal point of my seven-year-old mind. I knew more than most about the history of the Iron Curtain: what it was, and what it represented. To my parents, and me, it represented 'the system'.

As such, my single-minded goal was to 'bring down' the Iron Curtain, and, in doing so, release my parents from their persecution and free the people of the world from Communist subjugation! I wished for it so hard — every time I blew out candles on my birthday cake or tossed a coin in a fountain, it was to bring down the Iron Curtain. I honestly believed that if I thought about it long enough, and hard enough, I could bring an end to this oppression. And then, six years later, something incredible happened — the Iron Curtain fell! I wished for it to fall, and it did! It was a miracle! And it was all because of me! It got me thinking. If my thoughts could bring down the Iron Curtain, what else was I capable of? I could change the world! From that moment on, I was convinced that my thoughts had the power to manifest change, and this belief has stayed with me throughout my life.

Looking back, I can see this was an unusual way for a young boy to think. I knew I was different and the kids at school never let me forget it. After a while, I just embraced being different, and went deeper into *being* different. I accepted it, welcomed it and stopped fighting it. Eventually being different just became who I was, and the more secure I became around that, the more confident I became in myself. My parents encouraged me to be different too. They had always sat outside the system of what a typical Australian citizen looked like back then. They had gone against the grain and they fully encouraged me and my two younger siblings, Lenka and Filip, to do the same. Dad's favourite saying was 'Think different to make a difference'.

Ultimately, being different became an asset. It made me impervious to insult, teasing and offense, and steeled me from a very young age to not take things personally. My mother had a strong personality and insisted I take advantage of all the opportunities she and Dad had worked so hard to provide. This resulted in lots of arguments, berating and yelling, so I was already inured to verbal abuse. I endured it, and accepted it, because at the core of it, I knew her anger was born from love; that her heart was in the right place and that she wanted the best for me. This ability to endure criticism set me up well for a lifetime in business.

Mum the maverick

Mum did not have an easy life. When she was 12, her mother went in for a routine medical procedure and died on the operating table. Seven years later, when the Prague Spring erupted and violence broke out, Mum fled for London with nothing but a suitcase, two pounds in her pocket and a smattering of English. She found accommodation in a tiny bedsit on the outskirts of London, a low-paying job, and tried to make a new life for herself.

When the uprising ended, it was too dangerous for her to go home as the regime was punishing anyone who dared to return. She had the choice of going to Canada or Australia, chose Australia, boarded the ship with her husband, and landed in Melbourne four weeks later. (Yes, husband. While in London, the only way she could stay in her rental bedsit was if she had a marriage certificate. Ever the pragmatist, she married a Czech man staying in the room next door so they could both have a roof over their heads. When they stepped off the boat, they went their separate ways, without antagonism or enmity. It was a true marriage of convenience.)

By day she studied medical science at the Royal Melbourne Institute of Technology (RMIT) and by night, she studied English at TAFE. She chose science as it focused more on the numbers and less on the words. She befriended a fellow Czech student in the medical course who had better English than her. This lady became the human equivalent of Google Translate and every night my mother would take the translated notes home and study them in her own language. She graduated four years later with a degree in Biomedical Science and many years later would go on to set up her own laboratory business.

Dad the disruptor

Dad grew up in Shepparton on a fruit farm with his five brothers. Money was tight for them too. There was no electricity, running water or refrigeration and, while the Shepparton community was mostly welcoming, Dad and his family were more than aware that they were foreigners in a strange land. The boys tilled the soil, planted the seeds, picked the fruit and packed it up for shipment to the Melbourne markets. It was hard, back-breaking work but it was all hands on deck to make ends meet.

When Dad was eight, he contracted rheumatoid fever and spent a month in hospital. He went in with a fever and came out with a vision: he would become a doctor. The teachers at Shepparton High laughed at him. A doctor? Good luck with that. He was dux of the school but it wasn't a sandstone institution, so he didn't get accepted into medical school. He studied agricultural science for two years, and with the backing of one supportive teacher from his primary school days who believed in him from the beginning, he kept on trying. When Monash University opened their campus in Clayton, he won a place in their first medical school intake and became the first Albanian in Australia to enter university.

Mum met my dad in the corridors of the Alfred Hospital when she was working in a blood laboratory and he was working as a registrar. He offered her a job in his laboratory, and then asked her to marry him a few months later. In 1976, they travelled to Scotland so Dad could finish his surgical training under Dr Andrew Kay, the Surgeon General to the royal family. The hospital found accommodation for them in a freezing, cockroach-infested flat in the worst part of Glasgow. Mum was pregnant with me at the time and after she gave birth, tried as best she could to tend to this newborn on her own while Dad worked around the clock to complete his tuition. Mum always complained that I was a fractious, unsettled child, which doesn't seem surprising, given the circumstances.

When we returned to Australia in 1977, we settled in Hawthorn and Dad became an associate professor at the University of Melbourne, later Deputy Chairman and Acting Head of the Surgery Department there. He was a specialist surgeon at the Heidelberg Repatriation Hospital, and then became the director of the Victorian Public Health Research and Education Council.

Father of integrative medicine

Dad saw the power of integrative medicine long before most medical professionals. He understood the impact of nutrition, exercise and mindset on health and wellbeing. He was mystified that doctors received seven years of in-depth education about how to cure a disease, and one week's education on how to prevent it. He wanted to reverse that ratio. He was into prevention, not intervention. He couldn't understand why others in his profession didn't see that.

He told me of a time when he was doing his medical rounds with his colleagues and a supervisor. They assessed a Polish patient who'd just had a heart attack. Dad knew the Polish diet was heavy on processed foods and lots of red meat and yet the other doctors disputed that the diet had any role to play in the disease. They would poke fun at Dad and say, 'If he'd eaten a bit of brown bread this could have all been avoided.' It seems insane to think that was how doctors thought, but that's how it was.

Dad felt so frustrated at his inability to break through the system and was disappointed at how this hampered his progress in academia. He spoke often about how hard it was to beat their 'fix-it' medical ideology and wished they could blend the best of that world with the world of preventative medicine. This interest in integrative medicine put him on a collision course with the pharmaceutical industry in a battle that would last a lifetime.

The medical profession laughed at my dad, and it took 20 years for his work to be published. He subsequently went on to author over 300 peer-reviewed papers on integrative medicine, became the founding Dean and Professor of the Graduate School of Integrative Medicine at Swinburne University in 1996 and in 2009 established the National Institute of Integrative Medicine (NIIM). He is now widely considered to be the 'father' of Integrative Medicine in Australia. To me, he is my mentor, my inspiration and the ultimate disruptor.

Working hard

I have a prodigious work ethic, fuelled no doubt by my mother's formidable resilience and my father's relentless drive to educate the world on the powers of natural medicine. My working life started early. My first 'job' was babysitting my two siblings. I took this on when I was eight. Mum's instructions were as strict as they were brief: 'Don't answer the door.'

When I was nine, I delivered 40 newspapers a day and made seven dollars a week. When I was 11, I washed dishes at La Pizza Quadratta in exchange for five dollars a shift and a pizza of my choice. (Pizza was and still is my favourite food, so I was rapt.) The queue for their 'square' pizzas snaked out the door: an early lesson in how to create a point of difference in a commodified industry.

At the age of 12, I worked in the warehouse of Dynamo House, picking and packing bottles of essential oils to send out to customers. Stefan Manger was the enigmatic owner of this unique Australiana homewares business. He was a friend of my father's, and our family spent many weekends at his mansion in Eltham. This artistic outpost was a melting pot where artists, writers and activists would gather to eat, drink and create wonderful works of art. I was in awe of these exotic individuals and distinctly recall the wild hair and cherubic cheekiness of a young Michael Leunig drawing his caricatures and cartoons.

When I was 13, I worked for my Uncle Hismet's country fashion shops, a super successful business that attained legendary status in Shepparton. (It's still there, 50 years later.) I also worked for my Uncle Haset, a lawyer (and former chairman of SPC, Shepparton's largest company), filing documents for his legal firm. (The Sali family was industrious. My Uncle Sam ran a hugely successful trucking company and Uncle Alan was an early mentor and always had time to guide me and provide advice.)

When I was 15 I worked at a deli after school, cleaning out the fridges and closing up the shop. The highlight? Snaffling a couple of unsold sandwiches at the end of the shift. Like most teenage boys, I was always hungry. My dream job was to flip hamburgers at McDonald's. It was the coolest place to work, but the manager revealed to one of my mates that as he couldn't pronounce my name, he wouldn't take me on. I remember the searing burn of being discriminated against for something beyond my control and vowed I would never do that to another.

These jobs didn't pay much but I didn't mind. I derived great joy from working and valued the experience. I also received an early lesson in noticing how some employers valued me and how some didn't.

Mum and Dad frequently reminded us that they had worked their hearts out to ensure we had access to every conceivable opportunity. Their ethos was clear: work should be something you enjoy. Don't worry about the money — it will come. To them, money was the by-product of a job well done and the intrinsic satisfaction of doing the job well brought about happiness. Dad always said, 'It's not what you do, it's how you do it.' The purpose in doing something was everything. I inherited these principles and it taught me to focus on my actions rather than on the financial result.

A practical joker

Things changed when I turned 15. I still had the work ethic; I just chose not to apply it to school. Like many teenage boys, I was more interested in footy, fun and flirting. I was academically strong but behaviourally challenged. School bored me and getting bad marks didn't bother me. I just didn't see the point of school. I couldn't understand why or how algebra or *Othello* was going to affect my life and I couldn't get motivated enough to care.

I wasn't altogether lazy. I played a lot of sport: Football. Basketball. Cricket. Tennis. Skiing. Athletics. You name it, I was into it. I was a handy 190 cm, and fast as a whippet, so I was a valuable member of any team. (I could run 100 metres in just over 11 seconds.) I ran the first leg of the 100-metre relay in the state championships but jumped the gun three times at the finals and was disqualified. (Our previous times guaranteed us we'd lose anyway, so I figured we might as well get a running start.)

I squeezed as much as I could into my last year at school. I did six subjects instead of five and was equally uncommitted to all of them; I learned to drive; I had a girlfriend, and played endless rounds of street basketball with my mates at the local courts. I liked to party (a lot), and have a laugh. I wasn't a bad kid but I was cheeky and would play practical jokes. During the school church service, I'd bounce a tennis ball up against the wall, and catch it on the rebound. We'd snort and snicker behind our hands, the laughter all the more illicit for the fact we were in church. I'd push my mate into the procession of teachers as they made their way up the aisle: cue more uproarious snickers. When I was called on to read the psalm to the congregation, I'd read it with a particularly loud voice, seeing how far I could take it before being called out. It was hilarious watching my mates try to contain their laughter during the sombre silence of a church service. If there was mischief to be made, I was there.

My bad behaviour drove my parents to distraction. They had scrimped and saved to send my siblings and I to Carey Grammar, one of the most expensive high schools in Melbourne, and here I was, frittering the experience away. Mum nagged me relentlessly. *Do your homework. Stand up straight. Take out the rubbish. Do the lawns. Clean your room.* (She was so incensed with my messy room she once dumped all my stuff onto the front lawn and threatened to throw it out if I didn't sort it out.)

One day a bottle of tablets turned up in my bedroom. My first thought was 'Why are you putting me on drugs? I am not out of control.' 'No,' said Mum, 'But your hormones are. Take one of these each day and you'll feel a lot better.' I took the tablets (they were Swisse Ultivite) and, sure enough, I felt more energetic, less irritable and better able to manage the flurry of hormones that came with being a teenager. My equilibrium was returned, and my trust in my parents along with it. (This was my first contact with Swisse, or 'Suisse', as it was then known, and I distinctly remember feeling an intuitive connection with this brand; I still recall how nice the tablets smelled and tasted. This experience also piqued my interest in nutrition. If these tablets could help improve my mood so quickly, what else could these things do?)

Unsurprisingly I didn't do well in Year 12. I got low marks (62.75, in case you were wondering). Did I wish I'd worked harder? Nope, not really. Did I wish I'd got better marks? Yes, to please my parents. But I knew instinctively I'd find something I'd love and turn it into a success. I didn't mind working hard. When I did, I did well at it. I just wanted to work on something that made sense, had purpose and was useful. School didn't meet those criteria. I wanted to go to university but my marks didn't leave me with many choices, so I enrolled in an Arts degree at La Trobe, majoring in Law (to appease my parents who thought I might become a lawyer), Politics and Cinema Studies. The Cinema course, which was really the only component of the degree that interested me, had limited numbers and I didn't get in. When I told my mum I'd been denied entry, she rang the faculty head, gave them a blast, demanded they enrol her son, and hung up. It worked. I got a place in the course. As mentioned, my mother was rather formidable, and yet deep down, I knew her every action came from a place of unconditional love and a fierce desire to give me access to every opportunity she could provide.

Getting to the campus was my first challenge. It was in Bundoora, a two-hour round trip from Hawthorn. I bought a Datsun Stanza, (aka 'The Silver Bullet') off my Uncle Ludek for $800 and spent a further $800 on a car radio. It was worth it; driving to and from campus each day with Pearl Jam blaring at full tilt was my idea of heaven. (I still have the tinnitus to show for it!)

The La Trobe University campus was way out north, and way out of my comfort zone. This was not an Ivy League institution. It was a hotbed of political activity where the disenfranchised, the disengaged, the left, the greens, the feminists, and the socialists all came together to contest their ideals and compete to have their opinions heard. Many of the students came from disadvantaged backgrounds. This experience opened my eyes to issues of social class and I saw that not everybody got access to the same resources and opportunities that I had received. I got high distinctions in the Cinema Studies course without a lot of effort, mainly because I was learning about something I loved. This was another early lesson: if I wanted to succeed at something, I had to have a passion for it.

Give the gift of time

Time is one of the most valuable currencies we can offer those we love. I get this from Dad. He would come and meet me for lunch at The Agora pub on campus every week. He was incredibly busy with his work but he always made time to be with me. I have never forgotten that and it's why we are still so close today.

CHAPTER 2

VILLAGE LIFE

I've always loved the movies. My dream job (after failing to secure a job at McDonald's) was to work in a video store and maybe one day produce and direct movies, like Quentin Tarantino. My dad's family had a history with Village cinemas so when I finished school and was looking for a job, he lined up an interview with John Anderson, the CEO of Village Roadshow. The interview with John went well until at the end when he asked, 'What cinema would you like to start at?'

I said, 'Forest Hill.'

He said, 'That's a Hoyts.'

My first lesson learnt. Do your research.

In 1994, I started as an Entertainment Service Provider (or ESP) at Village Doncaster. As cutesy as it seems, the acronym had resonance. It totally represented what we were trained to do, which was to predict what the customer wanted before they even knew themselves — to think ahead and be of service so that we could deliver on the extraordinary, rather than just do what everyone else was doing.

I did a bit of everything. I was the guy who sold the ice creams at the candy bar, tore the tickets at the door, and swept the popcorn off the floor. I was the guy who stood at the back of the cinema watching the first five minutes of the film to make sure that the sound was up, the lights went down, and the film was in focus. I counted the money at the end of the night, locked up and set the alarm. I was that guy.

One of my early jobs was to compare our ticket prices with those of other local cinemas to ensure we were competitive. (This was pre-internet so it did take some sleuthing.) I did my research and noticed that the cinemas at Forest Hill (the Hoyts one) had increased their prices by 50 cents. This was news! This had to be reported! I rang my boss, John Iozzi, the National Operations Manager, and dutifully delivered the intel. Well, you'd think I'd discovered the cure for cancer. He told me in earnest tones how important that piece of information was, how it would ensure we remained competitive and how it would be acted upon immediately for the betterment of the wider organisation. I left work that night walking on air. I felt like I had been useful, that my actions mattered and that I had made a difference. This was one of my first lessons in business. Give praise.

The power of praise

Praise is an immensely motivating force. It's so easy to forget about the good things people do, and yet a little compliment, a thank you, or a moment of gratitude play a huge role in helping people feel valued. Even those who look super chilled and are highly accomplished need recognition. We're all hardwired to respond to praise.

Diversity rules

In 1995, I was promoted to the role of Candy Bar Supervisor and then Shift Manager. It was a more complex role but I loved the challenge of leading people and helping them find the right job for their personality. In 1996, the cinema industry underwent a major revolution when single-venue theatres became enormous multi-cinema complexes, or multiplexes. Village was at the forefront of this disruption and was instrumental in ushering in a raft of innovations. I was transferred to the Jam Factory, a newly built luxurious multiplex in South Yarra, a trendy suburb 6 kilometres south of Melbourne, and was stoked to be taking on a leadership role at this exciting time.

At the time, the Jam Factory had an unusual hiring policy in that they would only employ people with a creative arts background. If you were an actor, writer, dancer or director, you could get a job. As such, I was the first employee at the Jam Factory to have any cinema credentials, so it was quite a challenge to train up a team of people who had zero experience in cinema management. This worked in my favour because I was the only one who really planned on making the cinema their career. I wanted to *run* the movies. They wanted to be *in* the movies. This in turn made it easy for me to stand out and be noticed as most of the team were just marking time until they got their big break.

The Jam Factory opened my eyes to what diversity really meant. These actors and performers were more uninhibited, progressive, and curious than other people I mixed with, and while it was a little confronting at the start, I soon came to appreciate their flamboyant and expressive personalities, and quickly learned the values of acceptance, open-mindedness, and tolerance.

These creative souls were challenging to manage in some ways as they weren't motivated by the traditional methods that others responded to. More money, more shifts or management progression didn't inspire them to work harder, care more or do a better job. I had to find new and innovative ways to inspire them, and took great pleasure in trying to find the lever that would motivate each person, and then look for ways to use that lever. I worked hard to understand their unique personalities and the forces that drove them. I realised it had to be positive, rather than negative, reinforcement, so I rewarded those who did great work with a range of incentives: more flexible shifts, easier shifts that wouldn't tax them after a big show the night before, free movies, access to exclusive previews, or roles that were more amenable to their personality.

My apprenticeship

My job at the Jam Factory job was only part-time, but it was a deep-dive apprenticeship into how to run what would become a billion-dollar business, and I was so excited to have a front row seat. I worked with some great leaders during this time and learned a lot about how to manage such a complex and diverse array of personalities. Janine Allis, the founder of Boost Juice, was the General Manager of Knox Cinema at the time, and would become a leader from whom I'd gain a great deal of inspiration. With the right experiences, I knew I could replicate her success. Jacqui Perks was a Location Manager at the tender age of 20, and she inspired me to aim high too. Diane Moret was another exceptional leader. She was 45, a 'mother hen' to everyone, and an inspiring presence who empowered everyone to give their best. If you asked questions, showed initiative and owned your responsibilities, she'd give you the freedom to do your job as you saw fit. She gave swift, accurate and timely feedback on a regular basis so you always knew where you stood. She believed that if you got to the end of the year and you received feedback that was a surprise to you, then your leader had failed you.

Under Diane's leadership, I was exposed to all facets of operations and management and a wide variety of people from different backgrounds, personalities, and preferences, all of which gave me a fantastic foundation for how to be a general manager. I didn't even know what a general manager was until I started at Village and it was by sheer good luck that I fell into a role that enabled me to follow my interests, which, as it turned out, was pretty much everything that made the cinema business operate. I was curious about everything and everyone.

Merchandising master class

Watching the famous actors, directors and producers of the day go about the business of making and marketing their movies inspired me. I got an early master class in merchandising from Nick Giannopoulos, the star and producer of the Wog Boy movies. He'd come in to the cinema each week, pull me aside from what I was doing, and query why his posters weren't displayed, or cajole me to put up more posters or give them more prominence. He was charming and convincing and I gave him as much help as I could to showcase his films. Very few, if any, other producers went to this much effort to get cinema managers like me to help them generate awareness for their films. I admired Nick's work ethic and commitment, and I saw the impact of that merchandising too. When those posters went up, so did the box office receipts for his film.

I wrote the ads for the local papers, scheduled the movies, and keenly watched how the sales performed. I'd then use that data to tweak the weekly session times to see what impact it had at the box office. I managed the sales team and loved inspiring them to sell more choc tops, upsell a tub of popcorn or bring in a corporate group for a team-building event. I spent time in every division and immersed myself in all their activities. I found out what they were doing, how it was all interconnected, and tried to help them understand why their role was important and what was in it for them to do well at it. I learned that you couldn't expect people to do what you wanted just by asking them to do it. People needed to be led. That's what leadership was.

Most of the other managers weren't interested in doing these broad-based activities. They were specialists in one area and had little desire to step out of that square. I did. I wanted to learn everything so I took the opportunity to create relationships with these specialists to find out what they needed, and to learn more about how their area operated so that we could make it more efficient, deliver better results and have more fun. What's more, I was getting paid to learn all this. This part-time job offered me the best business education I could have hoped for.

In a world that often lauded the specialists, I very much valued the generalists and looked for this quality when hiring team members. A multi-tasker could step up when needed, help complete a task and often save the day.

Get an apprenticeship

Business is a craft and it needs to be learnt. You can go to university or do an MBA (both are good), but nothing takes the place of practical experience with those who know more than you do. If you can, get a job at a big corporate firm or even a small business with a strong mentoring program, and immerse yourself in everything they have to offer. You can get paid for an education that will set you up for business success.

How to create a new category

Legend has it that in 1997, when the Crown casino and cinemas in Melbourne were being constructed, Robert Kirby, the head of Village, walked past a disused storage area that backed onto the cinema kitchen, poked his head in, had a look around at the discarded office chairs along the wall and said, 'Why don't we turn this into a fully serviced luxury cinema?' So they did. They took three different categories – a bar, a restaurant and a cinema – and merged them to form an entirely new category of business called Gold Class cinema. The ingredients to create a new category were there: storage + seats + screen + service = an intimate cinema-going experience; it just needed someone with Robert's vision to connect the dots and capitalise on it. Gold Class cinemas became a raging success and redefined the industry.

The Love Seat was another classic Village innovation. It was just two seats next to each other, with an armrest that could be raised. Hardly revolutionary, but this innovation also created a new category of cinema experience and gave Village a marketable point of difference in a commodified sector. Deeming two seats without an armrest the 'Love Seat' was a stroke of marketing genius. Our patrons would frequently call in to reserve the Love Seat experience, to see which cinemas had the Love Seat, or if they could upgrade to the Love Seat. Little did they know, *all* the seats were Love Seats! It was a great example of how to use language to describe something that's *not* there and how to reposition an invisible feature as a tangible benefit.

(The Love Seat did create some challenges. Crown Cinemas was a 24/7 operation within a casino complex so people would use it to get some sleep, recharge their batteries and get back out gaming. Some 'outgoing' couples liked to use the Love Seat for other purposes. You'd be amazed at how brazen some people are.)

Taking three disparate ideas or categories and merging them to form a brand-new category, like Gold Class cinema, was what made Village excel (see below). This innovation practice was not new. Cirque du Soleil merged circus with theatre. Virgin fused the glamour of the music industry with planes and trains. Spanx merged Lycra with lingerie. We would go on to do it with entertainment and health at Swisse. But I learned the essence of how to do it at Village.

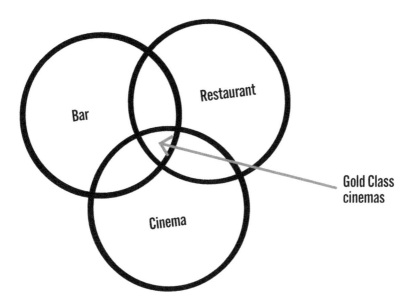

Merging three categories created a fourth category called Gold Class Cinema

People don't know what they want

Customers, and people in general, don't know what they want. Did customers ask for a cinema seat without an armrest? An in-cinema dining experience? Did they say, 'I've always wanted to watch a blockbuster movie in a cosy cinema, with a reclining chair that has a button that I could press that signals to a waiter to bring me a hot juicy hamburger and a cold, crisp glass of chardonnay without missing one minute of my movie'? No, people did not ask for that. They didn't know they wanted it until they saw it. And then they clamoured for it, and loved it. People don't know what they want, or need. Give them what *you* think they need, until the research or some other data point proves otherwise.

CHAPTER 3

THE CANDY MAN

'I want to become the National Candy Bar Stocktake Executive,' said no-one ever.

I did.

It wasn't the most exciting role, but that was the attraction. It was a chance to learn new skills and progress up the ladder. I had done some stocktake work, but this full-time role was a step up. I really wanted this job. I prepared for the interview by reading up on demand planning and sales forecasting and was ready to take any question they might pose. I was beyond thrilled when they offered me the role. When I asked how many people applied for the job, they replied, 'Just one. You.' No matter. I was stoked to get it.

This job required me to visit every Village cinema in the country, meet all the candy bar managers, spend time with each staff member to understand their role in the stocktake process, and help them be more efficient. On average, each candy bar lost around $1000 to $10 000 a week due to poor stocktaking practices. That may not sound like a lot for a global operation, but when multiplied out across the 30-plus cinemas in the Australian chain, and the hundreds across the world, that's a lot to lose every week. I took it upon myself to find a way to stem these losses. I always tried to think like the owner and treat the business as if it was mine. I figured if you always did what was right for the business, you couldn't go wrong.

Do what's right for the business

As a leader you'll be called upon to make thousands of decisions, most of which will affect someone, somewhere. You'll be pulled in many directions and be conflicted as to what decision you should make. These 'true north' decisions should be based on your values. For me, that value was 'do the right thing by the business'. When the right values drive the success of the business, everyone wins.

I set the vision for the team: 'We're going to have the most accurate candy bar stocktake in the world!' It was hardly a world-shattering goal, but I had to find a way to get them excited about it, because counting hundreds of boxes of stock in a dusty warehouse was pretty dull. I told them why we were doing it, why it mattered and outlined the impact it would have on the entire operation. I followed up with the team weekly to see if they were on track, and tried to be a good bloke about it.

True to Village form, the candy bar managers were diverse characters who all approached the job differently. I took their input into account, combined the approaches, found a new way that incorporated the best of all their contributions and created a brand-new system. By the end of the three months, I had developed a new stocktaking process, a revised manual that stepped people through the processes, and a set of policies to guide everyone on how to maximise candy sales. This manual became 'best practice' for how all the cinemas in the chain needed to do their stocktake.

When it was implemented, the $5000 average weekly loss of stock per cinema in the candy bar dropped to an average of $100 in stock loss. Multiplied out across all the cinemas we operated, this manual went on to save the company millions of dollars. It was still in operation when I left. It may still be in operation now.

That small, simple manual I introduced demonstrated the power of a well-documented system, and what was possible when you involved everyone in the process and brought them along for the journey. No-one wanted this job because it was hard, messy and detailed work. I had to really dig deep to learn about a type of process that didn't come naturally to me — but I wasn't after *easy*. I was after *hard*. I relished being put in uncomfortable positions because it increased my resilience, and I knew that eventually uncomfortable would become comfortable.

Do what others don't want to do

I wasn't drawn to easy wins. I liked to be dropped into difficult situations and told to find a way out. How I did that was up to me. But I had to find a way. I took on challenges at Village that no-one else wanted. These were ideal opportunities for me to step up, shine and get noticed. I also learned some valuable skills in the process. When a potential opening comes up that others turn down, even if it's an unpalatable role, grab it with both hands and run with it.

From routine to reinvention

After the stocktake role ended, I went back to working full-time at the Jam Factory and, while I enjoyed being amongst my team, I did miss the thrill and variety of being on the road, meeting new people and taking on new challenges. Life felt bland. University had finished, my relationship of five years had finished, and footy was over (my knees had given in). I worked a lot, ate more than I needed, put on weight and got a bit depressed. I was not at my best. Some of my mates said I was increasingly argumentative, judgemental, stubborn, late, jealous and an all-round smart-arse who needed to grow up. It was tough feedback to hear, but it was true. I had lost my mojo.

All my friends were going overseas so I thought I should probably go too. I needed to cut myself loose from what people thought they knew of me. I wanted to be free to explore parts of myself without others saying, 'That's not like you.' How did they know that wasn't like me? *I* didn't even know what I was like. I was leading an inauthentic life and I wanted that to change, so I put my Jam Factory job on hold, bought an around-the-world ticket, said my goodbyes, and departed for my big adventure. It was time to reinvent myself.

I backpacked across the United States, Mexico (well, Tijuana, just to say I'd been to Mexico!), Canada, Europe, England and Thailand. I started out as the shy traveller but as the trip went on, I became emboldened. I camped in canyons, slept on beaches, couch-surfed in warehouses, met new people, had a few romances, visited art galleries, theatres and festivals; I worked a bit, drank a lot, partied hard and saw the world. It was exactly what I needed.

I made a point of dropping into a cinema in every city I visited to see how they operated. I was passionate about cinema, and hungry to learn everything I could. When I am passionate about a topic, I give it my all. I found work at Warner Village cinemas in London, part of the global chain. It was interesting to see how different businesses within the same organisation operated. Some, like the London arm, focused on saving money, while others, like the Australian arm, focused on making it. I also did two weeks' work experience in Village's film production unit in Los Angeles. Our office backed onto the Warner Bros lot and I remember feeling so proud to be working for this Australian company that had made it big in the United States and it inspired me to think big with whatever I was going to do next. (I also distinctly recall noticing Nicole Kidman's promotional film poster for *Practical Magic* on the wall. Who knew she would play a key role in my life in later years?)

The traveller returns

I returned home a year later and I was a better man for it. Refreshed and reinvigorated, I had seen things, done things, and stretched myself to experience new and uncomfortable situations. Travelling on my own, meeting new people and having to rely on my own wits to survive had made me resilient. I was used to being uncomfortable now; it had become my natural state. Being back home felt easy. I had my family, healthy food, close mates, my car, and life felt good. This newfound worldliness and ease with myself inspired me to make the most of any situation that came my way. I was ready for new challenges.

I slotted back into the Jam Factory as a Location Manager. The place had doubled in size, and was the biggest grossing cinema in the country. I was hungry to progress so I applied for the role of General

Manager at Westfield Southland, a massive shopping centre about 30 kilometres south of Melbourne. I thought I was the perfect choice: I'd done my apprenticeship and paid my dues. But I didn't get the job. They gave it to my close mate, Jason Buesst. He was ten years older than me, suave, sophisticated, and wholly deserving of the role, but I was devastated. They 'didn't think I was ready'. When they gave me the news, I cried. I was really devastated. (I did not like to fail.) This was a defining moment. I never wanted to feel that way again, so I resolved to bottle that feeling of failure and use it to fuel my fire and work harder. I would not ponder why I didn't get the role, but focus on who I needed to become to get the next one.

Behind the scenes

I was a hands-on manager and took my responsibilities seriously. I didn't hide in my office or instruct from afar. I was on the floor, greeting the patrons and helping my team. As the Location Manager, I made a point of walking around the entire complex every 60 minutes to check in on the customers and to see if my team needed a hand.

One of my favourite things to do when the place was really pumping was to manage the ticket queue to ensure the line flowed smoothly so people could buy what they needed at the candy bar and get to their cinema on time. This also gave me the opportunity to greet every customer personally and make a connection. I would take the time to ask them a few questions about how their night was going, what film they were seeing, and sort out any agitations that may have occurred. If the candy bar was busy, I'd slot in behind the counter to help out, or clean up a spill to set the example and show the team that everyone was equal.

On one of my walks around the complex, I stepped into the kitchen where we made the choc-tops. We made them by hand back then and sold them by the thousands. It was a time-consuming and messy job and it required at least two people per shift in order to get it all done. One would scoop the ice cream, the other would dip the cone in the chocolate. On this day there was only one person in the kitchen. She was a grungy young woman who looked as if she hadn't slept for a few days. If I hadn't seen it with my own eyes I don't think I would have believed it, but after she dipped the ice cream in the chocolate, she ran her tongue around the rim of each cone to stop the chocolate from dripping down the side of the cone. When I asked her to stop, she looked at me in surprise, as if running her tongue over every ice-cream was a perfectly acceptable way to tidy up the dripping chocolate. I don't know how long that practice had been going on for, but if I hadn't been doing my regular rounds, I may never have discovered it. We had to throw all the ice-creams out of course and our patrons had to go without choc-tops that day. Walking the floor kept me in touch with how things really operated.

Be a generalist

There's a reason why General Managers are called General Managers. It's because they have a generalised overview of how everything works. I loved being the General Manager. I have a ridiculous curiosity about everything and everyone. I put this down to the Saturday afternoons I spent at Mangala Studios where I learned a range of skills that helped me develop my insight and intuition. To run a business, you have to understand every aspect of it, and know how each piece interconnects with the other.

CHAPTER 4

HOW TO CREATE A HIGH-PERFORMANCE CULTURE

The sheer scale of the Jam Factory meant you really needed to understand people and management to be successful. A typical shift involved managing at least 40 people, most of whom, as already mentioned, didn't take their job seriously. They were just marking time until the next audition. As such, the team would occasionally cut corners or not follow the correct protocol. Some managers were hesitant to address this bad behaviour or lacked the know-how to handle such situations, so I created a series of strategies that rewarded good behaviour and extinguished unwanted behaviours. I needed to systematise it to ensure these processes would stand up when I wasn't around.

These strategies were a mix of things that I had either observed in other leaders, thought of myself, or had come up with as a result of asking people about what would motivate them. Here is a snapshot of some of the strategies we implemented:

- **Clear goals.** We provided clear, concise, measurable goals for every employee and the tools to achieve them, which gave everyone clarity, purpose and something to strive for.

- **Regular communication.** We established a robust communication system and held regular meetings with pre-circulated agendas to ensure everyone had access to the same information at the same time.

- **Incentives and offers.** We offered cost-effective rewards that recognised great work and incentivised good behaviour. Rewards included positive reinforcement, flexible shifts, double pay on public holidays, higher paying shifts, training and development opportunities, and free movies.

- **KPI reviews.** At the end of each shift, we conducted individual KPI reviews with team members and discussed customer and team feedback, both positive and constructive.

- **Daily and weekly check-ins.** At the end of the week, all managers met with supervisors, set Key Performance Indicators (KPIs) and discussed individual performance.

- **Progress Reports.** To keep everyone informed, we provided the team with 30-minute updates and progress reports that highlighted how, or if, employees were meeting their targets.

- **Accountability.** We maintained detailed records about each team member so we could place them in roles that suited their personality, and track stated goals so that we could hold everyone accountable.

- **3-step warning system.** We introduced a fair warning system with three stages – green, amber, and red – to manage performance issues and give people advance notice if they were going off track. (The union would make its presence felt if proper processes were not followed, so everything needed to be done by the book.)

Breakout the whiteboard

In a world that values real-time reporting, there is still something to be said for using a good old whiteboard to keep track of your team's results. We used one at Village and it was instrumental in helping keep everyone focussed — not just on their own results, but on the team's results too. We kept track of everything — daily revenue, spend per head at the candy bar, payroll per-person per-hour, stock supplies, average ticket prices and more. This granular reporting gave us an instant snapshot of where we were succeeding and where we needed to improve. It gave structure to our performance reviews and informed our decision making. Most competitors didn't go to this level of effort to find the opportunities in the data — we did, and that's why we became one of the most successful cinema chains. It gave us our competitive edge.

As you can see, I lived and breathed the business. A 12-hour day was a standard shift, and outside of that, I'd spend countless hours thinking of different ways to improve our processes, raise revenue, reward those who came up with great ideas, cut costs and, most importantly, have more fun! People will always go that little bit further if they have a clear direction and are having fun. I always tried to be a good-humoured guy, deliver my directives with a smile and tell the team what a great job they were doing. I was genuinely interested in my team as people and made a point of enquiring about their lives outside of work. Importantly, these new processes were executed *consistently*, and the results were extraordinary. Morale improved, as did productivity. Everyone knew where they stood, what they excelled at, and what areas required improvement.

Give constant feedback

Which football team is more likely to win? The one whose coach comes out into the huddle at quarter time, addresses the immediate, urgent issues and then sends them back on the field with a game plan? Or the one whose coach says at the start of the game, 'Off you go, have a good time, see you on the other side.' The answer is clear. Business is the

(continued)

same. Don't wait for the end of the year to give feedback. Give it every day, on the run, in the hallway, or in the doorway. Let people know if they're on the right track or not, and give them constructive feedback if they're not so they can change direction.

Time to move on

In 1999, I was promoted to the position of Acting General Manager of Jam Factory and my pay went from $45 000 to $60 000 per year. I very much wanted the General Manager's role but the executive team didn't feel confident appointing a 22-year-old to a role that involved managing a $25 million business and 200 employees. This was frustrating as I could see what was needed to make the business successful, but I clearly had some blind spots that I needed to address. I was told that some peers didn't like the way I worked with them, and that some felt threatened by my leadership. I never got this feedback from my direct manager (as I was hell-bent on making them look extraordinary at what they did). It was often the person who was a rung above them that felt aggrieved. I figured it was because they could see me coming.

This upset me because my intention all along was to do the right thing by the business and to bring out the best in everyone. I responded to this feedback by doing what I had always done: let my actions do the talking, give my best and never give up. This attitude made me quite fearless. If a customer complained about me, or threatened to report me to a manager, I invited them to do so as I knew that everything I did was in service to the business.

On the surface, I was an assured and confident leader, but internally, I lacked confidence. I was still trying to find my feet as a leader of people and discover how to balance strength with ease. I was hungry to succeed, cared deeply about what I did and wanted to be good at my job. If I was to take the next step and be taken seriously as a leader, it was clear that I had to broaden my experience, address my blind spots, and find some new challenges. I needed to spread my wings and think big again. Melbourne was starting to feel a bit claustrophobic. Everyone seemed to know everyone. I knew it was time to move when I kissed a girl at a nightclub, and the next day she turned up for a job interview. Maybe I was kissing too many girls, or maybe Melbourne was just too small. Either way, I had to get out.

A bachelor in Prague

One of the things that made Village so exciting was the opportunity to work overseas. I had noticed that many of my senior compatriots would take up an international posting, come back and rise quite quickly through the ranks. I was ready for a change, so when the opportunity arose to become operations manager and open three Village cinemas across the Czech Republic, I put my hand up for the job and got it. I spoke rudimentary Czech and was looking for a big international adventure that would take me out of my comfort zone and make me feel uncomfortable again. This opportunity ticked all the boxes. The only downside was my new Czech boss suggested cutting my pay from $60 000 to $45 000 in line with the cheaper cost of living in Prague, while he, with zero cinema experience, took home a whopping $200 000. I felt pretty insulted and pushed back but still got the gig and maintained my existing salary. They needed my experience.

The first three months in Prague were the loneliest of my life. I didn't know anyone, my Czech was sketchy at best and the job of opening the first multiplex cinema in a country was far harder than I expected. It was tough working in a former Communist country, too. The generation who had grown up in the old system didn't ask questions, challenge anything or demonstrate interest. They needed to be told what to do every step of the way. It was learned helplessness on an industrial scale.

Three months prior to the opening of the complex, I had a visit from George Livery. He was the CEO of Village's European operation and was there to see how the project was progressing. The opening night was coming up and we were way behind schedule. George could see I really needed some support so he invited me to dinner just to chat and relax. I welcomed the invitation. I talked George through all we were doing. He had opened cinema complexes before and knew how challenging it was to introduce the multiplex concept into a new city. He reassured me that I was doing an extraordinary job and that I was on the right track.

He also asked me to visit and support the Village sites in Germany and Switzerland to share my knowledge of our systems. He in turn mentored me on how to build relationships and manage difficult situations with grace, and reinforced the importance of making time for people.

Cath Crowley was Village's European Operations manager based in London and she'd visit me every few weeks leading up to the opening. She also became a valuable mentor and taught me the power of structure, process and paying attention to detail. We worked hard, but partied harder. We both loved Powderfinger and had it blaring through the office as we worked.

Opening night arrived. We had met the deadline and the cinema looked amazing. We had 1000 of Prague's movers and shakers in the house and they all had a ball. I was still under the pump, trying to complete last-minute jobs. I spent the night rounding everyone up to get them to attend to their cinematic duties but it was hopeless. Most of them were socialising, some were imbibing and, as usual, the Managing Director was in hiding. We eventually found him in the back office, feet on the desk, reading holiday brochures to Casa Del Sol. He was moved on swiftly after that.

That same evening, I had a massive clash with the Site Manager. Despite spending weeks training the management team on how to handle the thousands of dollars in cash we took each day and how to accurately balance the till and store the money in the safe, I later returned to the office to find the cash room strewn with notes and coins, the safe open and the place in total disarray. I lost it and screamed at him at the top of my lungs for a full 15 minutes and then fired him. It was not my finest moment. I had been working from 7 am to midnight seven days a week for 90 days straight to bring this project to fruition and was not thinking straight. I regretted that outburst and resolved never to let my emotions get the better of me ever again. Firing the Site Manager was the right decision, but that was not the kind of leader I wanted to be.

A few months later I came back to Australia, was promoted to Regional Manager of a range of top-performing sites and complexes, and George and Cath would later join me at Swisse and go on to become some of my dearest friends.

These experiences were life-changing for a 24-year-old and altered the direction of my life. They also imparted a crucial lesson: our relationships shape who we are. The world is a small place, and the individuals we encounter in our youth, like Cath and George, often resurface in our lives many years or even decades later. (It's also a lesson to look out for those motivated teenagers who are in junior roles now. They are the ones to nurture as they will be the gun leaders of the future.)

CHAPTER 5

GETTING CLEAR

I arrived back in Australia in 2001 at the top of my game (well, for my age), and ready for the next challenge. Life in Australia moved more slowly than it had in Prague and everything felt easier. Everyone spoke English, the working culture was familiar and if I put my energy behind something, I knew I could make things happen. I had seen what communism looked like up close, and I realised how lucky I was to have grown up in a democratic country: to be able to speak freely, ask questions, think openly and strive to achieve my dreams unhindered by corruption or oppression. While my mother had talked endlessly about how lucky we were to grow up in a democratic country, I finally understood it.

I also understood that tyranny came in many forms, not just political. I had grown up watching my dad struggle against Big Pharma and the groupthink of academia and was determined to not be constrained by similar forces.

The time away had also crystallised my thinking. I now knew exactly what I wanted in life. My goals were clear:

- I would be financially free by the age of 30.

- I would own my own house and car and be debt free.

- I would only work with people and projects that piqued my passion.

- ■ I would work when I wanted, with whom I wanted, where I wanted.

- ■ I would have free and unfettered choice as to what I did with my time and how I lived my life.

To achieve my goal of financial independence, I would need to become the CEO of Village Cinemas. After that, I reasoned, I could do as I pleased.

Village drama

Village was in a state of flux. It was transitioning from a growth focus to a turnaround focus — turnaround being the act of 'turning around' a declining business to becoming profitable. Our revenues were falling and the business now required a CEO with a turnaround mindset. A new CEO had been appointed to make it happen, and it was my opinion that this CEO, a man in his late forties, was more focused on achieving a financial result no matter the cost.

I didn't believe that everything had to be sacrificed in the pursuit of profit. I recall a time when I was defending Jason, my old mate who got the job I wanted at Southland. He was now a fellow Regional Manager and had been going through a divorce. I explained that Jason needed some extra time to get himself back on track. As I recall it, the CEO bluntly said 'Zap!' and made a hand gesture of pulling a trigger. 'We need to make him redundant!'

I was shocked. 'What about all the years of great service he gave us before this flat spot?' I asked.

'If you want loyalty, get a dog,' he replied.

On another occasion, I asked him to deliver a pep talk to the Village team before the start of the Christmas season, which was the busiest time of the year. I remember him saying, 'For those of you having time off over Christmas and New Year, have a safe and enjoyable time with your loved ones. For those of you who are working, well, bad luck!' In my view, an attitude like that did not inspire loyalty. I saw this approach as a template for the kind of leader I did not want to become. The experience also taught me that we can learn as much from those we disagree with as those we don't. We all have flaws. Instead of dismissing those who differ from us, it's wise to use those encounters to discover who and what we don't want to be. Thankfully I had the support of Dimitra Manis, our astute HR director, who helped balance the situation out.

A duty to society

These experiences, contrasted with watching George, Cath, Dimitra and Jason deploy their exceptional leadership skills in such a positive manner, reinforced my intuitive belief that business leaders have a duty to prioritise their employees' wellbeing and happiness above all else. If we don't do that, what are we working for? If the very people we surround ourselves with are unhappy, unable to be their best and fearful of what every day holds, how on earth are we able to be *our* best, and how can we build a successful and thriving business for our stakeholders, customers and society at large?

I believe that unhappiness within the workplace can contribute to depression, anxiety, loneliness and general societal dysfunction, all of which is endemic in our society. We spend most of our time at work, and if we're not happy there, we have very little of chance of being happy anywhere. Regrettably, it seems predominantly Baby Boomer male leadership figures tend to push through with their antiquated ideals of what a workplace is meant to be and what a worker is expected to endure, with little regard for the repercussions of their actions.

I had to work with this Village CEO for many months and was constantly shocked at the way he appeared to treat his team and appalled at how he was amply rewarded for it. On the upside, I must give him credit for investing in his people. He set aside a budget for people to pursue professional development and encouraged us to use it. I was made aware of this option when I presented to him a series of strategies to assist with the turnaround. He criticised me for not presenting the financials to support my business plan proposal. He was right. I didn't include them because I wasn't confident with numbers. My financial skills were weak, and this prevented me from putting forward my case and getting the approvals I needed to execute my plans.

To rectify this, I enrolled in a finance course through the Melbourne Business School. It was a revelation, as was the leadership course I later took there that steeped me in the art of conducting 360-degree feedback. I met some important mentors at these courses, including one of the lecturers, Clarence da Gama Pinto, a man who would come back into my life at a critical moment years later. He taught me so much, including the life-changing belief that feedback is a gift, and that we must thank and reward those who have the courage to give it to us. He assured me that having these blind spots brought to my attention would make me a much better leader, and that *knowing* what people thought about you was far more powerful than *wondering* what they thought about you. He also encouraged me to embrace my Czech and Albanian background to become a more authentic leader.

With this newfound sense of confidence, I took on extra roles at Village. One of the most important tasks I was given was to fix up a range of underperforming sites around Victoria. This involved bringing in a team to rebuild a site from scratch and to turn around a loss-making enterprise.

I used this opportunity to apply my positive mindset and turn these 'problem' sites into 'challenge' sites. This simple language reframe turned the task into an exciting goal that the team could all get behind. I used my previously honed skills to create a group culture and the results were remarkable. The jobs got done more quickly, we delivered millions of dollars to the bottom line, we created a team-based culture that lingered long after I left the site, and, most importantly, we had fun.

Skill up

As my career progressed, it became clear that finance was not my strength, and this lack of knowledge began to stymie my progression. To close this gap, I went back to business school, studied finance and got the knowledge I needed to overcome this limitation. From then on, reading the financial reports became a sport and the source of many of our greatest opportunities. What aren't you good at? Identify it and do something about it. (Richard Branson once confided in me that he still doesn't know how to read a Profit and Loss statement. I *think* he was joking.)

A life-changing phone call

In 2003, I became the General Manager of the Jam Factory and a Regional Manager. Not long after, I got a phone call from Michael Saba, the co-founder and Managing Director of Swisse, offering me the role of Territory Manager of New South Wales. I was flattered that he'd thought of me as I respected him greatly, but politely declined. I was building my network in Melbourne and felt I was really going places at Village.

I was familiar with the brand as I'd grown up taking Swisse vitamins (and still was), and Dad had been recommending the brand to his patients for many years. Michael was friends with my dad and familiar with his break-through research and clinical work on integrative medicine. Like us, Michael is all about family, so it was no surprise that he would seek out my father to source the best medical care for his ailing mother. She had been on hormone replacement therapy (HRT) medication for menopause, and was suffering badly from a slew of other side effects that came from being on those drugs. She was frustrated that traditional doctors would try to assess her condition off the back of a 15-minute consultation. Dad spent over an hour with her on multiple occasions, took her off the HRT and replaced it with a regime of natural therapies. After just a few months, she recovered from all her ailments, never went back to HRT and lived a long and happy life.

After that life-changing experience, Michael asked Dad to advise him on conducting clinical trials, formulations and publications for Swisse, and that's how their mentoring relationship began. Dad was one of Swisse's first ambassadors: the words 'Formulated by a Professor' that featured on the bottle referred to him. Dad neither sought, nor would he have accepted, payment for this endorsement. He saw it as an act of community service and was dedicated to the elevation and expansion of what natural medicines could do. (Not long after, the laws changed so that doctors could no longer endorse medical products and Michael took the reference to 'Professor' off the bottle.)

Michael was a most hospitable man and loved to socialise, so when he had spare tickets to an event like the AFL or the Grand Prix, he invited Dad and me as a gesture of thanks. It was always a five-star event, with great seats, delicious food and wonderful wine, and Michael would be his gregarious self. I saw the joy he brought to others and thought, 'This man knows how to build relationships. This man knows how to bring people together.' It wasn't so much what he did — although he was always spectacularly generous — it was the way he made you feel, and he always made you feel special.

I also observed that he didn't seek anything in exchange for his generosity. His acts of kindness weren't based on a quid pro quo mentality. He firmly believed that doing good for others was simply the right thing to do.

New horizons

Ironically, not long after this job offer from Michael, my magic run at Village started to slow. I had become arrogant, I admit, and some peers and senior managers found me abrasive. My serve of humble pie was coming.

At the end of 2004, I applied for the role of Marketing Manager. I wanted to broaden my experience and needed to step sideways to go forwards in pursuit of my goal of becoming the CEO. I didn't have any marketing qualifications, but I didn't let that deter me. I thought my years of running cinemas, turning around under-performing sites and leading teams by creating a world-class culture would be of value. But alas, they were not. I didn't even get an interview. I was told, again, that I didn't have the experience. The new HR manager and I were at loggerheads too. We did not get along, and she hinted that my time at Village might be up and that if I wanted to grow, I had to go.

There were external factors at play too. Prior to the 'zap!' CEO, they had employed a 30-year-old CEO who'd started out at 18 as an usher, as I had, and this young gun hadn't worked out. So as an ambitious 26-year-old, hungry to succeed, it looked like I was unlikely to get a shot for a while. With lots of great people leaving around this time, and the values of Village changing, I knew I would have to look further afield to achieve my goals.

In early 2005, I took a business trip to China with Grant Moffit, a friend of my father's who knew I was seeking a change of career. This trip helped me see that there was life after Village and gave me a renewed sense of opportunity. I would return to Guangzhou, the city we visited, many years later and it would play a huge role in our success at Swisse.

Not long after I got back, I got another call from Michael Saba. We had gone to the footy together a few weeks earlier and I'd told him I was looking to leave Village if the right opportunity came along. (I was lucky that my dad had introduced me to Michael and I was conscious of leveraging any opportunity I was given, as I knew that luck and serendipity would only take you so far. I truly believe that if you want to succeed, you have to take action and capitalise on any situation that comes your way.)

Michael took me to lunch as he wanted to 'recommend' me for a job at another company. He asked me what I wanted in my next role and I launched into what could only be described as an impassioned rant. I told him how I longed to work for a company that valued culture and rewarded hard work; where people would be applauded for having a crack, where we'd be given clear goals, honest feedback, and the freedom to deliver on those goals. At the end of my rant, Michael smiled, shook my hand and pulled me in for his trademark hug and kiss on both cheeks. He said, 'That went better than expected. You just wrote your job description. Come and work with me at Swisse.'

I accepted his offer. It was time to move on. I could never have guessed that this was going to be the wildest ride of my life.

How Swisse started

People often ask, 'How did Swisse get started?'. Well, it all started with a potato cake.

Michael Saba, one of the two co-founders of Swisse, worked at his parents' fish and chip shop in the suburb of Airport West, 17 kilometres west of Melbourne. Stephen Ring, the other co-founder (and son of Kevin Ring, the original entrepreneur who brought Swisse — or Suisse, as it was known then — to life), worked at the Swisse office across the road. At lunchtime, Stephen would pop in to order some fish and chips

(continued)

and a potato cake. He and the Saba family struck up a friendship, and when Swisse needed an extra set of hands on the production line, several members of the Saba family, including Michael, aged just 15, would step in to help them out.

By 1988, sky-high interest rates (18 per cent!) saw businesses flailing, home loans defaulting, and people going bankrupt. It was a terrible time for many, and thousands of businesses went to the wall. One of them on the brink was Suisse, Kevin Ring's vitamin business. He'd started out as a baker, selling organic bread from his shop in St Kilda, and added pollen tablets as a sideline after a trip to Switzerland. He expanded into vitamins, employed more people, became a respected producer of high-quality vitamins and the business grew. But when the interest rates kept rising, he couldn't hold on any longer. It was either shut down or sell up. Stephen, his son, and Michael stepped in, bought the business off Kevin, renamed the business Swisse, and got to work.

PART II

CHAPTER 6

THE ADVENTURE BEGINS

I joined Swisse in March 2005 as Operations Manager. The company had 30 employees and an annual turnover of $15 million, 90 per cent of which came from two flagship products: Ultivite for Men and Ultivite for Women. I was excited to be there and keen to get started, yet from the moment I walked in, it seemed like everything that could go wrong did go wrong.

For a start, we had to delete SBS1, a topical crème for people with eczema and psoriasis. Despite popular belief, this product was not named after our multicultural TV broadcaster (SBS stood for 'sensitive beautiful skin'), and was one of our best-selling products. Customers raved about it. They wrote letters to us, letting us know how effective these crèmes were in reducing their pain and suffering and how much it had changed their lives. Reading these testimonials was a powerful reminder of why I transitioned from Village to Swisse. These products made a real difference and helped people lead happier and healthier lives.

The issues with SBS1 started when the health regulator instructed us to remove the therapeutic claims for eczema and psoriasis from the label. This was a major setback for us. These claims were crucial to its success. They explained the product's benefits to customers, and played a vital role in the marketing of the product. We'd conducted extensive clinical trials with scientists from Southern Cross University to prove these claims but, unfortunately, as the sample size used was not considered statistically representative, we were forced to drop the claims. Most products are only as good as their marketing, and as we were no longer able to communicate the benefits, people lost interest in the product and were confused as to whether it was the same product they'd bought before. Sales dropped off, and eventually the retailers deleted the product altogether. This was one of our more successful products so our profits took a massive hit. We could have commissioned a larger study to confirm the veracity of our claims, but this would have taken years to complete, and we didn't have the time or budget for it. We had to find a replacement product to make up for the shortfall in revenue, and we had to find it fast.

The challenges came thick and fast

To capitalise on the expanding weight loss market, we introduced TrimShot and CoQ10 under the 'ProvenSlim' brand. All the retailers asked, 'Why don't you call them Swisse TrimShot or Swisse CoQ10?' but Michael felt strongly that the Swisse brand should only represent multivitamins. He felt that if we sold other products that weren't multivitamins, it would confuse the message of our core business, and in turn affect sales.

We normally outsourced the making of all our products to a contract manufacturer, but on this occasion we brought production in-house, as we felt we could control the process more effectively and gain some economies of scale.

We engaged Dr John Gray, the American author of the international best-selling book *Men Are From Mars, Women Are From Venus*, to come to Australia and conduct a series of events to promote the products to our retailers. Women loved this book because it delved into the intriguing dynamics between men and women, and provided valuable insights into the complexities of romantic relationships.

As a rule, I don't like public speaking (I'm an introvert, which often surprises people), but when the topics are about culture, purpose or wellness, I feel totally energised and don't mind getting up on stage. Dr Gray and I spoke to thousands of pharmacy assistants around the country about relationships, fitness, nutrition and how all those factors contributed to a rich and satisfying life. The focus of the campaign was to help people feel better about themselves so they could feel confident in being their best for their partner. We explained how the product ingredients worked, shared with them our PR and marketing campaign strategies so they understood our unique selling points, and, most importantly, provided a deal sheet that encouraged them to order an initial allocation of stock.

Know thyself

I'm an introvert. This surprises people as they often see me in the newspaper kicking up my heels at a gala event and think I am the life of the party. I know myself well enough now to ensure that if I have to attend an event or deliver a speech, I allow time beforehand to meditate, and avoid scheduling something directly before or after that may require a lot of energy. I enjoy being extroverted but I need to have quiet time before and after to re-energise.

Dr Gray appeared on all the top-rating TV programs including *Today*, *Sunrise* and *A Current Affair* and received huge coverage in the mainstream press. The PR, training and sell-in events worked. The pharmacies pre-ordered over $2 million in stock, making it one of our most successful sell-ins to date. This was our first foray into hiring five-star celebrity ambassadors and we were stoked at the excitement this campaign generated.

The challenges began when people went in-store to buy the ProvenSlim products.

It started with the ProvenSlim brand packaging. If you walk down a pharmacy aisle, you'll notice that successful products have eye-catching packaging that 'pops'. Our packaging didn't. It faded into the background. We made the mistake of using a pale blue-and-white colour palette, which looked fine on the computer screen in the office, but in-store, under the fluorescent lights, looked wan and weak. The result? People couldn't find it on the shelf.

To add to our challenges, we had boxed the range to give it a premium feel. This didn't work well either. After even the mildest handling, the cardboard became dog-eared and creased, and looked as if it had been left out in the rain for a week. Now the product looked both pale and worn, and beaten up and bedraggled.

Test your packaging

It pays to test your product packaging design in-store before you roll it out en masse so you can gauge its impact in a real-world setting. The design might look great on the computer screen in your office but it may fade into obscurity amidst the sea of competitors and under the harsh glare of the store lights.

The TrimShot product itself also had issues. The 'directions for use' on the label were too complicated. It said: *'You can mix this product with water, yoghurt, juice, cow's milk, soy milk, almond milk, or anything really. You can even put it on your cereal! It's best with milk because it tastes better with milk, but if you don't like milk, which we know lots of people don't, then you can mix it with water. Either works. Your choice!'*

I am being a bit facetious, but the instructions were overly complicated, and if you did mix it with water, as first directed on the label, many found it tasted terrible. Had we said milk was the first and best option, it would have tasted better and people would have consumed it. But after their first taste with water, especially if they weren't used to the taste and texture of psyllium husk, they thought 'Yeah, nah, I'm not taking that again.'

The CoQ10 product drew unwanted attention too. It was a sachet filled with crystals that you had to mix with water. We hadn't quite mastered the delicate art of extracting moisture from the air, so if the product sat around on a shelf for a few weeks, the crystals would coalesce into fat clumps. When water was added, the clumps just floated to the top of the glass, like insoluble ice-cubes.

In short, the entire ProvenSlim range was a huge challenge. What had seemed like a great idea at the time — engaging Dr John Gray to be our first international celebrity ambassador — had directed widespread attention to a range of products that customers couldn't find, tasted terrible, or didn't work. And all of it happened on my watch.

Welcome to Swisse!

A doctor's endorsement

My challenges didn't end there.

A crucial decision all manufacturers need to make is to select the right sales channels for their products. (Whether you make computers, kettles or crisps, who you sell it to and who you *don't* sell it to are critical decisions that need to be considered with care.) In our case, pharmacies and health food stores were our primary channels. We were aware that selling through major grocery stores such as Coles and Woolworths would bring in large sales volumes, but we had to consider our existing retail base. They had made it clear that if we entered the grocery market, they would not be happy.

The obvious solution was to offer the grocers a different brand. This would give us the sales volume we needed from the supermarkets, while protecting the integrity of the Swisse brand sold through the pharmacies. To leverage this opportunity, we developed Evidin, a high-quality vitamin at a budget price point. The formulation wasn't as potent as a Swisse Ultivite, and it didn't have the premium price tag either, but it was a better-quality multivitamin than any other product in grocery. It was Swisse with a twist.

We knew from the ProvenSlim experience that a doctor's endorsement was powerful and could inspire people to trial a product. This was our goal. We knew that if people tried it, they'd love it and come back for more. If they stopped taking it, they'd notice the difference and come back to us again. Our products were a bit pricier, but we packed more active ingredients into each tablet, which delivered the results our customers wanted. It's why our tagline, 'You'll feel better on Swisse', was so perfect. People really did feel better after taking Swisse.

We chose Dr John Tickell as our brand ambassador to launch Evidin. John was a medical doctor and the author of the best-selling book *Laughter, Sex, Vegetables & Fish*, so he aligned perfectly with our product. Taking advantage of a recent change in advertising regulations, we were thrilled to be able to include his endorsement on our product labels. We sold in over $800 000 worth of stock to Coles, but despite the doctor's endorsement, sales off the shelf were slow. Then, literally overnight, the health regulator changed the law *again*, which now made it *illegal* to use a doctor's endorsement. The law did, however, allow us to sell through whatever stock was in market. We had to get ahead of this, and find an innovative way to remove the stock from the shelf but retain this coveted shelf space. Rather than discounting and selling through the stock at Coles, and risk losing the shelf space due to the slow sales, we positioned it to the Coles buyers that we had no choice but to recall the entire $800 000 worth of stock by a certain date. This would buy us some time while we came up with a new way to shift this stock.

After much debate, we came up with a new plan. We took the stock back from Coles, unpacked all the tablets, threw out the defunct packaging, and repackaged the tablets into white tubs, a style of packaging that had become synonymous with the Swisse brand. We plastered a big 'Play' button on the front of the tub to represent the 'play' button on an iPod, re-positioned it as a youth product and re-sold it back to Coles as Evidin Mark 2. We also hired two silver medal Olympians, John Steffensen and Elka Graham, to star in the TV commercials and let it rip. The campaign did okay — nothing spectacular — but it got us out of a very expensive hole and helped us retain that coveted shelf space.

Launching two versions of Evidin and the ProvenSlim range was a crash course in the challenges involved in bringing a new product to market, particularly one with no brand history or heritage. Despite all the significant resources we threw at Evidin, we still found it difficult to get cut-through. This insight highlighted the strength of the Swisse brand and reinforced how difficult it would be for a lesser-known brand to enter the market and compete against us. On the upside, we realised we had successfully built a moat around our Swisse castle, which afforded us the protection we needed to confidently introduce new products, explore new opportunities, and take risks with niche offerings. This awareness would inform and shape our future actions and, while Evidin did not survive, it provided us with this valuable lesson. We always learned from our experiences.

Don't invest in new brands too early

One of the two lessons we took from the ProvenSlim experience was that we should not invest in too many brands too soon. The Evidin launch also showed us that it cost us around $30–50 million to launch a new consumer brand in Australia properly. If your core business is not punching out enough money to pay for a new brand, don't launch a new brand. You could raise capital to fund it, but treat it separately from your core brand. The second lesson was that we should not develop products (e.g. CoQ10 and Trimshot) just to get a return on our manufacturing capacity. We should have been driven by what the customers wanted, rather than by what we could manufacture. (In any case, if we were manufacturing anything, it should have been multivitamins.) For us to become a market leader, we had to exit the manufacturing space and excel in our three core strengths: product innovation, marketing and sales. It's critical you understand what business you are really in and focus on that.

CHAPTER 7

A 'LEARN, GROW, IMPROVE' OPPORTUNITY

We made a lot of mistakes in those early days at Swisse, but Michael had a unique ability to see the best in every situation and turn those events into teachable moments. His attitude made these challenging experiences easier to bear. He believed, as I do, that words have the power to build people up, or the potential to drag people down. For example, rather than give the team 'feedback' on how they could do something better, he called it an opportunity to 'learn, grow and improve', which we all referred to as an 'LGI' moment. This LGI phrase was coined by one of our long-term team members, Musabek, the production manager. When something went wrong on the conveyor belt, he would say to Michael in his strong Kyrgyzstani accent, 'This experience will help us learn, grow and improve.' Michael loved that expression so much he used it in his feedback sessions as a powerful tool for reframing criticism.

These language modifications extended to the use of simple pronouns too. We never used the word 'I'. It was always 'we'. If something went wrong, no single person would be blamed. While the team leader would ultimately be responsible for the situation, the use of 'we' placed the onus on the entire team to fix it. (You'll notice I refer to 'we' throughout this book. 'I' am telling the story, but the success of Swisse was very much a collaborative effort.)

The word 'problem' was reserved for people with real problems, like those living in war-torn countries. 'We are lucky enough to live in one of the most peaceful nations in the world,' Michael would say, 'so we don't have "problems", we have "challenges".' Once the challenge was identified, he expected the individual to suggest a solution as to how it could be fixed, before raising it with their manager. (It's remarkable how creative people can be when they are given the freedom to find their own solution.) This reduced the learned helplessness that occurs in workplaces and gave people the confidence to take risks, be courageous and think for themselves.

The word 'staff' or 'employee' was replaced with 'team'. We didn't have 'departments', but 'areas of business'. We didn't work 'for' Swisse, we worked 'with' the company. 'Deadlines' became 'timelines.' ('No-one is going to die if we don't get things done,' he would say.) We didn't say, 'The sky is the limit,' we said, 'The sky is the beginning.'

We always aspired to deliver 'Benchmark standards' in everything we did, which was shortened to 'BM'. This provided a reference point for whether an initiative was setting a benchmark, which reminded us that there was always room for improvement.

Email salutations were given special attention. We replaced the words 'Dear' with 'Great day to you!' or 'Sensational day to you'. We even signed off emails with 'Celebrate Life Every Day!' Phone messages were scripted to ensure we greeted people with an upbeat vibe. My voicemail message said, 'Great day to you, we are busy making people healthier and happier so please leave a message and don't forget to Celebrate Life Every Day!'

The only time Michael insisted I change something was when I was on a short holiday. I left an 'out of office' message on my email. He did not like that at all. 'We are always on,' he said. I never left an out of office message again. (This may sound extreme in the current environment that promotes work–life balance, but the point Michael was making was that if you want to build a significant business, you have to be fully invested. This was the perfect advice for me, at that time. It reinforced our goal and the level of commitment that was required to achieve it.)

Words matter

We were highly particular about the words we employed to promote Swisse, both internally and externally, and offered the team a range of words to help them think about situations differently. The table below shows a few of the words we discouraged and their positive alternatives.

FROM	TO
I/Me/My	We/Team/Us/Our
Issue/Problem	Challenge
Execute	Deliver/Roll out
Constructive criticism/Feedback	LGI (Learn, Grow, Improve)
I forgot	I'll set a reminder
I'm exhausted	I need to rest/reset
Can't complain	Everything is going well
I'm busy	I'm having a productive day
Don't	I like it when...
No worries	Definitely/Certainly/Sure thing
Why not	Sounds good
But	And
Deadline	Timeline
Brainstorm	Blue sky
Running 10 minutes late	Running 10 minutes slow

In our experience, establishing a corporate language and culture typically requires about five years of consistent effort. (The real power came when the team members adjusted their own language to take full ownership of those values.)

Newcomers to the team found this focus on positive language a bit saccharine at first but soon discovered what a powerful impact it had on their day-to-day experience of working at Swisse. Errors, slip-ups and missteps were transformed into valuable opportunities for growth and it was this freedom to fail and take risks without fear of reprisals that formed the basis of our Swisse culture.

Michael and I had a lot in common. We were empathic leaders who both understood the power of language, and enjoyed bringing energy and laughter into the workplace. Having fun with words made the serious work of building a successful business a joyous experience, and when we are enjoying ourselves, we bring our best selves to the task at hand.

Don't 'just start'

The prevailing wisdom in the start-up community is to 'just start': to set up the website, hire that first team member, sign those share-holding agreements and bring in those investors. This advice is misguided. Yes, by all means, just start, but just start by *thinking* about what you are going to do, before you actually start doing it. Many irreversible mistakes are made at the start of an entrepreneurial journey — taking on the wrong investors, signing the wrong documents, and hiring the wrong people. These actions can, and often do, jeopardise your successful exit years down the track. Take your time, think about what you're doing and make a plan for how you're going to build the business. Starting with culture is critical.

The makings of a 4P culture

Michael's appreciation of culture, and the role language played in shaping it, led him to create the 'Ten Commandments of Health and Happiness'. This 'manifesto' encapsulated his core values. He believed that language and culture were intertwined, and when language was integrated into everyday workplace conversations, the culture thrived. The team found it challenging to remember all of the ten commandments and, as the tenets were very biblical in nature, some of the more secular team members found it a little confronting. To ensure inclusivity and accessibility for everyone, we distilled it into four values that simplified the core message while preserving the original intention. This symbolic gesture represented my style of leadership and breathed new life into our culture. The four new core principles (4Ps) were:

1. People

2. Principles

3. Passion

4. ... and then Profit.

We believed that culture was not just a set of words, but a set of behaviours, and that people needed to know how those values translated into everyday behaviours. When laid out simply, they became easy to identify and inhabit.

1. People

Our value of putting 'People' first acknowledged that success was achieved through their collective efforts. It meant we:

- respected each other and extended empathy and equality to all

- treated others as we would want to be treated

- celebrated difference and individuality and acknowledged contribution.

Sometimes things were defined by what they were *not,* which is why we also outlined what behaviours people should *not* engage in. This meant we did not:

- work in isolation or in silos

- gossip about people or denigrate others

- shift the blame onto others or be unaccountable.

2. Principles

Our 'Principles' were the guiding lights that determined how we made decisions. It meant we:

- gave accurate and timely feedback that was helpful and positive

- surpassed our 'Happy and Healthy' benchmarks

- acted with integrity and put the interests of our team, customers and environment first.

It also meant we did not:

- act in a dishonest manner

- display an apathetic approach to challenges

- make decisions to further a personal agenda.

3. Passion

Nothing happens without passion; it's the energy that breathes life into the values. Our value of doing everything with 'Passion' meant we:

- lived in alignment with our values and Celebrated Life Every Day

- went the extra mile to exceed expectations

- brought our best selves to every encounter.

It also meant we did not:

- shy away from challenging the status quo

- let emotion cloud our reasoning

- accept second best.

4. ...and Profit will follow

Putting profit last was controversial and confusing to many, but we knew that if our first three values were in alignment, profit would take care of itself. Our value of 'Profit' meant that we:

- worked collaboratively to create successful business results

- focused on the bigger picture when making decisions

- rewarded people who delivered great outcomes.

It also meant we did not:

- resist change or stymie progress

- waste resources, abuse privileges or be complacent

- become defensive.

● ● ●

I was truly inspired by this framework of culture and language, and saw it as a leadership fundamental. It made us stop and think about our words and behaviour before we said or did something. The best move I made in bringing the company forward was respecting and evolving this amazing heritage. We took the best of it and, as we grew, we adapted it for a much bigger team. Creating a constructive culture was our point of difference and a reference for how we'd always strive to do what was right, for the person and then the business, in that order.

CHAPTER 8

AN IMPRESSIVE INDUCTION

Despite Michael's belief that mistakes were an opportunity for growth, I believed that the challenges that I faced upon arrival – the packaging, manufacturing and marketing issues – needed to be addressed, and I needed to take responsibility for what was happening. Why were these issues occurring? What were we doing wrong? What did we need to learn?

Michael and Stephen were supportive of me during this challenging time and we all pitched in to solve this never-ending litany of issues. We acknowledged that some of these decisions had been made long before my arrival, but the fruits of these decisions were occurring under my purview; I was now responsible for them and it was up to me to address them. I felt the pressure to take control, maintain stability and demonstrate my leadership capabilities so we could start to deliver improved results.

When I started at Swisse, Michael devised a three-month induction process to school me in the 'Swisse Way'. This program enabled me to shadow individuals from every area within the business – marketing, sales, human resources, warehousing, logistics, manufacturing – and observe their daily routines to see how their roles contributed to the wider operation of the company. I also went out on the road with the territory mangers and met the pharmacy buyers, observed the customers, talked to them and asked them questions about why they did or did not buy Swisse. Interestingly, I was never invited to attend the finance meetings, and I was never given access to the Profit and Loss statements. I didn't know if this was an oversight, or whether Michael feared I would leave the firm and take the information to a competitor. I let it go, thinking he'd eventually share the information with me at the next meeting, but the next meeting came and went, and then the next, and still no access.

I eventually said, 'Michael, I appreciate that I'm new and that the finances of the company are confidential, but at what point will you share them with me? I need to know where we stand so I can see what needs to be done.'

He said, 'I'll reveal them in due course, but for now I want you to focus on doing what you think needs to be done. What do you see? What do you hear? What do you feel? Do that. Don't rely on the numbers to tell you what needs doing. Rely on your gut instinct, hone that and let that guide your decision making.'

Eventually he did share the numbers with me, but in hindsight denying me access was a profound form of management training. Any MBA worth its salt tells you that the first thing you must do is 'get the numbers'; that 'the numbers will tell you everything'. Well, that may be so, but those numbers may also cloud your judgement about what is happening right in front of your very eyes. This one act of counterintuitive training gave me the confidence to rely on my gut instinct. While the numbers provided valuable data, they did not always tell the whole story — and to rely upon them exclusively to make a decision was unwise. This induction was a wonderful start to my career at Swisse, and ignited a commitment to provide induction programs for all members of our team.

Don't rely (just) on numbers to make decisions

Not getting access to the Profit and Loss statement in the early part of my induction was gold. It forced me to ask questions, listen, learn from others, strengthen my gut instinct, and trust my judgement. Deep dives into data and financials are important but they should not be relied upon in isolation to make important decisions.

Stephen had a very different approach to business. He would wander into the office wearing board shorts, thongs and a T-shirt, say a casual 'hello' to whoever was there and then come into my office for a chat. You'd never guess he was the majority owner. He was very understated, and had a larrikin charm and charisma that endeared him to all. Stephen and I naturally aligned on various fronts, especially when it came to strategy and taking calculated risks. While he described himself as a gambler, the truth was his intelligence and tactical thinking greatly narrowed the odds, which increased his chances of success. He and Michael were an exceptional team and my arrival completed the triumvirate. After all my years of proving myself at Village, I had finally earned my place at the table and I was excited to become part of their trusted team.

Six months after joining Swisse, Michael and Stephen appointed me to the role of General Manager and doubled my salary from $130 000 to $260 000. I was stoked to be earning such great money at such a young age. Clearly, they saw my potential and didn't let my early missteps cloud their opinion of me.

To grow you have to let go

Swisse and Village operated at very different speeds. Village was a 24/7, 365 days a week business. We had thousands of team members, tens of thousands of customers coming through each day, and an endless supply of urgent situations that needed fixing. *The oven in Gold Class is broken. The safe won't open. The toilet is blocked.* I was constantly getting calls at 2 am to attend to something.

Swisse, on the other hand had a much slower pace, which I initially found unsettling as I was so used to running at full tilt each day. But this unhurried rhythm gave me time to absorb and reflect on what was happening. I was in my flow and could see very clearly where I could take this business.

I had spent a lot of time on the road gaining an informal education, but I was pragmatic enough to recognise that I had gaps in my leadership training and that in order to become the well-rounded manager the business demanded, I would need to do further study. I relished this opportunity to gain new skills. It would help me find solutions to the issues we were facing, and give me some time away from the office and the space I needed to reset my perspective.

I went back to Melbourne Business School, where I had learned those all-important financial skills years earlier. This leadership course was an extension of the course I had done on the 360-degree feedback process, and it delved into a cornucopia of topics:

- emotional intelligence
- ethical decision making
- purpose-driven leadership
- social responsibility

and provided me with a comprehensive understanding of concepts I had instinctively grasped but had not formally learned.

This course also reinforced my belief that culture was critical to the success of a company, and gave me the confidence to integrate the concept of culture into our workplace in a more formal and process-driven way. I knew I would have the support of Michael and Stephen to make these changes. But would I have it from the team? They were very set in their ways, and were already showing signs of dissent.

Who's the boss?

When I got back to work, I implemented some of the principles I had learned and, as I suspected, these changes were met with suspicion. 'Who is this new guy?' 'Why is he making all these changes?' 'Who does he think he is?' was the common refrain. My rise through the management ranks had rankled a few who thought they were in line for the promotion. I was in charge of the day-to-day functions of the business, and Michael, as well as Stephen, worked with me on the strategy and governance. After working closely with Michael for a time, it was obvious to me that a lack of structure and processes were holding the business back; that he had tapped out and had lost his passion for running the business on a day-to-day level. It didn't help that Michael was still taking meetings with many of the senior team, and was hearing their stories about how I was to blame for the woes that had befallen the company; all the usual gripes that occur when change is afoot.

We humans tend to favour familiarity and will go to great lengths to preserve the status quo. However, in our case at Swisse, change was imperative. We couldn't afford to continue with the failures and shortcomings that hindered our progress. We had to streamline communication, clarify roles, establish clear lines of reporting, and set up systems and processes that would enable our operation to thrive. The future success of the company rested on my shoulders, and I was responsible for the transformation. However, I realised that without the support and commitment of the team, my efforts would be in vain.

The leadership course helped me realise that there was a bigger issue at play. In short, the team did not know who the boss was. I was the General Manager, the official boss with formal authority, but Michael was the Managing Director, and in the office just one day a week. It was the old versus the new, and the team preferred the old. I quickly learned that a person cannot serve two masters, and the team at Swisse were now being asked to do exactly that, and it was creating confusion.

Stephen attended weekly meetings with Michael and I but he was very much the hands-off, semi-silent partner. Michael, however, was very much a hands-on guy, and he had his hands on *everything*. He was what Peter Gerber, the author of *The E-myth*, called the 'technician' – or indeed, the technician's technician. He loved getting stuck into every aspect of the company, and why wouldn't he? He knew more than anyone about how the company operated, and his passion for it was infectious, but how can a company grow when the knowledge, wisdom and processes are buried in the mind of one man?

Like many great entrepreneurs, he was a perfectionist, which occasionally led to micromanaging. He'd write long, detailed emails to the team dealing with an insignificant issue, or create amazing advertisements that would never get released because we'd miss the timeline due to all the last-minute tweaking. He'd want to sign off on everything, which absolved people of their ability to take responsibility for their actions. Nothing went out the door without Michael's approval. I shared the desire for excellence in everything we produced, however, I firmly believed that near perfection, rather than absolute perfection, was sufficient. The bottlenecks were challenging, but who was I to tell Michael what to do? It was his company and I was just an employee, but something needed to change. We needed to have a chat. I hoped it wouldn't be hard.

Strategy in the sauna

As it turned out, the chat wasn't hard at all. Fortunately, Michael was ready to leave the day-to-day management of the company to me. He openly admitted that his hunger to contribute to the expansion of the firm had peaked and he was pleased that he could finally hand over the reins to someone he trusted. He would still be intimately involved with the research and product development aspects, but he would remove himself from the daily decision making so that the lines of reporting would be clear and I could get on with the business of leading.

Michael and I still met up, but outside the office, mostly at the Park Hyatt Hotel in East Melbourne. We'd meet at 6 am, have breakfast and then head up to the gym for a sauna. I thought that was a bit weird at the start, but I think he was keen to help me curb my partying ways and thought a regular dawn detox might be a good way to do it. It was. I took the hint and cleaned up my act. Besides, I couldn't burn the candle at both ends and do what I needed to do. This job was all encompassing.

Our meetings covered a lot of ground. We talked about research and development, product innovation, team development, brand identity and science. Michael talked endlessly about the importance of having hero lines like we had in the Men's and Women's Ultivite Multivitamins, and how we needed to be very careful about any other products pulling focus from these. We also planned for what the future of Swisse would look like. I had big goals and Michael could see that I was hungry for success.

When Michael set an expectation of $50 million turnover, I said, 'Let's think bigger.' I knew Centrum had globally turned over $1 billion in revenue, and I knew we were better than them on every level. To my mind, there was absolutely no reason why we could not be the same size as them, or bigger. I turned to Michael and boldly proclaimed, 'Let's set our sights on $100 million and become Australia's number one multivitamin brand. Once we've achieved that, we'll build a billion-dollar global enterprise and become Australia's number one *natural health brand*,' which was a much more valuable and coveted milestone than just being the number one multivitamin brand.

We shook on that and I poured a cup of water over the red-hot glistening coals. The heat was being turned up in more ways than one, and I was up for the challenge. I loved setting big, bold goals, and considering we were only turning over $16 million at the time, aiming to build a billion-dollar business was more than audacious.

Start with the end in mind

If you want to build a business and sell it for the highest possible fee, begin with the end in mind and work backwards. If you start as you intend to finish, you'll get there quicker as you'll know what to aim for. In our case, we wanted to build a billion-dollar business. Business buyers use 'multiples' to value a business. They take the multiple (a number that varies by business sector, see table below) and multiply it by the business's EBITDA (earnings before interest, taxes, depreciation and assets — a simplified view of how much money a company is making) to determine the value of the business. We knew the multiple in our case would be around 10 to 15, which meant we'd need an EBITDA of $75–100 million to achieve a billion-dollar valuation.

When you know what you want, and can see it clearly, it's much easier to achieve it. If you understand how the multiples in your industry are calculated, you can identify the value of your business, get excited about what that means to you, and then put plans in place to achieve your goal. The key is to build a business you are passionate about and then the money will follow.

(Our multiple ended up being around 14, near the top of the range for our industry. For the record, a good result in any sector is to achieve 7 × EBITDA. As you can see from the table below, Swisse was at the top end of the quotient for every sector, including tech.)

Sector	Multiple
Professional services	5–12
Financial	7–12
Food processing	5–10
Education	5–12
IT and Digital	6–14
Energy, Power and Utilities	6–10
Transport and Logistics	5–10
Healthcare	6–14
Tourism	5–12

On the road

With Michael out of the office, I now had the chance to put my stamp on the company. We changed a lot of things: the management structure, the approvals process, and the recruitment criteria. In addition, we:

- empowered the senior management team to contribute to the strategy and gave them ownership of how those plans would be implemented. They'd never been given this freedom before and they responded eagerly to the challenges.

- shut down the manufacturing arm that had given us so much grief with ProvenSlim and SBS1, and focused on being a great product innovation, sales and marketing company, rather than a great manufacturing company.

- deleted old brands or brought them in under the Swisse banner, created more retailer promotions, found out exactly what retailers wanted and then harnessed our resources to give it to them.

- further improved our trading terms with our suppliers and customers so we had more time to pay those who made our stock, and got paid more quickly by those who sold it.

- hired first-rate creative agencies to create eye-popping, attention-grabbing point-of-sale posters, fliers and stands so that our in-store promotions were the first thing people saw when they walked in the retailer's door.

One of the most important things I did was go on the road and spend time with the territory managers to see first-hand the challenges they faced. This also gave me the opportunity to witness the consumers in action. What better way to gain market research intel than by watching the consumer pick the product off the shelf?

We discovered early on that you can advertise all you like, but when that 'ground zero' moment hits – when the consumer plucks a product from the shelf – it's the point-of-sale (and specifically, the point-of-sale on or near the shelf where the product is located) that makes all the difference. ('Point-of-sale' refers to a range of collateral pieces like posters and 'end caps' – the vertical display panels placed at the end of an aisle – that help a retailer draw attention to a particular product.) It's widely accepted by everyone in retail that the key purchasing decision is made when the customer sees the product on the shelf.

I spent time with the pharmacy assistants who stocked the shelves, learned what they needed and what we could do to make their lives easier. They were our 'first' customer and if we got them on board, we'd have a higher chance of being recommended to *their* customer. From the start, I made a point of sitting in on the meetings with the buyers from the pharmacies so that I could get a deeper understanding of their requirements. As a manager, attending these meetings was a pivotal decision. The buyers were impressed that the head of the company had taken the time to call on them, learn about their business and find out what they needed. This was not standard procedure. They were used to dealing with low-level account managers from the big pharmaceutical companies who had little autonomy and even less power to make decisions on the run. This worked in our favour because with me in the room, we could close a deal quickly, have the paperwork signed off and a pre-order placed before the competitor's rep had got back to their car. Now that we'd streamlined the decision-making process, and removed the brakes that had caused the bottlenecks, everyone was empowered to do things more quickly. The buyers appreciated this speedy decision making and it meant we got more deals approved.

Sit in on meetings

Our pharmacy buyers were not used to seeing the head of the company sit in on their meetings and were flattered that I took the time to find out more about their businesses. This helped turn around approvals more quickly, and it helped us build solid relationships that stood the test of time. These buyers understood our customers and the broader trends and offered us many pearls of strategic wisdom. If you can, meet in person with your customers as frequently as you can. They are the lifeblood of your business.

Our processes were being validated by retailers and our strategies were winning. Sales had increased by 100 per cent from the previous year, the mood was buoyant, everyone was excited at where we were heading, and, most importantly, our culture was thriving.

Hello Helen

I had a huge capacity for work and really enjoyed the challenge of re-booting this business, but I was losing myself in the job and needed to find some balance. Truth be told, I was a bit lonely too. I was tired of coming home to an empty flat with nothing but pizza and a cold beer to keep me company. I really wanted to meet someone, but nothing ever seemed to go smoothly or click in the way that I hoped it would. My last relationship had been a bit toxic and tempestuous and it did not make me feel good about myself. The residue of that experience made me question my self-worth.

My mate invited me to a nightclub for a few drinks one evening. I was non-committal. I was tired from a big week at work and planned on having a quiet night. But I knew I was unlikely to meet the love of my life sitting at home waiting for my pizza to arrive, so I went out. I am so glad I did: it was the night I met Helen. I spilt a drink on her (by accident, I hasten to add — it wasn't a strategy to gain her attention). She was gracious about it, ridiculously so, and we spoke for hours that night and connected on so many levels. I knew I just had to see her again.

A week later, we had a wonderful dinner at The George Wine Room in St Kilda, which reinforced that I definitely wanted to see her again. On the other hand, I didn't want to burden Helen with helping me get over that toxic relationship, so we tried being friends, avoiding each other, and even having a casual relationship. After six months of this, and with the added pressure of Helen moving to Brisbane for a new job opportunity with Virgin Velocity, we finally admitted that we couldn't resist each other. Helen quit her job in Brisbane after just three months, returned to Melbourne and I asked her to move in with me. She was only a few years older than me but light years ahead in wisdom, and wisely thought we should wait a while. Twelve months later, she moved in.

Coming home to Helen each night made work so much more enjoyable. I loved my job but it was relentless. We had big targets to hit and I was only as good as my last month's results, and if I wasn't hitting the targets, I was not doing my job. The worst part? I had set the targets!

The pressure was on, but coming home now was a joy. For a start, I had a reason to go home. Helen possessed the remarkable ability to transform a house into a haven and crafted a sanctuary filled with candles, cushions and home cooking that shielded me from the stresses and intense dynamics of the business world. She gave me the balance and strength I needed to take a step back and see the bigger picture. I could be a little blunt sometimes and her presence softened me. Her positivity was infectious and, with her strong background in senior marketing roles, she totally understood what my world was like and provided much needed advice and solace. We both shared a deep desire to make the world a better place. Our relationship was based on challenging each other and becoming more evolved individuals as a result of being together. She made me a better man.

She also believed, as I did, that our products had the power to bring positive change to the world. We believed that if we could all achieve happiness and good health, the world would be a better place with less suffering, and everyone could fulfil their full potential. Naïve? Maybe, for the cynical, but we believed it to be true.

Merge your passion with profit

People often ask me what business or industry they should get into. My advice is to not get caught up in what industry or sector you work in. Get caught up in what you love doing, merge it with what you're good at, and find a way to get paid for it. I never set out to be a vitamin salesperson but I was good at sales and I loved health, so it made sense to combine the two. You may be great with numbers. That doesn't mean you need to become an accountant or work in a bank. Go deeper. What do you love? What do you enjoy doing? Maybe it's football? If so, combine the two and merge your love of numbers with football and find a career in finance in a football club. Think laterally. Do what makes you happy. You will be better at it if you are.

CHAPTER 9

THE POWER
OF CELEBRITY

I thrived on the dynamic energy and passion that propelled the Swisse team during this exhilarating period of rapid growth. One aspect from my Village experience that was definitely missing, however, was the influence of celebrity power in driving sales. The movie business was sexy and the celebrity factor generated excitement about upcoming events: 'What's Brad Pitt really like?', 'When's the next Mission Impossible coming out?' and the inevitable, 'Can you get me some free tickets?'

I noticed this phenomenon when I talked to people at social events. I used to be able to wax lyrical about Hollywood and superheroes; now I was talking about health and wholefoods, and nobody was that interested. Here's how the conversations at a Sunday BBQ generally went now:

'So, what do you do?'

'I work at Swisse.'

'The embassy?'

'No, the vitamin company.'

'Gee, is that the time? Gotta run.'

And off they'd go.

If I managed to hold their attention for an extra moment, I'd try to keep the conversation going by finding out a bit about their health. I'd ask them, 'What vitamins do you take?' If they took anything, it was always Centrum. 'Why do you take that?' I'd ask.

'Because the champion runner Rob de Castella recommends it, so it must be okay,' they'd say.

The only reason they remembered what they took was because of the brand ambassador who promoted it. By this stage, they were inching to get away from me, fearful that I was going to ask them about their Irritable Bowel Syndrome or urinary tract infection, or worse. As the conversation went on, I could see their eyes widen a little, a look of fear come over their face, and they'd change the topic quickly to the weather or the footy — anything but their health.

These awkward encounters revealed people's underlying perception: vitamins were dull, a topic to be whispered about, an embarrassment. These chitchats also revealed to me what vitamins were *not*. They were not sexy, they were not acceptable topics of conversation, and they were not something people enjoyed taking.

After multiple conversations like this, I had a startling revelation! Vitamins needed a revamp, and not just Swisse vitamins, but *all* vitamins — *the entire industry needed a makeover.* We needed to make health and wellness an acceptable topic of conversation. The enormity of this challenge was not lost on me. How do you change the way an entire nation thinks about their health? And how do you do it on a limited budget? That's when it struck me. This wasn't a makeover; this was a *movement,* and we were going to lead it.

I knew what I needed to do. I needed to bring the cult of celebrity into the world of vitamins and make vitamins an aspirational topic of conversation. Centrum had brought a celebrity on board. So could we. We had a fraction of their budget so I knew I'd have to break the rules somehow to beat them at their own game, but I was up for the challenge.

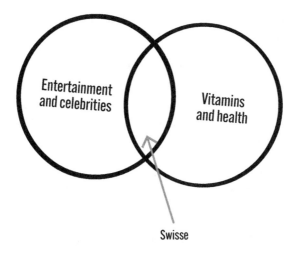

Swisse

Swisse landed where entertainment and celebrities met vitamins and health.

A formula for success

Our goal was clear. We needed to make 'health' aspirational. But how? I racked my brain to come up with new and innovative concepts. It was a challenging task. My dad wrote the dietary guidelines for the 'Life. Be In It.' public health campaign in 1975, and he told me later how hard it had been to change the mindset and movement patterns of a nation. I now had to do the same. But if the government couldn't do it with all their resources, we would need to get super creative to fulfil this mission. So, I did what I always do when I need inspiration and motivation: I hit the road.

I visited dozens of pharmacies around the nation to see what they were doing and how they were doing it. I walked up and down the vitamin aisle of each and noticed that while Swisse was shoved into the bottom corner of the shelf, Centrum had wall-to-wall coverage. This was not surprising. Centrum was a division of Pfizer, one of the world's largest pharmaceutical companies, and they spent millions on their advertising. Life-size posters of Robert de Castella hung from the ceiling. The end cap (often the first thing a customer sees when they walk into the store, which offers a significant advantage to those who use them) featured Robert holding up the Centrum bottle, his moustachioed face grinning from ear to ear. The catalogues at the front counter had Rob on the cover spruiking the benefits. The older demographic loved Rob, and with good reason: he was an outstanding bloke. But Centrum was not an outstanding product, by any metric, and that's what made this wall-to-wall coverage so confounding.

It was common knowledge that Centrum was an inferior product to Swisse. Their product lacked the therapeutic dosage that made our tablets so effective. That's precisely why customers kept choosing Swisse. Even the pharmacists said, 'Swisse sells itself. Once people try it, they stick with it.'

I said to one of the pharmacy buyers, 'If our product is so good, why do you give Centrum more shelf space than us? Do you make more money selling Centrum?'

'No, it has the worst margin of the lot,' she said.

'So why do you devote so much space to it?'

'Because we sell so much of it.'

'And why do you sell so much of it?'

'Because they advertise on television 52 weeks a year,' she said.

'I see. What else do they do that we don't?'

'They have Rob as their ambassador, which means we don't have to work so hard to sell it. The customer sees the poster and buys it.'

'What else do Centrum do that we don't?'

'They give us loads of posters and other point-of-sale material, and they come and set it all up for us,' she said.

Like Nick Giannopoulos with his *Wog Boy* promotional material, I realised. 'So, let me get this straight. Despite being an inferior product with low profitability, they sell more than anyone else due to their year-round TV advertising, their prominent ambassador, and abundant point-of-sale materials. And as a result, you allocate them the most shelf space throughout the store. Is that correct?'

'That's correct,' she said.

These were the simple yet profound reasons behind why Centrum had snared so much shelf space.

Now we had the formula for success. The only challenge was, we didn't have the budget to do a fraction of what Centrum did. How could we compete with their multimillion-dollar advertising budgets and their hordes of sales reps and merchandisers? If we wanted to take shelf space off Centrum, we would have to do things differently and find a way to beat them at their own game.

How often should a sales rep call on a retailer?

Sales is a delicate balancing act. Call too often, and you become a nuisance. Call too infrequently, you don't make an impact. As we grew, we needed to make sure that every store, and every sale within each store, was as profitable as could be. The table below shows the formula we used to determine the frequency of contact. Stores were graded (A–D) based on their sales.

Grade	Annual sales	Service
A	Extra high	Visit the store monthly (twice per month is optimal), plus weekly phone contact.
B	High	Visit the story monthly, plus weekly phone contact.
C	Medium	Visit the store bi-monthly.
D	Low	Managed by phone only though Swisse support office.

The numbers you use to calculate your sales contact formula will vary depending on who you deal with and what you sell. What's important to note is that you should have a sales contact guideline that lets your sales team know what's expected of them. This helped us manage our sales team's time and ensured that their efforts were funnelled into stores that could achieve the outcomes we wanted.

Borrowing from the beauty aisle

The advertising landscape for the multivitamin sector was littered with 'me-too' marketing campaigns. Strip out the logo for any vitamin advertising and it was indistinguishable from any other: same music, same script, same scenery. Other than Centrum, companies such as Blackmores and Nature's Own all used the same old health- and science-focused claims – quick fixes for specific health issues – to sell the product. They all followed the herd.

I invested significant time traversing the aisles of those pharmacies. Since I lacked access to financial data, this was my primary method for discerning how to persuade both retailers and customers to select our product. I'd stop the customer before they bought a product and ask them why they chose that particular product. It was an unorthodox research process, but powerful, and necessary. We needed to see how the sales process worked 'in situ' because numbers did not always tell you how or why people behaved in the way that they did. Being in-store, talking to the buyers and watching how real people bought a product did.

To the casual observer, I was aimlessly wandering down the aisle, but I was hard at work. This was my classroom, where all our investments in marketing, science, production and finance came together; it was the moment of truth when customers made their choice.

I was interested in what happened in the other aisles too, and in particular the beauty aisle. There was something different about this aisle. It took me a moment to realise the difference, but when I did it was blindingly obvious. It was the lighting! The fluorescent lighting in the vitamin aisle was bright, harsh and unforgiving. Conversely, the LED lighting in the beauty aisle was soft, diffused and flattering.

The merchandising and point-of-sale materials were different too. The big cosmetic brands like L'Oreal used supermodels such as Cindy Crawford, Kate Moss and Gisèle Bündchen as brand ambassadors. Their glorious faces were featured everywhere – on the posters, packaging, promotional stands, and price tags. Surrounded by all this aspirational beauty, you couldn't help but feel inspired.

Borrow from the best

We've never made any secret of the fact that we borrow from the best. Why wouldn't you? Companies bigger and better than ours have spent millions honing their craft. It would be silly not to see what others have done and try it out for yourself.

The lesson I took from this revelation was that health is our most precious asset and this is the true form of aspiration we at Swisse should be plugging into. Outer beauty was superficial; true beauty came from within, and when people were in peak physical condition it showed in their outlook and demeanour. These were the kinds of people we loved to be around. To my mind, this was the kind of holistic beauty we should aspire to, and I believed very strongly that we could play a role in helping people achieve that.

And that's when it hit me.

We needed to take a leaf out of the L'Oreal playbook.

We needed to make vitamins sexy.

We needed more celebrities ...

CHAPTER 10

WHO'S RICKY?

Choosing Ricky Ponting, Australia's cricket captain, as a celebrity ambassador to inspire women to buy vitamins may not have been the most obvious choice. After all, cricket is not most women's favourite sport.

So why pick Rick? Because to be different we had to 'do' different, and being paradoxical was part of that.

The strategy behind using Ricky Ponting as an ambassador was to inspire an unfit, uninspired middle-aged man to improve his health by motivating him to 'take what Ricky takes'. This, in turn, would motivate his wife to pop a bottle of vitamins in the shopping basket for him (and hopefully a bottle for herself as well) so they could cultivate a shared commitment to better health.

When we presented the Ricky Ponting concept to Dimi Papantoniou, the buyer at Priceline, she said, 'Who's Ricky?' That remark worried us a bit: if other buyers felt the same lack of engagement with our brand ambassador, the campaign could be an expensive failure. But I was certain this counterintuitive strategy was the right approach to take.

Making the deal

Looking back, it's easy to see how all those pieces of the campaign came together. At the time, it was like putting together a jigsaw puzzle without knowing what the final picture on the box was. Here's how the campaign unfolded.

Michael had already built a relationship with Simone Austin, the dietician from the Australian Cricket Team, so we knew the players were already using our products. We reached out to the team management to see if they were interested in being our partner. They were, but they wanted us to pay them a hefty $300 000 for the privilege of using the phrase 'Powering the Australian Cricket Team' in our advertisements. Given the relatively modest impact we anticipated we'd get from using this one tagline, we decided to forgo the opportunity. This experience, however, did spark a thought: If securing the endorsement of the entire cricket team came at such a high cost, how much would it require to enlist a single player, like Ricky Ponting?

We offered Ricky $250 000 per year to be our brand ambassador, and he agreed! It was still a big investment for us, more than we, or anyone in the industry, had ever spent on an ambassador, but it would give us more freedom to build campaigns around him than if we chose to sponsor the entire cricket team. It was a risk we believed was worth taking. With Ricky on board, the first piece of the puzzle was in place.

Now we had to get the pharmacy retailers on board. Many, like Dimi, the Priceline buyer, queried the logic of using Ricky, but when we explained our paradoxical strategy, they eagerly got behind it – so much so, we pre-sold over $5 million in stock, three times what we'd normally sell-in, before we had even started the campaign. Securing this large sell-in before the campaign began enabled us to de-risk the campaign, defray our advertising costs and go full-tilt with the rest of our plan.

Sell-in and sell-through

The 'sell-in' is the art of the sales and marketing team to persuade a buyer to *take on* a certain amount of stock. 'Sell-through' is the art of the sales and marketing team to *drive the sales* of that product so that it flies off the shelf. Our success came from being great at both, especially in helping our retailers with sell-through. This boosted sales and rewarded them for committing to buying so much stock in advance.

The second piece of the puzzle of getting the retailers on board was locked and loaded.

Now for the production of the advertisement. First up, we had to get cut-through with our TV commercials. Other than Centrum, the big brands focused specifically on the health claims about how it would help alleviate the symptoms of IBS or UTI. These campaigns were boring and completely lacking in aspiration. Our goal was to help the customer take that first step towards creating a healthy life. Once they took that first vitamin, they were on the road to being more mindful of their health. With our marketing budget mostly spent on Ricky, we couldn't afford to spend the standard $150 000 to shoot a 30-second TV commercial, so I had to pull in a few favours to cut costs. I approached Stewart Byfield, the creative director at our agency, and said, 'Can you shoot two TV commercials for $25 000 each?' He looked askance at me but agreed, knowing that success would lead to more collaborations. He was also a veteran in the field and took it on as an exciting challenge.

The third piece of the puzzle of producing the TV commercials on a budget was in place.

Now for the point-of-sale. We went all out and created the most stunning, impactful, and colourful merchandising collateral the industry had ever seen, and plastered the stores with wall-to-wall Ricky paraphernalia. We also instructed our team to go in-store and set it all up for the retailer to relieve them of this arduous task, just as Centrum did.

The fourth piece of the puzzle was complete.

'Can you recommend ... ?' is probably the most asked question in a pharmacy. We knew this to be the case, so we needed the support of the pharmacy team to recommend our product. (This wasn't hard as the pharmacy proprietor now had hordes of Swisse tubs stacked to the roof out the back and wanted to get rid of the stock as much as we did.)

All the pieces of the puzzle were now in place.

We didn't have the luxury of airing our ads on TV 52 weeks a year like Centrum. We did not want to do a slow drip campaign and string it out over months. We needed to make a big splash, be everywhere all at once, and completely own that mass audience for that small window of time during the cricket broadcast. I felt sure this unorthodox approach would work. Our competitors thought we were bonkers. The sentiment was, 'You guys are crazy. What a waste of money! Spending hundreds of thousands on a male brand ambassador. Placing all your advertisements in one show with a predominantly male audience. Shooting budget TV commercials. That's not how it's done.'

'I know,' was my response. 'That's why we're doing it.'

Now we just had to cross our fingers and wait for the results to come in.

What's the worst that can happen?

Let me be clear here. The Ponting campaign was a massive risk for us. We'd never spent this much on an ambassador, and we'd certainly never spent this much on TV advertising, let alone the mammoth amounts of point-of-sale stock we had created to support it. This was our biggest gamble to date and if it didn't work, it would be a very painful pill to swallow. That said, the biggest brands in the world had used this formula and it worked for them. They sponsored big events and worked with personalities that demanded huge endorsement fees. We were doing what they were doing, but going that step further by optimising the marketing strategy and creating a highly integrated campaign.

Michael, Stephen and I had all collaborated on the strategy and agreed it was exactly what we needed. As always, we applied our trusted decision-making litmus test by asking, 'What's the worst that can happen?' Yes, this was a big gamble for us, but we had mitigated the risk by getting such a big sell-in to start with, which covered our costs of advertising. But if the strategy proved unsustainable, we all agreed that we'd just scale back our operations, return to our humble beginnings and revert to the days of personally picking, packing and shipping the products to our loyal list of customers, akin to the roles Michael and Stephen assumed when they took over from Kevin Ring all those years ago. This 'worst-case scenario' planning philosophy guided us through all our major investments. If we could handle the potential consequences, we proceeded with confidence and went ahead and did it.

What's the worst-case scenario?

What's the worst that can happen? Plan for this because you'll probably end up there quicker than you think, and don't be surprised when you do. It's the nature of business. Can you live with it? If so, go ahead. If not, walk away.

The advertisements went to air and the campaign was a sensation. Within one month, sales of Ultivite for Men, our flagship product, grew by over 100 per cent. Sales of Ultivite for Women grew by over 75 per cent. (Considering we weren't even overtly targeting women in this campaign, that was an amazing result.) Within five months, sales had skyrocketed from $15 million to over $30 million. As we'd hoped, many women were so excited to see their men finally taking care of their own health, they decided to get on the bandwagon and switch from their existing brand to us.

Our tagline 'Tired? Stressed? You'll feel better on Swisse' began to get some serious cut-through. When I heard people on public transport jokingly respond to a friend's complaint about being tired or stressed with, 'You'll feel better on Swisse', I knew we were onto something. We hit the jackpot when Hughesy, Kate and Dave, Nova Radio's top-rating radio team, awarded our TV campaign the highly coveted, much-vaunted title of 'Most Annoying Advertisement'. I loved having this reverse compliment come our way. As far as I was concerned, there was only one thing worse than being talked about, and that was *not* being talked about. And *everyone* was talking about us.

An unorthodox approach

Our sales strategy went against everything that the traditional marketing playbook recommended. Our goal was to simply persuade the pharmacy assistants to purchase our product, recommend it to the customers and feel confident in doing so. We didn't mention anything to do with 'targeting a specific audience', or 'TARPS', or 'sell-through', or 'grocery buyers'. These pharmacy buyers weren't marketers and they didn't understand that kind of language. We needed them to firstly understand the sales proposition themselves, and secondly, sell the concept internally to the rest of their team. Our mission was to give them the ammunition they needed to help them convince the rest of their team that buying thousands of boxes of stock for their hundreds of stores was a good idea. We knew our sales pitch had to be simple, memorable and repeatable, so we ensured our key 'takeaways' were as clear and direct as possible:

- We're sponsoring the cricket.

- We've got Ricky Ponting.

- Customers will be asking for it.

- We will own the summer of sport.

- You will get bonus stock.

- You will get discounts.

- You've got to get behind this campaign.

This was the punchy sales pitch that the buyers could take back to their team and repeat without effort.

Learn how to sell

Selling strikes fear into the heart of even the most accomplished and confident person. The fear of being seen as pushy, aggressive or self-serving often underpin this reluctance. But selling is the essence of business. Nothing happens without a sale. Some are born with this innate ability to sell; it comes naturally and effortlessly to them. I was fortunate to be born with this gene, but I am not the sort of salesperson who can sell something I don't believe in. Natural medicine had been a part of my life as my dad had been recommending it in his role as a doctor and professor of surgery for many years, long before it became fashionable. Selling vitamins to help people become happier and healthier was a perfect fit for me as I talked about them all the time anyway.

Whatever you sell, it has to be easy for you to talk about with energy and enthusiasm. If you can't, or don't want to sell, you are simply selling the wrong product. Follow your passion and selling will become easy. If you want to be successful in business, you must master the art of sales.

Our groundbreaking campaign attracted attention and generated a month-on-month growth of 50 per cent. It was gratifying to see these outstanding results come in, particularly when so many had been critical of our strategy. David Ogilvy, the advertising guru from the 1950s, had a famous quote: 'We know 50 per cent of our advertising works; we just don't know which 50 per cent.' That was not the case for us; we knew precisely which aspect of our formula made the difference. We knew that placing a superstar at the centre of our advertising campaign, buying up the media for the duration of that one broadcast or TV show, and using point-of-sale material at the place of purchase dramatically increased our chances of success.

We finally had a formula for disrupting the market and were eager to replicate this winning formula in future endeavours.

CHAPTER 11

THE CREDIT CRUNCH NO-ONE SAW COMING

The success of the Ricky Ponting campaign came with some unintended consequences. After all, it's impossible to double your sales virtually overnight without it affecting other aspects of the business. The demand created by the campaign affected every area of the business: production, warehousing, logistics, finance, sales, marketing and merchandising. We were not unprepared, but we were taken aback by the success. We had to rapidly scale up to meet the demand, which required a significant financial investment. We were already investing everything we had in the growth of the business, and had always prioritised growth over profit, but this incredible demand for products put a strain on our cash flow.

The Global Financial Crisis (GFC) of 2007 didn't help matters. The GFC was a severe worldwide economic event triggered by the collapse of the US housing market. It led to a banking and credit crisis, widespread foreclosures, and a worldwide recession, which meant banks simply couldn't access money to loan their customers. Governments everywhere implemented large-scale interventions to stabilise financial markets and prevent further economic downturn.

The headlines in the news each day were terrifying:

- 'Financial Meltdown: Wall Street in Crisis as Lehman Brothers Collapse'

- 'Economic Tsunami: Global Markets Plunge'

- 'Stock Market Crash: Worst Crisis Since the Great Depression'.

I tried not to let these doomsday headlines get to me, so I put into action what I'd often read about and knew to be true. When there's a downturn, you don't cut back on adverting and branding; you double down on it. McDonald's, Apple and Amazon all famously invested in their brands during the GFC, as did Toyota in the recession of 1990, and Pepsi in the 1974 crash. They all had the courage to do what others were afraid to do and they prevailed. We would do the same. On the upside, advertising would be cheaper, there'd be less competition for attention, and we'd have more opportunity to stand out.

We just needed to get our heads around how the GFC would affect us. No-one knew what was going to happen next. In theory, health categories like ours tended to experience an *increase* in sales during tough times, as people could not afford to get sick or take time off work. And women, in particular, saw vitamins as an affordable luxury that made them feel good, similar to buying a lipstick or getting a massage. Our major concern, as always, was to ensure we had enough stock on the shelf to cater for demand.

The domino effect came into play. When the banks tightened up their lending criteria, it made it harder for distributors to get credit, so they stopped ordering stock. They normally held 12 weeks' worth of stock, but they were reducing stock holdings at the same time our product was selling out after just four weeks. So we had a compounding issue of the stock selling out way before their computers predicted it would and distributors not ordering as frequently, so we were out of stock all the time, all over the place. This was not a consumer demand issue, but a stock correction issue. It would take a few months to flush out, but we couldn't wait months for the computer ordering to catch up. We needed sales now. We doggedly nagged our distribution partners to ignore their computers, look at the actual sell-through and buy more stock. (Driving sales every day of the month no matter what was happening in the wider world became central to our culture, and a habit we would apply beyond the GFC.)

This lag had a terrible effect on us. Just as demand for Swisse products was increasing (thanks to the Ricky campaign), the shelves were gradually emptying, leaving nothing for customers to buy. We still had to cover the costs of the campaign, even though there weren't enough products on the shelf for customers to purchase. We were expanding rapidly, scaling up and hiring new team members to meet the demand from the Ricky campaign, but the revenue we were banking on to pay for this growth had slowed. It was a vicious circle.

To complicate matters, if the customer couldn't buy Swisse, they'd buy a competitive product, which meant all our advertising was driving our customers into the arms of our competitors. With orders drying up, we had no profit. We were growing the category from a sleepy 1 per cent to 10 per cent of total category revenue and everyone was benefitting, except us! (Marcus Blackmore should have been thanking us for doing his marketing for him!)

With this perfect storm of unfortunate events, revenue dropped by 50 per cent a month for the next few months. This situation drained what little cash we had left and gave Michael, Stephen and I many sleepless nights. Our bank funding was maxed out and we did not have unlimited cash to keep this boat afloat.

Control the controllables

Whenever we encountered challenging situations, we had a powerful mantra that would inform all our actions: 'control the controllables'. I learned this from my father. No matter what was happening in the external world, we needed to focus on our internal world, and do what we could to manage our circle of influence. We couldn't do much about the worldwide recession, but we could control our reaction to it.

Ask for better trading terms

The first thing we did was ring our suppliers and ask for better trading terms. It was low-hanging fruit. The worst that could happen is they say no. We contacted our contract manufacturer, Lipa, and they were happy to extend our terms. This brought us much-needed time. It was always in our culture to think of our suppliers as partners. Just as we worked hard to be retailers' number one natural health brand, we also wanted to be our suppliers' number one client. We'd invite them to our big VIP events, celebrity meet-and-greet events and treat them to a great time. We'd get in front of them as frequently as we could, visit them at their facility, express our appreciation for their business, and most importantly help them grow their revenue on a massive scale. While this was not done for transactional reasons, if or when we needed something, we hoped that the bond we had created would stand us in good stead — and, more often than not, it did. Relationships are everything.

Thank your suppliers

Let your suppliers know you appreciate their work. Supplier relationships should be treated as partnerships as you will need each other along the way. We often took our suppliers out for lunch, regularly updated them on our plans or treated them to a VIP event to say thank you for their work. Treat suppliers with the respect so when you do need a favour, they will be happy to help you out.

Launch new products

Secondly, we needed to launch new products, and lots of them. Ultivite was our best-selling multivitamin. If we were to launch another vitamin, Michael feared the consumer would be forced to make a binary choice, Ultivite or the new product; but we still needed to launch new products to stay relevant. Michael was reluctant to do this as he didn't want to cannibalise our best-selling product, but Stephen and I felt we needed to satisfy consumer needs. We'd been pushing Michael on this for a while, kept up the pressure and he finally came up with an ingenious solution. He said, 'Let's keep the Ultivite as the master vitamin product, but let's create a sub-product called Ultiboost that people can take, in *addition* to Ultivite, for specific needs like joint pain, gut health or immune support. So instead of consumers needing to pick Ultivite OR Ultiboost, they could now take Ultivite AND Ultiboost.'

This was a solution to a marketing dilemma we had been grappling with for many years and it offered many benefits. It enabled us to leverage our underperforming Clinicals range (a wide range of high-quality products that focused on providing support to the seven most common health ailments people face) by re-branding them as 'Ultiboost' (see below). To achieve this goal, we reduced the pack size, lowered the price, and repurposed them as a Swisse product, all without negatively affecting Ultivite.

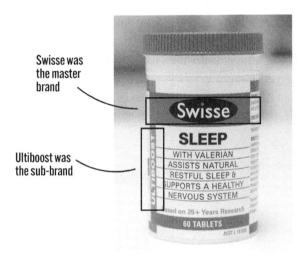

Re-branding our underperforming Clinical products as Swisse Ultiboost was a marketing masterstroke

As a result, we could offer the market a wide array of new products. It was Michael at his best. (This scenario represented how we operated. We didn't see problems, we saw potential; the Clinicals range, for example, was a failure but we didn't see it as that. We saw it as a 'misfire', and an opportunity to launch a new innovation.)

Incentivise your retailers to recommend you

Retailers can't sell something they don't understand, so help them learn more about your product by making it easy for them to access training materials. We provided our retailers with Swisse IQ, an online training portal that delivered on-demand product training, and rewarded those who completed the training with certificates, badges and complimentary Swisse products.

Conduct continuous coaching

Lastly, we fostered a culture of 'continuous coaching' amongst the team. This type of coaching was often conducted on the run, which ultimately, and ironically, laid the foundation for our future success. In times of extreme stress, often the first thing to go out the window is the commitment to culture. But that's exactly when you should be focused on it most. If you have a crisis you will 'drink deeply from the cup of culture', so you need to move quickly to fill it back up.

CHAPTER 12

THE CALL FROM COLES

We were running fast, borrowing from Peter to pay Paul, and growing quickly. We were hiring people at a rate of knots, all of them united by our culture and commitment to our purpose. We knew what we were capable of, but we just needed to make sure we brought everyone on the journey with us so they could embrace the vision too. Our goal was to help the team see their own potential so they could fully express that and be of service to the business, the culture and, in turn, one another.

At this point, we had already achieved our goal of beating Centrum to become Australia's number one multivitamin brand, and we were stoked to achieve it! We were never one for sitting on our laurels though, so we then set our sights on the next goal, which was to become Australia's number one natural health brand, a much bigger, more prestigious and more valuable category than just multivitamins. To achieve this, we needed to beat the market leader, Blackmores, and to do that, we needed to go into the major grocers, and, in particular, Coles. Blackmores were five times bigger than Centrum, and turned over around $300 million to Centrum's $50 million in Australia, so taking them on was a David and Goliath challenge.

Blackmores and Nature's Own had five to ten times the shelf space we did, and we knew that if we had that same amount of space, our sales would surpass theirs by a significant margin. The key to unlocking our full potential and achieving remarkable sales figures was to secure a larger share of the prime shelf real estate in pharmacies. But the pharmacies were reluctant. They had deep connections with the big vitamin brands and were not about to take space away from those long-standing, successful products without proof that we could achieve the same level of sales success.

That proof would need to come in the form of sales data from a reputable source such as Nielsen or Aztec. To get that data, we'd need to get ranged in Coles, make the requisite sales, and then go *back* to the pharmacy, show them that sales data, and get the shelf space we deserved. It was a heck of a way to go about gaining more shelf space in pharmacy, but that's what we needed to do. Why did we need pharmacy so badly? In a word: margin. We made significantly more profit in pharmacy than we did in the grocers.

I then received a phone call from the head buyer at Coles. We were expecting this call: Coles did not yet stock Swisse, but it did stock Evidin and ProvenSlim, two of the problematic products endorsed by the two Dr Johns a few years earlier. We knew Evidin and ProvenSlim were struggling and that Coles was going to delete them. We also knew they had seen the results we were getting from the Ricky Ponting campaign and would probably want a slice of the Swisse action. We were ready for them to range Swisse, but it definitely needed to be on our terms. Our highest priority at this point was to keep our pharmacy partners happy; they were the bedrock upon which our success had been built and we did not want to upset them.

The success of our plan relied on us securing the same amount of shelf space as Blackmores, which would be achieved by implementing our comprehensive marketing plan, and by offering a broader product range. This would, in turn, fuel overall category growth in both distribution channels, appease our pharmacy partners and establish a formidable presence in Coles.

The $30 million order

Our pharmacists were terrified that they would lose vitamin customers to the major grocers. We patiently explained that our massive investment in TV, print and billboard, our product innovations, and partnerships with renowned celebrities would attract an entirely new customer base — individuals who had never purchased vitamins before. We anticipated that a substantial portion of these new customers would also choose to buy our products from pharmacies, which would equal or exceed the number who shopped at Coles.

Stephen was on board with the strategy and pushed for us to be in Coles. He was the voice of reason who could see that this was the only way to become the number one brand in the category. Michael was less enthusiastic. The truth was, we didn't have much choice. Coles was going to stock us with or without our approval. They owned an online pharmacy store and said that they'd work out a way to get our product no matter what. We needed to act now to get the best deal possible. I took Michael through the strategy and the numbers (that finance course came in handy!) and he reluctantly agreed to let us sell Swisse to them.

This was a once-in-a-lifetime opportunity to strike a deal with Coles: one that would shape our future success. Stephen, Michael and I rehearsed this meeting countless times, and strategised every move. Failure was not an option.

We knew what we needed from them: end caps, catalogue support to drive sales, a massive commitment to buying stock in advance, and a full team on deck to make it work. We had told them for many years prior that they could not have Swisse, which frustrated them, but now the time was right for both of us. We set the terms and they agreed and it was a fair deal for everyone. It's worth mentioning that while it was an *important* meeting, it wasn't a *difficult* meeting. We both knew what we needed from each other and both sides were committed to success. (If you have a difficult meeting with a retailer and it feels forced, or it feels as if one is coercing the other in some way, it probably won't end well. This tension may indicate that it is not the right time to be doing business with that retailer.)

We expected the initial order to be in the vicinity of $3 million. The order we got was for $30 million! For just one order! We nearly fell off our chairs. We weren't expecting our first Swisse deal with Coles to be of this magnitude.

As tempting as it was to accept this colossal order, we proceeded with caution, took the middle ground and halved it to $15 million. This was still a massive order for us, equivalent to 50 per cent of last year's worth of pharmacy sales, but we knew that placing too much stock with one retailer could cause all sorts of havoc down the path. (Having too much capital investment tied up in stock sitting on the shelves can place a significant strain on a retailer's cash flow and can create a negative 'vibe' about the product that is tying up all that cash.)

The whole team was pumped. Our strategy was vindicated, dividends could be distributed, and, most importantly, we could supercharge our growth. The timing was perfect. If Coles had not rung us then, we would have had to *ask* them to range us, and the order and in-store support from Coles would have been significantly smaller.

The Bank of Coles

The trading terms were ideal too. Lipa, our contract manufacturer, generously granted us 120 days to settle the payment on the first order and Coles promptly paid us within a mere 45 days. It was a gift. Coles had unwittingly become our benefactor, subsidising our entire operation. With this free credit from the Bank of Coles, we had newfound freedom. We could push boundaries, move faster, and reach greater heights than ever before.

As it happened, we had been a bit ambitious with the order, and this created some issues. We thought (or hoped) we'd sell $15 million worth of stock in three months, and so did Coles, but it actually took 12 months to sell. Despite incurring significant marketing costs to expand our category and maintain strong partnerships with the pharmacies, the sales in Coles didn't quite justify the massive investment we had made in marketing. (We had also paid out dividends, which created cash flow pressure. If we'd sold 12 months' worth of stock in three months, as we'd hoped, this situation would not have arisen. In hindsight, we should have not paid dividends at that time). As a result we had no option but to seek out Woolworths to tap into new market opportunities and generate more revenue. We presented to their team and gained a standard opening order of $2 million, a far cry from the stupendous $30 million opening order from Coles. On the upside, Chemist Warehouse would finally give us as much shelf space as Blackmores, so our goal to secure more shelf space would be achieved. It was a high-risk strategy but it was the only way to go about it!

How to negotiate with the major grocers

The best time to deal with a new sales channel such as Coles or Woolworths is when you don't need a new sales channel like Coles or Woolworths. If you can get them to come to you, as they did after they saw the success of the Ricky Ponting campaign, you will be able to negotiate a much better deal. That's easier said than done of course, but that's the only way.

If you are dealing with the major grocers, you have got to come with your best game. Their decisions are all data-driven, and their buyers are incentivised to be incredibly ruthless and only care about one thing: profit. I treated every negotiation with them (and everyone) like a game of chess. I knew our worst-case outcomes and knew exactly what we wanted and what we were prepared to give away to get it, all before we stepped foot in the door. I also knew their every move and all the counter-moves and every contingency that all those permutations would create. I loved this part of strategy planning.

If your goal is to go into the major grocers, do your homework before you go, be prepared, and don't leave anything to chance.

Our marketing was gaining attention and its success cemented our relationship with Coles. They wanted in on the other deals we were doing with their competitors and were now open to all sorts of promotional opportunities. It was so gratifying to see our relationship with the buyers morph from combative to collegiate. They knew our motto was always win-win and they trusted us to have their best interests at heart. For example, if they had too much stock we'd take it back; if we had slow-selling lines we'd swap them for better-selling new products; and if they wanted a promotional program, we'd be only too happy to tailor one to suit their customer. No matter what challenge they presented us with, we would find a solution. This 'can do' attitude was embedded in our culture and we became known for going the extra mile to help our retailers achieve their goals.

Buying into the business

In June 2008, not long after the Coles deal, Michael and Stephen offered me the role of CEO. I was thrilled to accept it. I was 32, and my salary was now an impressive $300 000; more than double what I had started on a few years earlier. I felt truly recognised for the work I had put into Swisse, and really appreciated the way Michael went about remunerating me. I never had to come to him, cap in hand, asking for more. He always initiated these salary conversations and I appreciated that my efforts were acknowledged. This also aligned with my values of letting my actions do the talking, and I would apply this philosophy when it came to pay-related matters with our team.

Stephen and I worked more closely during this time too. He would come into the office in his board shorts, have a chat, listen to our strategies, give me some sage advice, and, like Michael, became a mentor to me. He was 20 years older than me, a hugely experienced business leader, and a fantastic sounding board who would help me take the business to the next level.

I was further humbled when the guys offered me another 5 per cent stake in the business. This offer came just after I became CEO around 2010. (I had already been offered a 5 per cent share for $750 000 back in 2007, just after I'd become General Manager, so this felt like a further vote of confidence in what I was doing.) I took out a loan of $2 500 000 to pay for this second tranche, which equated to 15 times EBTIDA. Their confidence in me fuelled my passion and I was determined to honour the trust they had placed in me.

It was game on. We had a remit from the founders to move fast, take things to the extreme and keep momentum up. We were helping people live happier and healthier lives, and I was being handsomely rewarded for my efforts. Best of all, we had refined our recipe for success with the Ricky campaign, and had created a purpose-driven culture that had made all this possible. Our goal was to become the number one natural health brand in Australia. To achieve it, we couldn't just do what we'd done before. We'd need to double down on everything and give 100 per cent of our energy and focus to make it a reality.

Go all in

I don't do things by halves; I don't dabble and I don't do side hustles. Once I set my mind on a goal, I do whatever it takes to achieve it. Many entrepreneurs get bored quickly and move on to the next project before they've finished the current one. Resist the temptation to move on. Stick with the one idea and take it to its fullest expression. Go all in.

CHAPTER 13

GET SONIA

We now had the formula for marketing success, but we didn't quite yet know how to sustain it. We didn't need to reinvent what we'd done, we just needed to get better at what we were already doing, refine the process, keep all the elements relevant to our audience and maintain the momentum.

To become Australia's number one natural health brand, we needed to achieve these three goals:

1. consolidate our core customer base in pharmacy

2. bring new customers into grocery

3. bring in customers who had never previously bought a natural health product.

To achieve this, we needed a similar but different version of the Ponting campaign that had been so successful: a campaign that would leverage the learnings we had made but attract a new audience. In short, we needed a 'female Ricky': a personality who was fit, fun and fabulous, a woman at the top of her game and an aspirational role model. I conducted a poll of one and asked my mother what her favourite TV show was. 'Dancing with the Stars,' she said.

I watched the show and it was clear that Sonia was the star and was the key to its success. She was beautiful, healthy, had an awesome sense of humour and, to cap it off, was a superstar ballroom dancer. I checked in with Dimi, our Priceline buyer, about having Sonia as an ambassador and she was more excited than I was. That was a great sign. I rang Sonia's manager, eager to discover if this deal would be of interest. It was, and, even better, she was already an avid user of our products. We signed her up within a week. We didn't have a big marketing budget so we did everything we could to make the most out of what we had.

In those early days, our marketing budgets were minuscule compared to those of our cashed-up competitors. As such, we had to be very careful with how we allocated our advertising budget. For example, we were very strategic about where we placed our billboards. We wanted the retail buyers to get behind the Sonia Kruger campaign and to give them the impression we were bigger than we were. We knew that their buyers travelled a lot for their work, so instead of taking billboards out across the nation and diluting their impact, we took out billboards on major freeways near their homes and at the entrance to airports so they'd see the billboards on the way to the terminal. It worked. We'd come into the buyer meetings and they'd say, 'Hey, I saw the billboards. You guys are everywhere!' Mission accomplished. (We didn't know exactly where these buyers lived, by the way. We just knew through general chit-chat what suburb they lived in, and from there we could extrapolate approximately what route they might take to work.)

Ballroom blitz

From a TV advertising perspective, we wanted to replicate the model we had used at Channel Nine and feature the star of the broadcast in the advertising during the show. In hindsight, we should have done some more research before signing the Sonia deal as we assumed we'd be able to seal a similar deal to what we had with Channel Nine, where Ricky fronted the advertising campaign during the cricketing broadcast. But Channel Seven was not nearly as accommodating. They advised us that the industry had never permitted the star employee of a leading lifestyle program to appear in an advertisement during the show and that we'd need approval from the BBC, the program's central owners, to allow it to happen. They also doubted our comparatively small media spend would justify the merits of having one of their most valuable superstars on board. (If they were going to commit one of their biggest stars to a 'break the rules' advertising campaign, they would have preferred the advertiser to be a major player, such as a car company or insurance provider, who would spend considerably more on the advertising than what we were planning.)

I met with as many network executives as possible, presented our strategy and tried to convince them our plan was beneficial to them. I emphasised our long-term commitment, not just with Sonia and *Dancing with the Stars*, but with future initiatives as well. We finally got the BBC's approval to use Sonia in our TV commercials during the broadcast, and we promptly committed to a $1 million media spend. This bought us one 30-second commercial per week during *Dancing with the Stars* and a further 20 commercials to air during *other* programs throughout the week. It was this last point that bothered me. We wanted *all* the commercials to appear during *Dancing with the Stars*. We'd done that with Ricky within the cricket broadcast, and we were sure that this was a key factor in its success. I did my best to convince them that our way was the best strategy, but they were unmoved. The only thing to do was to let our sales results do the talking. They needed hard evidence and hard data would be the only way to convince them.

Unlike Channel Nine, who let us buy our media directly with them, Channel Seven insisted that we go through their recommended media agency, which meant the agency would get 10 per cent of the $1 million media spend, as we needed to satisfy their risk management committee. I said, 'Please let us buy the media direct. The 10 per cent will go straight to your bottom line, and we'll get our extra airtime.' They said, 'We can't take on this risk without the payment insurance offered by an advertising agency.' I'd heard it all before and I knew it could be done. I said, 'Channel Nine did it. Why can't you?' But the network was not for turning. Buying media on this scale directly had never been done before and we were considered to be serious disruptors to the sector. This desire to do it our way later inspired us to launch Noisy Beast and again with Strat, both integrated agency services that would become Australia's market leading independent operations.

Listen to your instinct

The campaign went to air and sales were okay, but with the investment we were making, we needed to see much bigger sales. I was frustrated with myself. We shouldn't have given in to Channel Seven and allowed our commercials to be dotted throughout the schedule, but we did. I went against my instinct, and paid the price. There was moderate growth — around 10–15 per cent, which was adequate for other brands, but certainly not enough to cover the costs of our advertising investment.

We met with Channel Seven, showed them the sales reports to prove that the campaign had not made the necessary impact for our spending to be sustainable, and asked them to reconsider. Our positive and relentless message that this strategy was good for everyone eventually sunk in. They finally agreed and allowed us to place all our TV commercials within the *Dancing with the Stars* broadcast, as originally requested. We also asked them to permit Sonia to promote a prize featuring an all-expenses-paid trip to London to watch the UK taping of *Dancing With The Stars*. We always looked for new ways to do things and give our audience interesting and fun ways to engage with us.

Share the data

If your suppliers aren't delivering on the agreed results, as the TV network wasn't for us, let them know. Show them the data, tell them what you expected to achieve and work together to find a solution. The key is to share the data so they can understand your point of view.

To their credit, Channel Seven agreed to the deal, and lo and behold, the campaign took off! The impact was immediate. Sales skyrocketed from 10 per cent to 30 per cent and then 50 per cent. While this was a great result and we were all relieved at how we had redeemed the situation, the sales *still* did not fully cover the advertising expense.

This was a big lesson. I learned to not let others, like TV network executives, dictate our campaign media strategies. I had assumed those executives knew more than I did about what we needed to succeed. Following the herd is a sure-fire route to failure, and it was a costly lesson for me to learn. However, it served as a powerful prompt to trust my gut and have faith in my own judgement. From that point forward, I made a solemn commitment to back our strategy and work hard to constantly improve our winning formula.

On the bright side, we successfully fulfilled our three-part goal: we had consolidated our core customer base in pharmacy, brought new customers into grocery, and attracted new customers who had never previously bought a natural health product before, all of which subsequently increased everybody's customer base. The whole category grew by 15 per cent per year, five times faster than it had since I started at Swisse. (Even our biggest customer, Chemist Warehouse, who was unhappy about our decision to go into Coles in the first place, said that our strategy to grow the category was the best thing we'd done.)

Our strategy had worked. We did not just grow our slice of the pie; we expanded the size of the actual pie, and gave all the pharmacies the opportunity to have a share of it, at no cost to them.

It was truly a win-win-win for everyone. The customer, *all* the retailers, and us.

Exclusivity is the key

While the Sonia campaign solidified our reputation for delivering results to retailers and created significant momentum, we wanted to make it as successful as the Ricky Ponting campaign. We wanted to top what we'd previously done, learn from it, and put that into play to improve our next campaign. We thrived on this constant search for excellence. Our research into how to make the next campaign better revealed that we needed to focus on our prize promotion support.

Our post-campaign research found that the all-important promotional posters we'd had printed up for the 'win tickets to see the *Dancing with the Stars* in the UK' promotion did not get used by all the stores, and if they did get used, they got buried amongst all the other competitive point-of-sale material around it. The second issue was that the retailers didn't really get behind the prize promotion or recommend our product because they knew that every other retailer had access to the promotion too. They didn't feel the promotion was created just for them, which was true, so they didn't feel invested in it, or take ownership of it, which meant it didn't work. This 'LGI' moment taught us that we needed to create *exclusive* promotions for our retailers.

Baptism by fire

It's a little-known fact, but the Health and Beauty categories at Chemist Warehouse are worth more than the Health and Beauty categories of Coles and Woolworths combined. They are a powerhouse retailer and, as such, if you're not stocked there, you're not in the game. I thought the grocers were tough to deal with but they had nothing on Chemist Warehouse.

My first meeting with them occurred in mid-2006, shortly after I assumed the role of General Manager. It was a trial by fire, marked by lots of shouting, finger-pointing and chest-thumping histrionics. Trying to impress these demanding buyers with our sales strategies felt like an insurmountable challenge, but these intense encounters did not bother me in the slightest. They were a walk in the park compared to the relentless nagging and verbal lashings I had endured from my mother throughout my life. Her colourful language and relentless persistence to help me maximise my potential had prepared me well. I viewed these confrontations with the buyers as a chance to earn their respect, redouble our efforts and excel. I, and in turn our team, loved rising to the challenge and doing things that others said we couldn't do.

Michael and Stephen, with many years of wisdom under their belts, encouraged us to see these explosive meetings as a compliment. They'd both say, 'If they didn't believe in you, they wouldn't get so angry with you!' I'd also learn later that your first meeting with Chemist Warehouse was always the hardest as they saw it as a test to see how committed you were. It was our culture to always see the positive side in every situation, work hard to find a solution and seek a win-win result for everyone.

The principle of 'not taking things personally' became a hallmark of our culture and a deeply ingrained principle. We continually emphasised to our team that a challenge or tough negotiation was not a reflection of our worth or collective efforts. Instead, it was a chance to deploy a strategy to secure the best possible outcome for everyone.

This made our team resilient and helped us navigate through many difficult situations.

Over time, as the trust grew and the relationship deepened, the Chemist Warehouse team rightly mellowed. They were, and are, still ridiculously tough and demanding, and it takes a lot to impress them, but they are an extraordinary partner. If you did a deal with them, they honoured it to the letter and delivered the best sales results by a mile. Getting to that result was a journey, but a most rewarding one. We eventually became their biggest customer, and they ours. Simply put, we enabled each other's success.

Learn from the best

The Chemist Warehouse annual event for their top 100 suppliers was legendary. No expense was spared to create an unforgettable experience. Good food, a glamorous location, and a sneak peek into what they had in store for the year ahead made this a must-attend event. They invited charismatic speakers to ignite our enthusiasm and remind us why we should give them our very best deals — and the speeches from senior management provided a not-so-subtle warning about what would happen if we didn't. ☺

I received my first invitation to this event in late 2008. It did not disappoint. Harold Mitchell, the larger-than-life media mogul whose company Mitchell and Partners was responsible for most of the buying and selling of media space in Australia, spoke at the event. (Remember the 10 per cent fee that went to the media agency in the Channel Seven deal? That 10 per cent pretty much went to Harold.) Renowned for his love of wining and dining, he seemed less than qualified to talk about health, but he did showcase a very interesting promotional concept that he'd initiated for *Huey's Kitchen*, a daytime cooking show fronted by the ebullient chef Iain 'Huey' Hewitson. The segment was sponsored by Nature's Own, one of our key competitors.

During the show, Iain would air a two-minute in-show segment spruiking Nature's Own vitamins to a captive audience of over 400 000 viewers. Chemist Warehouse was Nature's Own's exclusive partner in the promotion, and they'd load up the stores with large quantities of stock, provide voluminous quantities of point-of-sale materials, and give extensive coverage in the catalogue, which was a central plank in the promotional platform. It was a hugely sophisticated campaign, and it delivered a big result to Nature's Own.

We set up a meeting with Chemist Warehouse and told them straight out: 'We want what they've got. How can we get it?'

They said, 'It's a journey.'

We were up for it. Here's what we did to get it.

We ran another Ricky Ponting TV campaign during the summer of cricket. It was an exclusive (note that word, 'exclusive') promotion for Chemist Warehouse. The ads only ran during the cricket broadcast. (We'd learned that lesson from our *Dancing with the Stars* experience: *don't* dilute the exposure by sprinkling the advertisements throughout the week.) We spent $2 million on TV, billboard and print advertising, with 80 per cent dedicated to promoting our brand and products. The remaining 20 per cent went toward a competition to win a money-can't-buy prize (a trip to London to watch England play Australia in the Ashes) and a raft of marketing initiatives to promote that competition.

In return for the exclusivity option, Chemist Warehouse agreed to give us extra coverage and prime position in the printed catalogues; more, and better located, floor space; and a commitment that their individual store managers would recommend the product to customers. They also guaranteed that our stands would be prominently positioned, fully stocked at all times, and protected from other unscrupulous merchandisers to prevent our stock from being shifted to the bottom or top shelf or out of sight altogether.

Chemist Warehouse committed to buying $5 million worth of stock to support the campaign, enough to cover the cost of sponsoring the cricket, which de-risked the entire campaign. More importantly, that big stock sell-in ensured we would never run out of stock, that we'd have the best representation at the point-of-sale, and that Chemist Warehouse team would be as incentivised to sell our product as we were.

We were ready to launch.

CHAPTER 14

CRACKING THE CODE

The campaign launched and whoosh! Sales took off like a rocket. In fact, sales doubled. We'd never seen anything like it. Through continuous iteration, refinement and adaptation, we had discovered the precise combination that consistently yielded exceptional results. Our modus operandi was to find out what worked, keep that, drop what didn't work and keep going. Our dedication to finding the optimal mix was the driving force behind our ability to deliver outstanding outcomes for our retailers.

How prizes and exclusivity drove sales

We partnered with Chemist Warehouse to launch a series of exclusive promotions. One hugely successful campaign was the exclusive promotion we held during the Australian Formula 1 Grand Prix. (This campaign occurred quite a bit later in our Swisse journey, but it's worth mentioning here as it demonstrates clearly how our success was not due to one critical factor or strategy, but was the result of a combination of a wide range of integrated factors. When combined, they delivered a result that exceeded the sum of their individual contributions. As we delivered more and more campaigns, we got better at finetuning the components to generate better results.)

The pitch was simple: buy a Swisse product and win the chance to attend the Italian Grand Prix, get VIP access to the track and have dinner with the legendary F1 driver Mark Webber. This was a pretty impressive prize by any measure and the racing crowd loved it. This promotion resulted in an 88 per cent increase in sales. It was one of the top redeeming promotions in our history.

To get access to a promotion like this, the retailer had to commit to a significant pre-order and marketing/co-op package. (A co-op package refers to the cash a manufacturer like us gives a retailer that they then spend on promoting our product via end caps, advertising and catalogues. It's most often calculated based on a percentage of sales). As a guideline, the value of the media spend was always equal to or greater than the value of the order received from the retailer, and always included a 'money-can't-buy' experience linked back to either the ambassador or TV event.

Don't underestimate the power of celebrity

Swisse was the challenger brand. We were a minnow compared to the Centrums and the Blackmores of the world. As such, we had to think different and be different. Instead of spreading our advertising out over a year like most big brands, we hired big-name celebrities, bought out every advertising slot we could afford in the selected program, put the celebrity in the advertisements that aired during the program, and offered the retailers exclusive prizes and promotions so they'd get behind us and recommend us. This was the birth of our flywheel model. It was an all or nothing move. But it worked, and by continuously improving the model, we were able to take on the giants.

The flywheel unleashed

The flywheel was a process that seamlessly integrated all marketing elements within our campaigns. This flywheel was a step-by-step process that not only enabled our team, partners and suppliers to understand our distinctive marketing approach, but also served as the catalyst for our departure from conventional methods, which ultimately led to outstanding results.

Don't follow the herd

Our flywheel sell-in/sell-through model enabled us to compete with the bigger brands but with a fraction of their budget. When you are operating in a new or challenging market, it's often tempting to just follow the leaders and assume that what they are doing must work. Don't fall into this form of groupthink. Try to establish what works best for you — do your own research, challenge the status quo, test a new concept and use the results to develop your own flywheel. Launch it, test it, refine it. Even when you experience success, don't get complacent or rest on your laurels. Aim to constantly improve everything you do to deliver a better result.

We used this approach in our sales pitches to help the buyer understand our advertising process. When people could see how it worked, it made the sales process smoother, which meant they bought more stock.

This is how we explained the flywheel to our retailers and partners. We:

1. *Connect Swisse with large-scale TV events:* This makes us unmissable. We support the advertising with print and billboards to engage viewers and connect with consumers and retail partners.

2. *Source partnership associations and sponsorships:* These connect with the consumers and retail partners.

3. *Engage ambassadors that connect with our media events:* These generate the earned/owned media mentions and elicit the support of our consumers and retail partners.

4. *Launch multi-platform 360-degree advertising campaigns:* These campaigns drive awareness of the media event, the sponsorship partnerships and ambassadors, and drive in-store traffic.

5. *Amplify our events, sponsorships, partnerships and ambassador associations:* Our strategic PR plan integrates all these elements to create a streamlined, multimedia attack that generates earned media and social shares.

6. *Guarantee an exclusive retailer commitment:* Before any marketing spend is committed, the retailer commits to a joint business plan and buys enough stock to own the advertising campaign with an agreement that the stock sells through.

7. *Provide high-quality, impactful point-of-sale material:* Every campaign is supported with posters, decals, gondola ends (a type of display fixture to showcase merchandise) and other high-quality point-of-sale material to drive in-store purchase.

8. *Appear within the in-store catalogues:* We leverage co-op dollars to appear prominently in the store catalogue and use email newsletters to drive traffic.

Everyone wanted in

'We want Ricky too,' said the Priceline buyer. They wanted to be next in line to take advantage of our marketing flywheel. This comment made me laugh for a few reasons. One, because it came from Dimi, the buyer who had never heard of Ricky a few years earlier, and secondly, because over 90 per cent of Priceline's customers were women. To be fair, Dimi was only doing what her (male) bosses asked her to do. They were cricket tragics, had seen the success we'd had with our Ricky campaign and wanted in on the action. These seasoned executives had succumbed to the cult of celebrity. The fact that Ricky had zero appeal to their core audience of women was irrelevant. This just proved how seductive celebrity really was (and why more women should be in senior management, especially in workplaces with a predominantly female audience).

As always, we turned this challenge into an opportunity by offering Priceline a partnership with the reality dating show *Farmer Wants a Wife* and the Australian Open tennis over the next 12 months, both of which were much more aligned with their female audience. To secure these exclusive promotions, they agreed to:

- provide over and above product representation at the point-of-sale

- get behind our new product development program and stock our new products

- commit to a significant stock buy-in.

This would ensure they'd never run out of stock, that our marketing and advertising costs would be covered and that the sell-through results would be rewarding.

Off the back of this campaign, Priceline that year grew as fast as Chemist Warehouse. We became the talk of the industry and the subject of much speculation: 'How are they doing this?' 'How does it all work?' 'Surely this kind of spending can't last?' This exclusivity factor created an undercurrent of competitive tension, with all the retailers fighting to see who could get the next Swisse promotion. It was the ideal scenario for us, as it drove the all-important sales and marketing outcomes for our retailers, and ensured the whole industry grew. Everyone was winning.

Movie magic

While attending a trade show, I ran into a friend from my Village days who specialised in creating unique promotional and merchandising deals. The premise he presented to me was simple: 'Buy any Swisse product and receive a free ticket to a movie'. I loved the concept. We presented the idea to Coles, and they enthusiastically embraced it, and agreed to run with it. We supported it with TV and catalogue advertising and a range of in-store point-of-sale collateral that featured our product alongside the stars of the movie. What a great combination.

It was fun to see my past and present careers of Hollywood and health come together to create this deal.

We occasionally ran competitions that offered a major cash prize, sometimes as much as $1 million. This idea came from a Chemist Warehouse buyer. She said it in jest and was visibly shocked when we took her up on it. It generated a lot of interest and was one of our most popular competitions. We were always up for trying something new and different.

Don't be complacent

Don't wait for competitors to do something to spur you into action. Be on the front foot, innovate, do something different.

The pressure was intense

TV was always the glamour vehicle that convinced a retailer to be a part of our campaigns. The retailers *loved* being on TV and they also loved the sales that came with it. I still did most of the media buying and as a result, I had to make sure that every advertisement we paid for actually got played on TV. I would sit up watching each show to ensure the TV commercial went to air, or I'd record the show and watch it back the next morning before work. That might seem a bit obsessive, but we really, *really* needed that TV commercial to air *during* the show — not before it, not after it, and certainly not on another day. The TV commercial was the sun around which all the other flywheel elements rotated. Without that, the rest of the campaign would struggle to achieve the heights we knew we could achieve. It was a vital cog in our marketing machine.

So, you can imagine my dismay when, in week one of the *Farmer Wants a Wife* campaign for Priceline, the TV commercial *did not go to air*. I was ropeable. Without that all-important commercial airing, the flywheel fell apart. It was the TV network's error but I still had to face the client and explain what had happened. We took responsibility for it and worked hard to put the campaign back on track the following week, but this was just one of a hundred mini and major crises we were dealing with every day. It was high pressure, go go go, all the time, and we were constantly on call to put out the spot fires that occurred. There were so many interconnected moving pieces that it didn't take much to upset this finely tuned flywheel.

TV works

I used to laugh when I saw those red stickers emblazoned with 'As Seen On TV' stuck on random products in the supermarket, as if the very act of being on TV gave it a stamp of approval, but there was some truth to that. TV was, and still is, the most powerful medium for influencing buyer behaviour. Social media has of course been a phenomenal tool in driving engagement, but I believe online advertising is a little over-hyped. It generally costs us a dollar in online advertising to generate a sales dollar. In my opinion, nothing beats TV for driving brand awareness and sales. Digital marketing is obviously a major marketing tool and is evolving rapidly, but even so, it's very difficult in Australia to attract one million people online to watch whatever you are advertising, in one sitting. TV delivers this daily.

For example, in later years when we had further refined our flywheel model, we ran a price promotion for Woolworths and showcased the offer via The Voice, one of Australia's highest rating reality talent shows. The results were instant, and incredible. Before the TV commercials went to air, sales were, on average, $450 000 per week. After the TV commercials went to air, that figure rose to $2.5 million per week, a massive five-fold increase. Who said advertising (and a solid price promotion) don't work?

The pace of growth at this time was intense. We had a rolling series of campaigns for retailers being launched back-to-back, so we were under the pump all the time to deliver on our promises, while at the same time trying to hold the retailer accountable and have them do their bit. We were still a small team, and we were all a bit 'tired and stressed', but the thrill of achieving our long-held goals gave us the energy and passion to keep going. Our uplifting, purpose-driven culture always got us through. People loved working at Swisse, and we made sure we rewarded the team every time we had a small or large win. It might have been a simple word of praise in recognition of a job well done, a prize awarded around the themes of nutrition, mindfulness or movement, a team outing or access to a VIP event to acknowledge the team's unwavering commitment to our 4P culture.

On a personal note

Helen was so tolerant and understanding of what I was going through, which only made me love her more. She understood the business, had worked in corporate life and knew the demands and pressures that came with it. But gee, I was pretty hard to live with. On the upside, our success gave us the financial stability to buy our first house, a beautifully renovated three-bedroom home near the Yarra River in Melbourne's inner east. It was a beautiful old schoolhouse with a rustic charm and, because it was on a main road, we got it for a good price. We bought a sausage dog, Floella, as a companion for Helen's cat, India, to add a bit of colour and movement to our lives, and we came to love those two little creatures as if they were our surrogate children, which in some ways, they were. Coming home to a hug and a belly rub was the highlight of my day. I enjoyed the cuddles with the dog too. ☺

In April 2009, on a warm autumn day, Helen and I got married at Morningstar Estate, one of the most beautiful wineries on the Mornington Peninsula. We had 150 of our closest family and friends attend, hired a Cat Stevens tribute singer to entertain us, and my crazy Albanian family busted their best traditional dance moves until the wee hours of the morning. We had a blast. When we exchanged vows, we said 'the best is yet to come' and we believed it. We had found our perfect life partners. Helen was everything I had been looking for, and more.

Our journey to become parents started at this time. Like many young couples, we thought it would be easy, and we'd have lots of fun trying. Unfortunately, it wasn't that simple. In fact, we had no idea how hard it would be.

CHAPTER 15

GAME ON

By late 2009, the business was humming and we were hungry to expand. We worked hard to innovate and come up with new products, new campaigns, and new initiatives. We were never complacent. Our mission at Swisse was to make people healthier and happier and so we worked hard to develop a product for everyone, from toddlers to pre-teens, pre-natal to post-natal, from the over-50s to over the hill. We wanted to have something for everyone.

A winning team

Off the back of the success of our cricket campaigns it was time to double down and move into winter sports. If we wanted to reach the widest market possible, we'd need to find a way to connect with the games Australians loved to play all year round. Australian Rules Football (AFL) and Rugby League were the obvious choices as they covered most of the populous mainland states. After much discussion, we chose AFL over Rugby League as the latter was being hit with so many controversial issues. (We wanted to de-risk as much as possible, and, while no sport was quarantined from the vicissitudes of daily life, we felt AFL was the safer route to take.)

The next question we had to address was, 'What team or which player do we approach to be our ambassador?' I would have loved nothing more than to have Hawthorn as the face of our brand as I was a die-hard Hawthorn supporter and wanted our captain, Sam Mitchell, or the mercurial Cyril Rioli, but I knew that it had to stack up as a business case. Stephen felt the same about Essendon; he was a massive Essendon supporter and wanted James Hird, who was coming off a very impressive stint as a commentator and was about to become Essendon's coach. Fortunately, Michael, Stephen and I were all aligned in our quest to choose personalities that would match the customer we were targeting and drive sales.

In the end, we engaged Tom Harley, the former captain of Geelong which, at the time, was one of the league's most successful teams, and Tom Hafey, the super-ripped 78-year-old coaching great who was renowned for bringing the concept of elite fitness to the game. We also enlisted Karmichael Hunt, who had excelled in Rugby League at the highest level and was about to embark on doing the same with AFL. We wanted to appeal to as wide a supporter base as possible.

Generally speaking, I deliberately kept my distance from our celebrities so I could keep objective. To me, these celebrities were our valued business partners: ordinary individuals who happened to excel in their respective fields and were actively involved in helping us achieve our desired outcomes.

Don't vampire the brand

This was all in line with our long-standing policy of not allowing any one celebrity to dominate, polarise or overshadow the brand. To allow one personality, sporting or otherwise, to become so identified with the Swisse brand would risk them 'vampiring' the brand. We had learned from the Ricky campaigns that if Ricky had a bad day, it could quickly generate blowback on Swisse. Some of the customer feedback, sent via voicemail or via the website, was amusing. The gist of it was, *Ricky Ponting, out for a duck. Swisse's fault. Ricky Ponting steps down as captain of the Test team. Swisse's fault.* You had to laugh.

While we didn't mind that much — we were getting great cut-through — we did make a note of it for the future. It's a fine line to walk because the whole point of an ambassador is to align their brand with yours, but not so much as to consume it. We had a stable of brand ambassadors, which meant that if one personality became problematic, we were able to switch the focus to another personality to minimise the negative effect. When the media storm died down, we'd shine the light on that person again.

Loyalty was a two-way street. Our personalities were like family and we knew that everyone goes through ups and downs and challenging times. We did not want to be one of those companies that dropped their talent the minute they had a misstep.

Hedge your bets

To de-risk, we placed lots of bets and hedged every one of them. We did that by:

- regularly launching new products
- having lots of ambassadors
- ensuring our retailers paid for their stock before the advertising began
- following up our sell-in with the sell-through.

De-risking was the name of the game.

Breaking barriers

Our audience, like our team, was hugely diverse in age, gender, health and ethnicity, so we wanted to make sure everyone was represented in our ambassadors.

In 2011, we were particularly proud to engage Evonne Goolagong Cawley, the champion tennis player from the 1980s. She won seven Grand Slam singles titles, including four Australian Open championships, two Wimbledon triumphs, and one French Open victory, which also made her the first mother to claim the title since 1914. She is a trailblazing feminist and one of the greatest players of her era. At the time, Evonne was the only First Nations person fronting a national TV campaign and we were thrilled we could shine the spotlight on such a great player and her heritage.

How to choose a celebrity ambassador

Selecting the right celebrity ambassador to represent us was crucial to our success. We used a checklist to ensure every person we chose aligned with our values and embodied our 'Celebrate Life Every Day' attitude. We also wanted our ambassadors to feel privileged to have been selected and needed them to feel genuinely excited about the appointment so that they could authentically promote Swisse at all times. Here's some questions to consider when selecting a brand ambassador. You should aim for a 'Yes' in all categories except the last one.

Ambassador checklist

Are they connected to a TV show in which we would like to advertise?	☐ Yes	☐ No
Will their presence help us connect with a specific target audience?	☐ Yes	☐ No
Are they #1 in their field?	☐ Yes	☐ No
Do they have a strong social media following?	☐ Yes	☐ No
Do they represent the values of health and wellbeing?	☐ Yes	☐ No
Do they believe that vitamins and supplement help maintain good health?	☐ Yes	☐ No
Do they have an upbeat and sunny nature?	☐ Yes	☐ No
Are they authentic?	☐ Yes	☐ No
Are they connected to any other competing brands?	☐ Yes	☐ No

CHAPTER 16

A TOTAL TEAM EFFORT

Our focus now shifted to the people of Swisse. It had to. We were growing at a rate of knots. We'd gone from a team of 30 in 2005, to 40 in 2006, 50 in 2007, and 70 in 2008: we'd more than doubled in under three years. Finding quality people was always one of our hardest challenges. We paid well over the market rates for great people, and preferred to work with fewer people (and pay them more) than hire someone who may not fit in. Our team had to be open-minded, love change and be prepared to share their ideas on how we could improve upon what we were already doing. What we had done in the past was good, even great, but we needed our people to be relentlessly driven to make Swisse even better. Constant improvement was always our goal. Our culture was our primary superpower that separated us from every other company in the sector, and it created a team bond that transcended the normal day-to-day commitment that most employees had for their workplace. We hired the best and brightest and they gave so much because they loved what they did and what the company stood for.

Our marketing was our secondary superpower. Competitors tried to replicate our marketing but they never got it right. How could they? There were so many interwoven elements that unless you were involved in the intricate planning and production of the campaigns, you would have no hope of unlocking the code. The competitors looked at it through the traditional marketing lens of the 4P's of marketing:

- What were we doing with the Price?

- What Promotional plans did we have going on this month?

- Where were we Placing the advertisements?

- What Products were we selling?

They'd pore over our campaigns, looking for the one strategy that made us the stand-out performer. What they failed to understand was that our flywheel was so much bigger than the sum of its parts. They also overlooked the key elements that made us successful:

- we'd only advertise in a TV show using the talent from that show

- the stock sell-in was specifically timed to coincide with the TV advertising

- the retailer needed to pre-order the stock to get the exclusive rights to the campaign

- the retailers were emotionally and financially invested in the campaign succeeding and would support the sell-through of the campaign with all of their marketing assets.

They also couldn't have matched the sheer volume of ambassadors we engaged, which totalled over 300 at one point. Most would also struggle to find a creative team of the calibre we had, who truly understood how the flywheel worked. Our advertising agencies were instrumental in helping us implement our marketing flywheel plans. Most traditional agencies didn't understand our model or would try to get us to use their systems. Eventually, we created our own agency to produce the Swisse work, as it ensured we could create our campaigns in a way that worked for us.

Our flywheel enabled us to compete with the biggest brands: Centrum, Nature's Own and Blackmores. When I first started at Swisse, they had monster advertising budgets that we couldn't hope to match, but we eventually found a way to beat them at their own game. (And we would go on to have advertising budgets that far exceeded theirs.)

Practise what you get right

To reach our aim of becoming a billion-dollar enterprise and secure the top spot in the natural health industry, we had to concentrate on reinforcing our existing strengths and maintain an unwavering commitment to what we had already perfected.

Like an NBA basketball player who practised for hours every day to bag a shot from the three-point line when it really counted, we too needed to practise what we got right – to get better at what we were already good at. Why spend time on things you aren't good at when you can focus on what you excel at and get brilliant at that? By all means, look at what you don't do well and always seek out others to help you identify your blind spots, but to really maximise your full potential, you need to double down on what you do well.

As a team, we were good at a few things. Firstly, we hired emotionally intelligent leaders who embraced our values. This approach fostered a team of individuals who took pride in their work and embraced a performance-driven culture. Secondly, rather than hiring those who had a particular skill set or technical expertise, we hired those who fitted in with our culture: the kind of people who would smile, say hello to each other, stop what they were doing to have a conversation, listen actively and help each other out when needed. At the core, we hired people who really liked each other, who got on well together and had similar values.

Thirdly, we encouraged questions and accepted that not knowing everything was perfectly fine. 'LGI' became our mantra and our focus was to help our team evolve, grow and flourish. Feedback played a crucial role in our culture, and we encouraged a 360-degree approach where improvement was sought without fear of repercussions. This led to a team that embraced change, reinvented themselves and inspired others to do the same.

Every new team member was made aware that embracing change was a necessary part of our fast-growing company's success, and we were unapologetic about that.

Culture of kindness

People loved working at Swisse as our commitment to culture brought out the best in them, and deep down we all wanted to be our best. It gave everyone a purpose. Success felt good, and practising being successful became a habit. Our positive language and mindset inspired the team to make our customers healthier and happier.

We created a workplace where acts of kindness, risk-taking and courage were rewarded. We encouraged paying it forward. Michael led the way here. Notoriously generous, he would regularly pay for the coffees of everyone in a café, or put down $200 to pay for the groceries of the person behind him in the queue. (When I got married, he bought up the entire wedding registry.)

Paying it forward didn't have to be about money. It could be any act of generosity: walking someone's dog if they went away on holiday, helping them fix the photocopier, or complimenting someone for a job well done. Or it could simply be taking the time to smile at someone or make them a cup of tea. It wasn't about how much was spent. It was about cultivating a generous mindset.

Creating a healthy culture was a priority and took precedence above all else, including the business plan. It was a constant topic of discussion. We reported on it regularly and this had a material impact on our success. Unsurprisingly, when our culture was off, so were our KPIs. Our culture truly was the heartbeat of our organisation.

Looking back, our journey may have seemed audacious, but it was a revolution in the making. We disrupted the status quo and transformed health into an aspirational lifestyle. Our impact went beyond the boundaries of marketing; it empowered individuals to take charge of their wellbeing. The world was a better place when we cared about our health because from there, we could care for others. That started with caring for those you worked with. They were our family.

Focus on culture

Your personal brand is what people *say* about you when you leave the room. Your culture is what your team *do* when you leave the room. Set up your values and ensure everyone knows what they are so that when you are gone, your team act as if you were there. Creating a culture will take your business further and faster and motivate your team to be more loyal and work harder and for longer than any pay rise will ever do. It becomes part of your corporate intellectual property that competitors can't copy.

The language of numbers

Taking that finance course at Melbourne Business School all those years ago was one of the best things I ever did. I wasn't a natural with numbers and I really had to work hard to understand the minutiae of how the money flowed. Numbers are the language of business, and if you don't speak it, it is impossible to communicate your position, or argue your case.

This financial knowledge, coupled with my instinct and ability to see the bigger picture, fuelled my passion to uncover the hidden stories behind the numbers and identify untapped opportunities. I spent hours reviewing our spreadsheets searching for gaps, patterns and anomalies. It was within those white spaces that the true potential resided. When I stumbled upon something unseen by others – an opportunity for a new product, a unique formulation, or a different price point – it sent a surge of excitement through my veins, like a jolt of adrenaline. This is what made business thrilling for me. Numbers had once been my greatest weakness; now, they were my greatest strength.

How to find white space opportunities

If you're looking for a niche to enter or want to find an untapped area of potential – what we called a 'white space opportunity' – do a deep dive

(continued)

into the data: review your sales figures, read a trend report, or download an industry white paper. Even better, augment that research by talking to your customers or store buyers to find out what matters to them. It will always be the sum of all these inputs that will inspire innovative thinking. If you can't afford to pay for industry trend reports, explore the websites of global advisory firms for their free white papers on what they believe the future holds. They'll unveil insights about trends and innovations that you can apply to your business.

Through constant testing and refinement, we discovered anomalies in customer behaviour that enabled us to maximise our revenue. For example, to determine the most efficient product size versus price point, we conducted a test on one of our detox supplements, one of our most popular products.

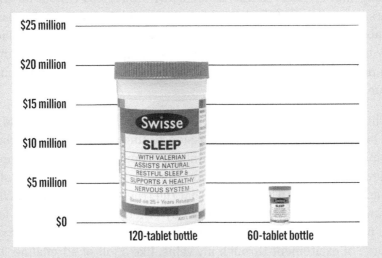

120 tablets vs 60 tablets

We compared the sales of the 120-tablet bottle (which sold for $35) with the 60-tablet bottle (which sold for $20). Surprisingly, the larger bottle outsold the smaller one despite its higher price. This discovery was significant because it indicated we could increase the number of tablets in a bigger bottle, which would then lower the cost of goods through economies of scale, and increase our profit. It also meant the consumer was using our product for four months instead of two. That meant they would get the maximum impact from the product, which increased the likelihood that when it came time to replenish the product, they would choose us again.

It also meant the product would gain a better point-of-sale presence, get more shelf facings, and attract better marketing, and it lessened the likelihood of the product running out of stock, all of which enhanced sales.

To formalise this process within the business, and to build systems around it to make it sustainable, we assembled the team every month to meticulously review the figures and explore the untapped opportunities that lay buried in these numbers. These campaign reviews became a team sport. Every area of the business was involved, and we had huge fun trying to out-pitch each other to see who could come up with the best ideas. No stone was left unturned, no idea left unexplored. It was a collaborative effort aimed at staying ahead of the game.

CHAPTER 17

RUNNING FAST

From 2009 to 2011, we went on a hiring spree. We were running fast and needed people who could not just keep up, but take the lead. We had all our ducks in a row: we were advertising 52 weeks a year, had a rotating roster of five-star celebrities, a powerful flywheel, a thriving culture, exceptional product formulations, and a world-class team. All hands were on deck and aligned with the mission of reaching our $1 billion target and making billions of people around the world healthier and happier. But first, we needed new team members, and lots of them.

It's no secret we employed a raft of family and friends whose company we enjoyed. We became (in)famous for it. I've hired so many people from school, Village, family, friends of family and friends of a friend, that going to work often felt like I was going to a Sunday BBQ. People thought it was hugely unorthodox to hire people you liked or loved to work alongside you. I never understood that. You spent half your life at work. Why wouldn't you want to spend it with people you already knew you liked? Besides, our recruitment process almost always delivered a much more effective outcome than when we used the traditional method.

Our unique culture was not for everyone. Some thought we were a cult. They'd come to work and see people laughing, smiling, and genuinely enjoying each other's company. 'How could everyone possibly be so happy?' they'd ask. 'How could everyone actually *enjoy* coming to work each day?' The culture eventually became self-curating. People would join and within a month or two, they would know, as did everyone around them, that this was, or was not, the environment for them. People would then leave of their own accord and be replaced with people who were more aligned with the culture. Some people just love being miserable, so they were much happier going back to work somewhere miserable to be surrounded by other miserable people. Misery loves company.

Of course, working with family and friends could be challenging and get complicated. Hiring friends meant that they might witness a side of us at work that we'd rather keep hidden. But what does that say about us? It says that we're one person at home, and another at work. I wanted people to feel free to be their authentic selves at work and embrace their true selves, flaws and all.

Michael had a rule: we needed to be tougher on family members than any other team member. I later extended this to friends as well. It sounded harsh, but it was crucial for our team not to feel compromised when working alongside family or friends. And surprisingly, it worked. Did we let people go? Did we have disagreements? Did we make tough decisions? Absolutely. However, our cultural values guided us throughout any conflicts or difficult conversations, and we always prioritised people over profit.

(If someone is unhappy in their workplace, it is best for them and the rest of the team that they move on. Yes, it's better for the business but ultimately better for the team member to find a culture that resonates with them. We always helped those who left to find new opportunities elsewhere that were more suitable to their needs and goals.)

Work with people you like

If you want to save potentially millions of dollars in recruiter fees, and minimise the likelihood of a hiring misfire, seek out people you already have a relationship with as the source of your new employees. You want to work with people whose company you enjoy, so why not choose to work with family and friends. To keep things fair, we made a point of holding these people to a higher standard than others. Once you have a great culture go a step further and incentivise your team to do the same so they can tap their network for new team members.

Hiring Helen

As sophisticated as our flywheel was, we lacked serious marketing clout. Marketing was now a multidisciplinary science that required a deep understanding of the traditional mediums — TV, print, press, radio, catalogues, co-op promotions — coupled with an in-depth knowledge of the digital tools — data science, analytics, social media and influencer marketing.

We needed a fresh face; a person who not only understood all those modalities, but who also knew how to work with a small marketing team, and even smaller budgets, and accepted that most of our limited advertising funds would go into paying for the TV media. We needed a person with a unique blend of skills to take our marketing to the next level, a person who understood our culture and appreciated our unorthodox approach to just about everything. Turns out the person we needed was hiding in plain sight. The person we needed was my wife.

Having worked at big companies such as Flybuys and Virgin Velocity, Helen knew how their systems worked, what excellence looked like and how to transfer those learnings to our company. Back when we were a small team of ten, 20 or 50, communicating our vision and being involved in decision making was a breeze. But now, with our team size growing rapidly and revenue doubling year on year, every decision carried significant weight. It could either propel us to new heights or send us crashing down.

To take our strategy to the next level, we needed a framework to ensure that the decisions we made were the right ones. It was no longer about individual involvement; it was about implementing efficient systems at scale. Helen joined Swisse in September 2009 and one of her first tasks was to conduct three much-needed reviews to help us establish where we'd been, where we were now and where we needed to go. The first examined our internal processes, the second our position in the natural health category, and the third, our reputation with customers and retailers. These reviews were instrumental in shaping our brand fundamentals and gave birth to our three-word positioning statement: Premium, Proven, Aspirational. This statement became the ultimate filter that guided all our product marketing decisions and assessments.

We also took a reflective deep dive. For our marketing to be authentic, the company had to reflect inwardly what it was projecting outwardly. If our external image was built on those three words of Premium, Proven and Aspirational, what three words did our internal team culture need to embody? We identified Mindfulness, Movement, and Nutrition as the core internal values that would guide our team.

The result of this work meant we now had a values platform that the team could use to make decisions. It meant I could let go of the need to be everywhere all at once, playing every instrument and singing every song. Now I could step up to the podium and conduct the orchestra, which meant our team of talented 'musicians', each a virtuoso in their own right, could play their instruments without supervision. I'll stop with the analogy.

The foundation that Helen created enabled us to hire at scale as we now had a common platform that helped everyone understand our values, which in turn guided the decisions people made. Unlike the early days when Michael needed to see and touch everything that went out the door, which caused bottlenecks that prevented growth, we now had a streamlined process that empowered everyone to make decisions without seeking formal approval or guidance.

Still trying...

On a personal note, Helen and I were still struggling to conceive. Despite undergoing our fourth IVF attempt, the doctors couldn't determine the cause of our infertility. Helen continued to stay strong and resilient and endured the process with grace. But I can't deny that this journey to parenthood was challenging and upsetting. We both felt the desire to become parents and were committed to the journey. It put any challenges we had at work into perspective. Helen was characteristically stoic during this time. IVF is extraordinarily invasive; daily injections, hormone fluctuations, painful surgical procedures, and the emotional toll of yet another negative pregnancy test. Her composure and resilience were remarkable. Other than me, no-one would have known what she was going through or appreciate the depth of her strength. Being the quintessential English lady, she embodied the 'keep calm and carry on' philosophy to the fullest.

Our people were our greatest asset

By June 2011, we had almost 100 on our team and nearly $100 million in revenue. When we reached this goal, we celebrated with the team and had company-wide gatherings that made sure everyone knew their contributions were recognised and rewarded. We used our values of Nutrition, Mindfulness and Movement as pillars for how to acknowledge their hard work. We offered meditations at 3 pm with a leading coach, access to a personal trainer and dietician to create personalised health programs, a day off every month (if there was no public holiday in that month), time off to attend our community fundraising days, free gym access and much more to reward and thank everyone for their hard work. Having these defined values made it easier to come up with exciting and innovative recognition programs that constantly reinforced what we believed in. We were a tight-knit team and I knew everyone by name. We enjoyed creating these outstanding results and we enjoyed each other's company even more.

I'm often asked why Swisse was successful. The answer is easy: it was because of our people. Coupled with our culture and our pursuit of excellence, we were a formidable force. What did the pursuit of excellence actually mean? It meant we hired people who were not only great at what they did, but people who truly loved what they were doing. We took the time to ask people about how they wanted to spend their time. We'd ask, 'What do you really like doing? What lights you up? What do you do in your spare time? What do you like reading, watching, listening to?' We wanted them to find their passion and bring it to the Swisse table so they could fulfil their potential. It also meant we held them accountable; we were firm but fair, and rewarded them with above average financial rewards, offered them outstanding working conditions, and, importantly, encouraged them to bring their whole self to work.

We had yet to reach our goal of being Australia's number one natural health brand. While we could achieve the title for a week or two at a time, we weren't *consistently* number one every week, which is what we wanted and needed to be. We were just hitting our stride and were hungry to see how far we could grow. We just needed more people to help us do it!

Just another day at the office

Swisse was renowned for being a fun and exciting place to work. Where else could you come to work and meet a celebrity? We often invited our ambassadors to attend and/or perform at our team functions. These appearances resulted in a surge of communications from within the company to the team's social media network, and this not only increased our reach and impact within our own community, but it also helped fill our pipeline of future employees. Everyone wanted to work at Swisse. You were expected to work hard, but we guaranteed you'd have a fun time doing it.

These events had a dual purpose. The team got to have a great time, but so did the ambassador. They saw our culture in action and witnessed first-hand what a fun-loving and authentic team we were. The ambassador often shared this experience with their own network, which meant our Swisse culture was broadcasted far and wide to their many millions of followers.

Two people for the same role

I was still managing the grocery and key pharmacy accounts, buying the media from the networks, and coordinating the talent and sponsorship program, all of which took up a lot of my time. As much as I enjoyed these roles and was good at them, the team was getting bigger and I realised my time was better spent leading them and setting the strategy, rather than getting caught up in transactional details.

I needed to hire a range of people to take on all these important roles. These were critical roles that I could not just give to anyone. Finding the right people for the right roles was difficult, and we didn't have time to waste so we initiated an unorthodox but highly effective hiring policy of recruiting two people for the same role. My process was to hire a highly experienced person from a company bigger than ours, but from within our industry, as this ensured we had someone with an in-depth understanding of the market and its dynamics. I'd also hire someone who had no industry experience, but possessed exceptional talent in their respective field. Hedging our bets like this allowed us to mitigate risks and maximise our chances of success.

Unsurprisingly, this person was often sourced through the Swisse network of family and friends. By adopting this strategy, we not only saved significant recruitment fees (recruiters charged $30 000 or more to recruit a senior executive), but we also expedited the hiring process. Existing employees knew our company values and could vouch for the candidates. This approach created a culture where like-minded individuals attracted other like-minded individuals. It was a fast and effective way to find great people and we rewarded those who referred people to us with a generous cash bonus.

This policy made us one of the most productive and efficient companies in our industry, if not the world. Salaries would run at an average of 7 per cent of revenue, which is when we'd run at our optimum. The challenge was to keep hiring at the rate our revenue grew.

Sometimes, we didn't even wait for a job to come up. If we liked someone who was great at what they did and they shared our values, we created a role for them. We figured they'd pay for themselves eventually.

We hired for attitude and trained for aptitude. Most people can learn a new role, but it is a lot harder to learn to be a good, kind person.

Finding the right people

Magically, the right people we needed to take on these roles were in close range. (I truly believe that if you are in flow, the universe will always provide.) As our campaigns and scope of business became increasingly complex, we needed a numbers person who could give us the depth and detail needed to keep our retailers accountable. I had just the person in mind: Adem Karafili. I'd known Adem since I was five years old and had always admired his charisma and ability to 'keep your head when all about you are losing theirs', as Rudyard Kipling said. I socialised with his sister Violetta, attended his wedding, and knew his extended Albanian family well. (We Aussie-Albanians all seem to be related in some way!)

He came on board in 2009 and instantly became part of the fabric of the business. From the get-go, Adem was fantastic. Finally, we had someone who truly understood numbers. He used to say, 'If you put shit numbers into a report, you'll get shit out.' (He liked to swear, did Adem.) He did shock people a little when he started shredding reams of files that had been stored in the back office. He stood at the shredder, leafing through report after report, mumbling to himself, 'What the f...k,' 'What a f...g idiot,' 'What the f...k is going on here?' 'That's not very H and H Adem,' we'd say to him good humouredly. (This was our way of letting him know that we took our cultural values of Health and Happiness seriously but could do it with a smile.) He'd grimace, apologise and promise to do better. Expletives were not quite part of our corporate culture, but at the same time we did encourage people to bring their true self to work, so we found a compromise in the form of a swear jar. We put it on his desk on day three of his arrival. By day four, it was full. ☺

To his credit, Adem embraced change and strove to become his best self. He revolutionised our financials and integrated the flywheel into our systems, ensuring the right balance between revenue and cost.

Thanks to his efforts, we gained the confidence to focus on what we knew worked, with a system and process that ensured no opportunity was missed. His natural leadership style made him a dependable resource. When I was on the road, I could rely on him to keep things steady. He came to embody everything our culture represented. I can't overstate how crucial Adem's contribution was to the success of Swisse. As our 'second in command', he played an instrumental role in driving the growth of the business. We could not have achieved what we did without him.

Sales superstars

With that key role taken care of, I turned our attention to finding a pair of sales superstars to head up our grocery and pharmacy accounts. After having got to know her over many years, we hired Dimi from Priceline to take on the pharmacy role. She'd worked at Chemist Warehouse before that, so she was well-versed in the world of pharmacy retail. We also hired Leigh Small, my best friend from childhood, to take over the grocery role. We had been opposing captains on our Under 12s footy teams and had been friends ever since. He never ceased to remind me of what a stand-out I had been on the field — not because I was good at getting the ball, but because I was the tallest on the ground and wore a helmet. (Mum made me wear it. How embarrassing.)

Leigh had worked extensively in the supermarket sector selling yoghurt and dips so he was the perfect person to help us manage the grocery channel. I did ponder whether hiring my best friend made good business sense, and wondered if being his boss would change our relationship, but considering we'd already hired my wife, sister, brother, brother-in-law, cousin and countless other family and friends, I couldn't see why this wouldn't work out equally well. Besides, what could be better than us all being on a mission to make people healthier and happier together? Leigh and Dimi became an extraordinary team and were responsible for a huge chunk of our sales success.

We also hired Andrew Milligen, or Milligenius, as I called him, as the head of IT and Analytics. I worked with him very successfully at Village.

Nominative determinism must really be a thing as Andrew truly lived up to his nickname. He was a genius at turning numbers into meaningful stories that helped us spot trends and opportunities in the data before the rest of the market did.

Having Helen on board allowed us to promote Aaron Fitzgerald, our existing marketing manager, to the position of General Manager. In those early years, his exemplary contribution made it possible for Swisse to achieve what it did, as did Nahla Saba's, Michael's sister. She was an integral part of Swisse's founding success and was central in laying down the foundations for what would become our unique recruitment process and the subsequent cultural superpower that resulted. Her extraordinary empathetic management style enabled her to be there for everyone, no matter what was happening.

Every time I was able to release myself from the day-to-day of running a particular area of the business, we became better as an organisation. The trick, though, was releasing myself at the right time to the right person. We had a number of false starts with this transition process. It was either too early in our growth trajectory or the person taking over the role would not respect how we did things, and often totally ignored what was going well and changed the way we did things for the sake of making us the same as other big companies. Our goal was to achieve a seamless fusion of Swisse's proven strategies with successful elements from other approaches, while improving upon them with each iteration.

The A-team on board

With Aaron's oversight, Adem's attention to accounting, and Andrew's dexterity with data, we finally had the A-team needed to take us to the next level. Coupled with the marketing expertise that Helen brought to the table, we were able to become the data-driven company we needed to be. They all had a huge role to play in helping us keep track of everything we did at store level. Our campaigns were complex with many moving parts. Getting our numbers right was crucial and accountability from all parties was a must. We looked at what sold, who sold it, when and where. The team had spreadsheets as long as my arm that documented the stock levels, sales and profitability on a store-by-store basis so we could see at a glance how each store stacked up against the other, whether our sales promotions were working and what new opportunities could be uncovered.

This functionality was important. We needed to prove to our retailers that our elaborate campaigns added up. If we could show them what worked and what didn't, they were 100 per cent more likely to approve another campaign. The days of guesswork using rubbery numbers were over. This attention to detail enabled us to hold the team members, including the retailers, to account. The data does not lie.

Doing things differently

The last piece of my role that needed to be delegated was the media buying. Normally we bought our media directly from the TV networks but if this option wasn't available to us, we'd supplement it by getting an agency to process the media spots we had carefully hand-picked. It was a super important task that couldn't be delegated to just anyone. We were buying around $15 million per year across the three major networks and various other support media, so we had become a significant buyer — not yet in the realm of Toyota, Coles or Coke, but, for a home-grown family business, we were a player.

We offered the role of Sales and Marketing Director to Adam Hilton, a superb media professional who was previously the commercial director at Channel Ten. He declined the role and let it be known he had ambitions to run his own media agency. He offered me a 50-50 stake in that business but I declined that offer and promptly let him know that while I couldn't partner with him personally, Swisse definitely could. We introduced him to our creative agency and our digital marketing agency, and suggested that they collaborate to offer a unique media buying/creative/digital marketing agency. This was partly in response to the fact that we could no longer buy media directly from the networks (they were concerned we did not have the debtor insurance that most agencies had, which would protect them and ensure they got paid) and we saw the need for an independent media agency who could do it for us.

That trio of companies united to become Noisy Beast, with Swisse as its anchor client. The beauty of this partnership was that we now had an agency that understood the Swisse way, the flywheel and the interconnected nature of all the pieces of our marketing machine. They were able to model their services around the way we did things, rather than the traditional agency way. When we'd said to Stewart Byfield, creative director at our agency, a few years earlier, 'Please look after us on these early jobs and we will look after you in the future', we meant it. We didn't know how that future would look but we appreciated that he trusted us enough to know that we were an organisation that stood by its word and that somehow, an opportunity would arise and he would be part of it. (Noisy Beast went on to become one of Melbourne's most innovative, highly awarded and largest independent agencies.) We learned a lot from this collaboration and in my years after leaving Swisse, I would apply those lessons to form Strat, a progressive integrated agency specialising in retail and ecommerce that would go on to achieve even greater success. Our disruptive approach to doing business better and differently did ruffle some feathers in the advertising sector (and other sectors!), but if you're not upsetting someone somewhere, you're not pushing hard enough.

The opportunity to hire good friends kept coming. We hired Wade Porter, one of my best mates from high school, which released me from the critical role of leading our New Product Development team. We also hired Jason Buesst, another ex-Village mate. (Jason was the suave dude who got the job at Southland that I had desired so much – the job I cried over when I didn't get it.) He firstly headed up our logistics team and then took over our skin care division, which went on to have spectacular success.

CHAPTER 18

MELBOURNE CUP MADNESS

In 2009, Channel Seven offered Stephen and I tickets to the Melbourne Cup. I wasn't a big horse person, but I've always loved the spectacle of Australia's richest horse race (well, it was the richest race, until The Everest race came along – a cautionary tale that even the strongest brands are always under threat). For the uninitiated, the Melbourne Cup is a renowned annual horse race that takes place on the first Tuesday of November in Melbourne. Often referred to as 'the race that stops a nation', it attracts a wide range of famous and infamous celebrities along with the regular punters who want to kick back, have a drink and enjoy a day at the races. The race started back in 1861 and is now one of the most prestigious horse races in the world.

Stephen and I stood on the balcony, sipped our beers and looked out over the 90 000 people in attendance. It was a glorious scene. The sun was shining, the track glowed a luminous green, the crowd was dressed to the nines, and joie de vivre emanated from every corner of the track.

Just below us was The Birdcage. This was where all the corporate marquees were located and where the captains of industry, socialites and sports stars came together to eat, drink and network. The logos on the marquees glittered in the sunlight. Emirates. Lexus. Myer. These global brands represented the best of the best. The idea came to me in an instant. I pointed to The Birdcage below and said, 'We need to be in there. We need to have a Melbourne Cup marquee and we need to be in prime position in the front row. If we are to become a mega global brand, we need to position ourselves alongside these other mega global brands.' Stephen looked at me and smiled. He was used to me coming up with these grand plans and loved spurring me on to think bigger and better. We had always borrowed from the best, and if this was what the best did, then we'd do it too.

He and Michael were totally supportive of the plan but we all agreed it had to be done properly. This would be a major investment for us and we couldn't afford to put a foot wrong. This marquee would place us not just on the national stage, but on the world stage. We'd always had the vision of taking the business global. We weren't quite sure how that would happen but here was an opportunity that would help us get closer to it.

Our ambition was audacious: to establish Swisse as the premium lifestyle brand, first for Australia, and then the world. I liked to think big. Why not? If you only achieve half of what you set out to do, you're already further ahead than if you'd just aimed for something small.

Is Kim K coming?

None of us were experienced in hosting a huge sponsorship event like this. These big events are multifaceted, logistically complex operations that demand careful planning, resource management and contingency preparation to ensure its success.

We needed a talented media maestro with experience in branding, sponsorship, media, PR, hospitality and event management who could pull it all together. We searched far and wide and came up with the perfect character: Mitch Catlin. And what a character he was. He had been the creative brains behind the Myer marquee and knew how these big events operated. Myer were unmatched in transforming corporate hospitality into earned media. I read a raft of newspapers every day and saw each year how many millions of dollars in media mentions the Myer marquee made. No-one did it better.

I invited Mitch for a coffee, complimented him on what a great job he had done for Myer, and offered him the role to put our 2011 Melbourne Cup marquee together. He said yes instantly. We were thrilled. Our grand plan to transform this event into a masterful marketing opportunity was one step closer to reality.

(I later asked him what made him accept our offer and he said that it was because I had told him what a great job he had done with Myer. No-one had ever told him that before. Never forget the power of praise.)

We created a spreadsheet and carefully selected a range of ambassadors who we felt would best represent us at the Cup, and then matched them to a specific demographic and Swisse product. Celebrities who graced our tent that year included Ash Hart the supermodel, Lleyton Hewitt the tennis player, Sally Pearson the Olympic hurdler, champion cyclist Cadel Evans, and the Grande Dame of Hollywood, Joan Collins. What an eclectic mix!

But our trump card, the celebrity who was bound to create an uber-sensation, was none other than Kim Kardashian. She was at the pinnacle of her fame. She had over 10 million Twitter followers, her reality show *Keeping Up with the Kardashians* was at its zenith, and her tumultuous marriage to Kris Humphries was on the rocks, which constantly put her in the headlines.

We'd negotiated a watertight contract to confirm her appearance, but as the event drew near, I did lose some sleep wondering if the drama in her personal life would preclude her from coming to the event. We had spruiked her appearance for weeks prior to the event and were really relying on her to be there. In typical Mitch style, he had expertly chosen Stakes Day, which was the last day of the Melbourne Cup Carnival, for the day of Kim K's appearance. This ensured that we had the full attention of the media, which created a perfect setting for drama and the coverage that was bound to follow. But, as Stakes Day drew near, it became clear that Kim's marriage to Kris was imploding and that it was highly unlikely she would come.

We needed to turn this uncertainty to our advantage, so we strategically placed stories in the media that fed into the 'will she come/won't she come' hoopla. (If you can't beat 'em, join 'em!) These stories were not fabricated. We genuinely didn't know if she would turn up. Everywhere I went, people asked, 'Is Kim coming?' I didn't know. No-one knew. I don't think Kim knew. All we knew was that the mystery and intrigue surrounding her attendance was generating more coverage than the entire Melbourne Cup event.

The Kim frenzy hit its peak when I received a text from Mitch the morning of Stakes Day: 'She's not coming.' That threw us into a spin. What do you do when the biggest celebrity in the world – the guest you've been spruiking for months as your star attraction – doesn't turn up? We had to turn this challenge into an opportunity, and quickly. The minute we heard she wasn't coming, we had a life-size replica of Kim made from corflute, a type of corrugated plastic that is strong and lightweight and easy to transport. When the moment came to introduce Kim to the crowd, we unveiled the corflute cut-out and announced that since we couldn't have Kim herself, we'd have the next best thing. The crowd roared with laughter and applause. I ended up doing TV interviews with the corflute cut-out, had drinks with 'her' at the bar, and placed bets with 'her' at the bookies. The media lapped it up. It was priceless.

To top it all off, we didn't have to pay Kim her appearance fee. We calculated that the earned and shared media coverage generated by Kim's frenzied non-appearance was worth around $2 million, which effectively subsidised the cost of the entire Melbourne Cup sponsorship event.

Affordable influencers

Hiring a world-famous star to endorse your product is out of the realm for most small businesses. But hiring a micro influencer with a small (but engaged) audience could be a good starting point. Check out the extensive range of influencer platforms to find out who is available, the kinds of products they endorse and how much they charge. You may find them more affordable than you think. Better still, review your existing customer base to see if there is a person of influence that already loves your product and could become your ambassador. Whoever you choose, they must genuinely love your product and exude authenticity.

The Melbourne Cup marquee marked the ultimate evolution of our flywheel. All the pieces were in place and provided the perfect backdrop for what was possible. Our goal was to use this event to generate as much PR as possible, pin it on the flywheel and let it rip. We had the country's biggest sporting event, the world's biggest celebrities, controversy, drama, glamour and tension — all of this fed into our flywheel, which generated millions of dollars in earned media coverage, which in turn generated more coverage. The event was outrageously successful and really put us on the global map.

If people didn't know about Swisse before the Melbourne Cup carnival, they sure did afterwards. All that coverage, hype and goodwill meant people could see we were a fun-loving yet aspirational company, a company that didn't take itself too seriously, and all that contributed to the brand we were working so hard to build.

Bringing Mitch on board meant I could hand over the coordination of the talent and sponsorship marketing work. Like all the roles I'd transitioned away from, I'd wait until I'd found the right person and then hand it over. If you have the courage and humility to hire people better than you, the business can only get better.

Now that these key hires were completed, I could finally release myself from the day-to-day management of the business and focus on the big picture of becoming Australia's number one natural health brand and prepare to launch Swisse onto the international market.

'Could you live in a caravan in Byron Bay?'

Stephen had made it increasingly clear that he wanted to sell the business and cash out so in 2012 I stepped in and offered to buy another 5 per cent of his shares. The price? $7.5 million. Ouch. I'd bought my first 5 per cent in 2008 for $750 000 and my second 5 per cent tranche in 2010 for $2.5 million and now I would be the proud owner of my third 5 per cent tranche. Although each was at a 15 times EBITDA multiple, those purchases all seemed like bargains now. Yes, 15 times EBITDA was a lot to pay at the time, and I could have declined the offer and watched someone else buy in, or I could back myself, purchase the

(continued)

shares and just get cracking on making the company as valuable as I knew it could be.

I consulted with Helen about buying more shares, and opened the conversation by asking, 'Could you live in a caravan in Byron Bay?' (This was before Byron was the salubrious hangout for the rich and famous it is today.) If this investment went badly, living in a caravan would be our only option! She looked at me, smiled, and said, 'So long as I'm with you, I don't mind where I live.' The love of a good woman is priceless.

I took out another loan, bought the third tranche of shares, and now owned 15 per cent of the company. This significant investment, plus my home loan, meant I now owed the bank nearly $13 million. You could say I was fully invested.

CHAPTER 19

HOW TO INNOVATE

I'm often asked how we came up with such great ideas for new products, promotional ideas, and PR campaigns that broke the mould and garnered so much attention. In short, it was our passion to always do better that drove us on! In the dynamic realm of retail, staying ahead meant being innovative. We understood the importance of:

- consistently introducing exciting new offerings

- creating exceptional product formulations

- ensuring that we always had something unique and captivating to present to retailers.

If the campaign idea didn't send tingles down your spine and make you think 'wow', it didn't make the cut. In short, we strove to continually improve and outdo the last thing we had done. We thrived off coming up with new ideas. Our culture demanded it.

Our inspiration for innovation came from a variety of sources. Travel. Trade shows. Trend reports. Sales data. Market research. Talking to retailers. Watching customers in action. All these data points coalesced and we funneled those insights into our New Product Development meetings.

Attending industry trade shows kept me in touch with innovations in the retail world. The big shows for us were the natural health shows in the United States and Europe that focussed on raw materials and the finished products and, whilst travelling, I would regularly visit the best retailers outside of our industry to see what they were up to. I liked to cross-pollinate learnings from different worlds. This is when true disruption happens. The most important part of attending these trade shows was visiting the best retail stores in the world's most innovative cities – Los Angeles, Paris, Singapore and London. I would walk up and down the aisle, talk to the customers, ask them questions and speak to the retailer about everything they did – the packaging, point-of-sale, shelving displays and merchandising. I immersed myself in this global creativity and it sparked new and innovative ideas that I brought back home and put into action.

Delving into the data was another important input for me and the team. We'd devour our internal performance reviews, trend reports and data packages from the world's top futurists, management consultancies and industry associations. This data often unearthed a new white space opportunity.

I consumed news of all genres, from politics, sport and business to culture, art and fashion to see what was hot, new and happening in the world. This opened my eyes and my mind to original concepts and fresh ideas. My mission as the leader was to share my sources of inspiration and innovation – management books, motivational podcasts and inspiring blogs – so that the team could generate their own creative connections and locate new possibilities for disruption, and ultimately embed this disruptive sentiment into our culture.

Our New Product Development meetings were the powerhouse forums in which all these data points would merge, and where our new product formulations would emerge. The leads from each area of the business – product, sales, marketing, research, IT, finance and science – would present the results of their own research and contribute their unique take on the topic at hand. We invited contributions from a wide-cross section of the business, because we knew that innovation worked best when you had a diverse group of people in the room, each pulling and pushing in different direction to create the best idea. I enjoyed attending these meetings. After culture, this is what got me up in the morning. Some of our best ideas were germinated at these meetings.

The commodification of creativity

We used the principles of 'design thinking' to bring structure to this seemingly chaotic accumulation of creative inputs. Design thinking is an innovation process that uses a range of data sources to find out what users really want, and then harnesses collaboration and iteration to bring that idea to fruition. This process will sound familiar as we were already applying it as part of our creative process, albeit unconsciously.

How did design thinking translate into real world actions? We deployed the process to:

- find categories in which we were not represented

- locate gaps or niches that had not been covered

- uncover a price point opportunity that would open a new market.

Our ability to unite a range of data points and funnel the resulting insights through our design thinking process delivered us many successes. Who knew products like Cranberry, Liver Detox and Deep Sea Krill Oil would be so popular? We discovered these at a series of trade shows in the United States, tested them out in our NPD meetings, introduced them to the Australian market and they sold like wildfire. 'Hair Skin Nails+' and 'Sleep' were another two popular products that defied expectations.

It's very difficult to codify creativity but our design thinking process helped us get pretty close to achieving this, which enabled us to excel in product development. We'd launch ten products simultaneously, twice a year: the first batch in March and the second in September. We carefully monitored sales and eliminated the two poorest performers. It was akin to basic A/B testing, where you create one advertisement, evaluate its performance, make a single adjustment, run the revised version, and compare the results. Through this iterative approach you gradually find the best-performing advertisement.

While most companies applied this principle of A/B testing to their online or print advertising, we were doing this at scale, with nutritional products, in a highly regulated and competitive market. This iterative process produced 20 unique products each year and had thousands of moving parts. It was heady stuff. People often asked us how we innovated – well, that was how we did it. It was challenging, but that was what made us unique. Our culture inspired the team to embrace change, innovate and to do the things others didn't want to do. This is what created our point of difference.

The three steps to unleash retail innovation

Our New Product Development team kept the retailers' shelves filled with novel and exciting formulations by following a three-step formula (see below).

1. **Focus on the core**: this involved adding line extensions to top categories (introducing new products or variations within an existing product line or brand family), and improvements and revisions to existing products.

2. **Iterate and expand the core**: we looked at what core products were selling well and added new products based on extensions to those popular products.

3. **Innovate into new values-aligned categories**: once we had the core products established, we hedged our bets by leveraging the strengths of the core products and expanded into new areas.

The three-step formula to new product development

Our Deep Sea Krill Oil product was a major success and showcased how our new product development process functioned. We introduced it in May 2010 as a part of our core range. In 2011, we 'extended the core' by introducing new formulations such as the 4 × Strength Wild Krill Oil and Wild Neptune Krill Oil. In 2012, we used our strength in the natural health category to diversify into other business areas and 'expanded beyond the core' by launching our Superfoods, Sports Nutrition, and Skincare ranges.

Within two years of launching, the Skincare and Superfoods ranges each turned over around $10 million. Three years later, each turned over $30 million. (Some said that us going into skincare was like L'Oreal going into vitamins. It wasn't quite the same. They tried and failed. We went into skincare and succeeded!) Despite their later success, these products had a poor start. We commenced advertising before the product was on the shelf, an error that we would repeat later on that would cost us dearly – a story I will cover later in detail – but once the flywheel to launch these products was in motion, they became hugely successful.

Commit to continuous improvement

Our commitment to continuous innovation and product development secured us more shelf space, excited our existing customers, and attracted new customers. The retailers loved that they had something new and different to offer, and we supported them with a range of promotional incentives to stock the products, which generated higher sell-ins/sell-throughs, buy-in and greater engagement. Everyone won. Stephen, Michael and I met constantly to discuss how these plans and the wider goals of the business would be achieved. We met for breakfast at the local café, spoke daily on the phone, attended conferences and trade shows together and spent countless hours refining the strategy to ensure we all had buy-in on major decisions and that we were all invested in working towards a common goal. It was a true team effort.

Grow the core

One of the most frequent questions I get asked is, 'How can I get started in business?' The best advice? Find a product that's profitable, make that your core product, and use it to fund the early-stage growth of your business. Don't launch other products until you've established this core product. You can (and must) hedge your bets later on by 'extending the core', and piggyback off the success of your existing line by 'expanding beyond the core', but at the start, focus on creating a superstar 'core' product and grow from there.

Survival of the fittest

People often asked how we chose what products to advertise on TV. We relied on real customers buying real products to determine what products we would promote on TV. When we had that sales data, we'd identify the top performers, create a new commercial to promote those products, release the advertisement, wait to see how sales went, review the sales data again, and then repeat the process. Once we identified the products for promotion, we sprang into action to produce the TV commercials. While traditional shoots typically took six weeks, we completed ours in less than ten days. This data-driven approach significantly improved our capacity to maximise the return on our marketing investments.

We could also move quickly because we had such great support from our agency creatives, our contract manufacturers, and our retailers who trusted us with our crazy, but now proven, strategies. We all played a role. Michael was responsible for researching the formulas and ingredients and I focused on the speed of launch, the product sell-in to retailers, and market positioning. We created a product plan that spanned the next three years which enabled us to roll out a plan way in advance and create economies of scale.

This commodification of creativity led to explosive results. At the start of this innovation experiment, we'd get five out of ten products right. Then we'd get seven out of ten right, then eight, and eventually nine out of ten would become proven performers and superstars in their own right. When we got to this point, the business was humming like a finely tuned car. We knew that releasing new and innovative products was critical to securing more shelf space. How quickly did we ramp up? Below is a snapshot of how our NPD program contributed to our fast-paced rollout of new products. We were fast to market when launching new products. We had to be: retailers (and customers) demanded it.

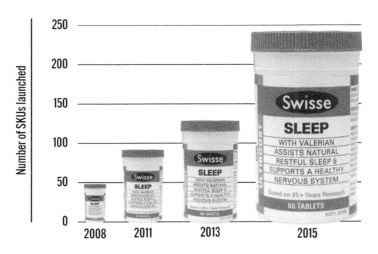

The number of new SKUs launched by Swisse, 2008–2015

We needed this design thinking process to work as it gave us our competitive edge. Without that, we'd quickly become just another natural health brand. It was this commitment to endless learning that set us apart. Some companies live by the motto, 'If it ain't broke, don't fix it'. We lived by the motto, 'If it ain't broke, fix it anyway!'

CHAPTER 20

CULTURE AND COMMUNICATION

Yoga. Massage. Complimentary gym membership. Personal trainer. Chef-cooked meals. Fully stocked pantry. In-house dietician. Meditation coach. Naturopath. Celebrity VIP events.

This reads like a blurb from the brochure of a five-star luxury health resort. It was in fact a slice of life in the day of a Swisse team member. We wanted to keep our team happy and knew that providing perks like these would make work feel more like home. Productivity experts talk about work–life *balance*. We preferred to call it work–life *integration*. We wanted people to feel as comfortable at work as they did at home, so we did everything we could to make work feel more like home. The heritage of this largesse began over a decade earlier.

It all started with lunch.

A home away from home

The tradition of providing the team with a daily meal began when Swisse consisted of just Michael, Stephen and a handful of people working out of the office in Airport West. Michael's parents ran the takeaway shop across the road and when Michael started work at Swisse, his mother would cook up a beautiful hot lunch of Lebanese delights like baba ghanouj, tabbouleh, falafel and shawarma and bring it over to feed the Swisse team. They all stopped work, sat down at a communal table, broke bread and talked about things other than work.

Michael told me what an impact these small but incredibly powerful gestures had on the team, so when I took over as the leader at Swisse, we made sure this tradition continued. We were a family and we wanted our family to be happy and healthy. While a fully cooked lunch and these other little luxuries may seem out of a place in a corporate office, we wanted our team to know we appreciated their efforts and dedication. This concern for our team extended to the office layout too. We engaged one of Australia's foremost architecture firms to conduct our office fit-out, with the design brief stipulating that every desk have a view of a window and access to natural light. Our people spent a lot of time at work. If we could make that place a more enjoyable place to be, everyone won.

People always commented that after a few months of joining Swisse their loved ones said they were in a much better mood at home, less stressed and better people to be around. Why shouldn't work be as good a place to be as home? We saw no excuse for why workplaces should be anything short of this. I believe business leaders have a duty to society to prioritise culture and to create harmonious workplaces, and that governments should provide tax incentives to companies that make the workplace a purposeful, inviting and nurturing place to be. Imagine what kind of innovative and creative methods companies would find to keep their team happy if they had a financial inducement to do so? Imagine how much better our society would be if we all had workplaces that put culture and people first? If business leaders did the right thing, it would enhance company performance *and* make for a better world.

We were dedicated to building an exceptional culture but it went up a notch when Cath Crowley joined. Her expertise in operations and training, honed through her roles at Village (where I reported to her when I was working in Prague) and Mecca Cosmetics, made her an exceptional Director of People and Culture. Cath's attention to detail and commitment to our shared vision were instrumental in shaping our culture, communication, and business plans. We had always had these plans in place but with Cath's arrival in 2011, she took them up to the next level. These three plans formed the foundation of our strategy and became our touchstones for how the organisation would run. I'd meet with her most days to discuss the progress of our culture. While she initially found managing family members particularly daunting, her contributions were outstanding, and she became a trusted adviser.

1. The Culture Plan

Our Culture Plan was a formal document for how our culture was created and rolled out across the organisation. It was built around our four key values and consisted of a range of different initiatives:

1. *People*: building our capability

   ■ an induction program

   ■ Health and Happiness (H+H) Days off

   ■ product and sales training

   ■ Weekly Savvy Sessions

   ■ diagnostic training

   ■ leadership programs

   ■ weekly team lunches

2. *Principles*: upholding our wellness philosophy

   ■ monthly 'lunch and learn' sessions

   ■ meditation training

   ■ book club

   ■ movement coaching sessions

   ■ wellness week festival (twice a year)

   ■ paid gym membership

   ■ free yoga classes

3. *Passion*: celebrating and connecting

- social and wellbeing events four times per year

- one family day per year

- mid-year party

- end of year party

- volunteer day for the Celebrate Life Foundation

- $1 coffee donation option

- invitations to VIP retailer events – Olympic launch, Grand Prix, Spring Racing, the 'Celebrate Life' Foundation Ball

4. *Profit*: ensuring value for all

- international relocation and secondment opportunities

- succession planning

- 'Swisse Stars' award prizes

- gratitude cards

- job matching and salary benchmarking

- recruitment referral bonus scheme

- rostered days off.

Development plans

Honouring development plans was an important aspect of keeping our team culture buoyant. Our surveys showed that continuous learning development plans were one of the most important drivers for why people chose one workplace over another. That's why we initiated our Savvy Sessions. These Friday afternoon get-togethers provided continuous learning opportunities for the entire team. It was not unusual to have a leading sports star talk about their Olympic win and then the following week be given a tutorial in the history of Chinese culture. These events were a fun, affordable way to bring people together, share expertise and be upskilled.

Training

Every team member received a training and development budget, which ranged from $3000 to $30 000 per person per year. This enabled everyone to further their expertise, close their skill gap and develop into the best versions of themselves. (You'd be surprised at how often 'personal development' was ranked as the key motivation for staying with a company.)

Pay

We treated pay reviews seriously. Cath and I would go through these line by line and review the manager's recommendations to ensure fairness across the board. The salaries were benchmarked against industry data, aligned with performance, and meticulously conducted to ensure people were rewarded for their achievements. Our aim was to pay employees in the upper twentieth percentile of market rates, which reflected the company's growth and commitment to rewarding excellence. We knew money wouldn't make people stay if they were unhappy to start with, but we also knew that pay was a recognition of effort and would make them feel valued and appreciated. It's not enough to have the intrinsic motivators covered. You need to have the extrinsic factors covered too.

Awards

Our efforts to create a world-class culture did not go unrecognised by the wider business community. In 2012, we were nominated in the Australian *BRW Magazine* as one of the 'Top 25 Best Places to Work', we were named an employer of choice by the Australian Business Awards and Australian Human Resources Institute, and several Swisse executive team members were listed in the top five of their respective categories for the *CEO Magazine* Executive of the Year Awards. I was runner up for CEO of the Year, the Health and Pharmaceutical Executive of the Year as well as *GQ Australia*'s Entrepreneur of the Year and Cath

Crowley was awarded HR Executive of the Year. The company was also recognised as *BRW*'s Private Business of the Year (turnover over $100 million). To this day, Swisse is still an employer of choice.

Team surveys

We routinely conducted team surveys to see how we were going as a company. These were anonymous so they gave us a true measure of the team temperature. They were remarkably effective in revealing what we were doing right and what we needed to improve upon. Here are the twelve Employee Satisfaction Indicators we surveyed:

1. role clarity

2. motivation

3. satisfaction

4. intention to stay

5. role conflict

6. job insecurity

7. stress

8. intra unit teamwork

9. intra unit coordination

10. area level quality

11. organisational quality

12. external adaptability.

Our Culture Plan was a formal framework outlining how our company's culture was established and implemented. It defined us and gave everyone a common purpose that united us during the good times, and the challenging times too.

2. The Communications Plan

As we got larger, people's roles got more specialised and it became harder and harder to communicate in the way we had in the past. When you have under 100 people on your team, it's reasonably easy to know everyone's name, have everyone attend meetings and connect with them on a one-to-one basis. As we grew, we needed to change the way we communicated, increase the cadence of our meetings, and create more formalised induction programs. Here are some of the initiatives we created to streamline our communication and keep the team happy:

- **Weekly one-on-ones:** These one-hour meetings were conducted with my direct reports. We'd talk about how their team was going and then how they were personally tracking. I'd provide input and feedback on how I thought they were performing, and they would do the same to me. It was a two-way channel. These meetings were diarised to ensure they did not get missed.

- **Weekly executive team WIPs (Work in Progress):** I was already meeting with the team in our one-to-one sessions, and got together quarterly for a couple of days as a team but on Stephen's advice, I initiated these weekly group meetings, and the results improved dramatically.

- **Fortnightly Health and Happiness (H+H) Huddle:** This was a town hall–style meeting held on Tuesday mornings to share updates from different areas of the business. Whoever was in the office would attend and it would be an opportunity for a few of our general managers to present what was happening in their area to the team. This was a great way to ensure ideas, events and initiative were cross-pollinated across the wider team.

- **Senior team monthly WIPs:** These meetings provided our senior managers with a platform to discuss important matters and foster independent leadership. We deliberately made these meetings an 'executive-free' zone so that the senior team could take ownership of issues and forge autonomous thinking. This played a huge role in succession planning, which meant the pipeline of future leaders was always fully loaded.

- **Quarterly CEO updates:** These were conducted to communicate the business's progress, reinforce values and culture, and maintain transparency with the team. I had so much fun doing these. I'd crack jokes, share the wins (and the losses), regale them with tales from being on the road and remind them of the bigger picture of what Swisse was doing and why. We also filmed these updates so that they could be distributed around the country and world.

- **Quarterly Team H+H News:** This evolved from being a casual update from me into an important hard-copy publication that kept the team informed of all the important developments happening within the company. As my travel schedule increased, and I was out of the office for three weeks out of four, this newsletter became an integral tool for keeping the team updated with how the company was tracking.

- **Quarterly team planning workshops:** These sessions allowed the leadership team to focus on strategy, culture and communication planning, all vital for achieving our business objectives. These sessions often became passionate as they became a forum where people could test their ideas out and have a robust yet safe conversation about the merits of those ideas.

- **Twice-yearly performance reviews:** We set up these reviews to ensure my reports had direct access to me on a one-to-one basis and could use the time to get feedback from me on areas of importance, check in on their career development and share their team's progress. The same would happen with every reporting line throughout the business.

- **Annual conference:** This was the highlight of the year for everyone. We put a lot of work into making these both educational and motivational. We hired the best speakers, booked out the top hotels in the most luxurious resorts, treated the team to extravagant dinners and great parties and invited our brand ambassadors for some VIP power. We did some work too, but the point was for the team to kick back, relax and enjoy some time with their colleagues.

There's safety in numbers

Stephen's guidance and mentorship at this time became increasingly invaluable. He possessed a remarkable instinct for understanding both the business's growth requirements and my personal development needs. Recognising the limitations of one-on-one sessions with my team, Stephen said, 'The individual won't feel comfortable challenging you in that setting. As the boss, they might feel intimidated, and you won't get honest feedback.' He encouraged me to schedule meetings with the wider management team where the 'safety in numbers' factor meant the team could challenge me without fear. This would ensure diverse perspectives and dissent could be shared collectively.

Too busy to talk?

When talking about the cadence of communication I am reminded of this famous quote from Gandhi: 'I have so much to accomplish today that I must meditate for two hours instead of one.' The same must be said for communicating with your team. When everyone is working flat chat, taking time to have a meeting can feel like you're cutting into people's productivity. However, the opposite held true. Just as Gandhi meditated more when busy, we worked hard to communicate more when we were busy too. During our turnaround phase, we often met weekly instead of monthly, and monthly instead of quarterly. Keeping the lines of communication open during even the busiest times was critical to success.

In the spirit of our commitment to give and receive 360-degree feedback, I saw these meetings as chances to openly admit when I messed up, made the wrong call, or overlooked something. If leaders can't own their errors, the team won't either. Our thriving culture valued honest and transparent communication, and, as the leader, I took it upon myself to set the example and lead the way.

3. The Business Plan

The third pillar was the Business Plan. This was a personalised roadmap for growth and development. We combined the Culture and

Communications Plan with individual aspirations, and crafted unique career plans for each employee. These one-page plans aligned with our values, crystallised our priorities, and provided a clear vision of what we aimed to achieve as a team. It was each person's own personal blueprint for success.

CHAPTER 21

GOING INTERNATIONAL

With a firm grip on the Australian market, our ambitions turned to global expansion. We sought a world-class event that could catapult us onto the global stage in a spectacular way. The 2012 London Olympics provided the perfect opportunity, and our audacious move to become a broadcast partner in the event marked a defining moment for us.

The Olympics

Sponsoring the Summer Olympics was a significant yet calculated risk for us. We initially tested the waters by sponsoring the Winter Olympics as it was a more cost-effective proposition (i.e. cheaper), but we soon realised that if we wanted to make a global impact, we needed to go all out and sponsor the Summer Olympics. Securing sponsorship wasn't just about putting up the money. Our products had to undergo a rigorous testing regime to get the approval of the nutritionists and the medical directors of each sport and meet the stringent standards of the Australian Olympic Committee. After jumping through a few more hoops, forgive the pun, we became proud sponsors of the 2012 Australian Olympic team. These milestones solidified our position as a premium supplement provider, enhanced our reputation and positioned us for growth.

In line with our goal to have a product for everyone and to appeal to as many demographics as possible, we shot over 60 different TV commercials (our competitors would shoot one or two, at best) and created a dynamic media strategy to ensure they all got used in the right order and at the right time. We had a couple of interesting challenges that required some delicate massaging. For example, the four members of the 400 metres relay team all took our vitamins, and were widely expected to win the gold medal, but didn't. The cycling champion Cadel Evans was meant to compete, and win, as he was the reigning Tour de France title-holder, but had to pull out as he was so exhausted from winning the Tour. (Not a good look, considering he was also taking our vitamins!) Our marketing was incredibly agile. When the Opals, led by a very young Liz Cambage, started winning, we'd change our media schedule almost overnight to include the TV commercials featuring her. In addition, the sporting public had cottoned on to what we already knew and that was our Paralympian teams were punching well above their weight and had captured the imagination of the world. Because we'd shot so many TV commercials in advance, we were able to shine our marketing spotlight on them, all of which gave them, and us, incredible cut-through, goodwill and customer awareness.

The Olympics was a huge turning point for us, and was as integral to our future success as our first Ricky Ponting campaign was to our initial success. Importantly, it propelled us to become consistently ranked as Australia's leading natural health brand and established our brand as a major player in the Australian media sector. The market was in awe of our strategy. They thought we were a one hit wonder, but this continued success proved we were anything but.

The success of this endeavour not only laid the groundwork for Project Gold (more on that later) and the creation of the Noisy Beast agency, but also fuelled our ambition for global expansion.

Going global

The Olympics really put us on the map. We had been a well-known brand nationally but now we had massive brand recognition on a global level.

This international awareness, coupled with our successful expansion into subcategories such as Superfoods, Natural Skincare and Sports Nutrition provided us with the confidence to take the next logical step: launching Swisse onto the international market. Australia had served as our foundation, but to continue growing, we had to explore new horizons.

Finding the right person to head up our international expansion was a challenging task. This person would need to have:

- exceptional sales skills

- a deep understanding of our culture and products

- the ability to navigate complex negotiations

- a willingness to live a nomadic lifestyle

- the expertise to represent us at the highest echelons.

After an exhaustive search, we found the perfect person in Ulrich Irgens.

I met Ulrich when we were exploring the probiotics sector for Australia. Our New Product Development team had spotted this as a huge area of growth for us and Ulrich was the global lead for Danisco, one of the world's premium suppliers of raw materials for probiotics. He pitched for our business, and encouraged me to meet him at a trade show I'd often attend in Las Vegas so we could find out more about what Danisco did. He then connected us with a contract manufacturer who specialised in probiotic manufacturing and took us on a tour of the Danisco raw material–producing factories in Madison, Wisconsin. I saw how hard he worked to achieve an outcome for his clients and thought he would be the ideal candidate to lead our international expansion. I subsequently offered him the role of Head of International for Swisse, and he accepted. It was a win-win for everyone: for him, for us, and for Danisco, who would get Swisse as a lucrative new customer.

Meanwhile, we needed to establish what country we would expand into first. China was our first choice because:

- it had a market of over 1 billion people

- the region was nearby and easy to get to

- they valued natural medicine, clean and green formulations and aspirational branding

- they would pay a premium to get them.

Our next goal would be to find an investment partner in China.

Be prepared to travel

You can build a $100 million-dollar business by selling just to the Australian market, but if you want to build a billion-dollar business, you will need to expand internationally as Australia is just too small to generate that kind of revenue. This is great news for those who love the thrill of travel, the adventure of opening new markets and exploring new cultures. But be prepared. It will mean long-haul travel, many months away from home, missed birthdays, weddings and anniversaries; airport hotels, bad food, jet lag and deep pockets to fund the mission. (I am not joking when I say that if you want to conquer the United States or China, you should set aside at least $50 million to establish your brand.) That said, even if you want to build a $10 million business, you will need to be on planes and flying around the country to meet with your customers on a frequent basis. Relationships need to be built face-to-face.

The China syndrome

We had done enough research to know that while it would be tempting to launch into China on our own, navigating the complex maze that is the Chinese culture would be fraught with risk. Their rule of law, culture and general market conditions were, and still are, literally worlds away from how we operated. Taking on an investment partner was the ideal way to gain fast traction for our first foray into international expansion.

Fortunately for us, Ulrich knew everyone in the industry and introduced us to Biostime, one of China's leading manufacturers of baby formula and other supplements. Ironically, they were based in

Guangzhou, a vibrant and bustling city I had visited ten years earlier with Grant Moffitt when I worked for Village.

We flew to China and met with Luo Fei the CEO, his brother Jackson, the sales director, and Laetitia Albertini, the head of international business. They greeted us warmly and we got down to the business of finding out if they could partner with us to distribute this probiotic product throughout China.

We were confident this product would sell well in China for a few reasons. Firstly, there was only one major brand in the natural health category that had a strong voice and personality: Centrum. We wanted to be the other. Secondly, the price of vitamins in China presented a profitable opportunity. To illustrate, a fish oil product that sold for $20 in Australia could fetch $50 in China. As such, we saw a huge potential to make a sizeable margin. Lastly, we were a clean and green premium brand that represented an aspirational lifestyle so we were perfectly positioned to become an influential player in the Chinese sector.

Unfortunately, after several meetings, lots of false starts and close calls, the Biostime board declined to partner with us. They wanted to stay focused on baby formula, and decided we were not the right fit for them at this time. We were disappointed. We had spent time getting to know them, and felt their culture and ethos were the right match for us. But alas, the universe had other plans in store for us. Like all things in China, relationships are paramount and it would take time to build an authentic relationship. We stayed in touch with Biostime and focused on implementing plan B for our international expansion. No matter what we did, or what happened, we always had a contingency plan in place, and if plan B didn't unfold as expected, we'd turn to plans C, D and E. We never let any setbacks stand in the way of achieving our goal.

One door closes, another one opens

After we got back from China, we received an invitation to attend a meeting with PGT Healthcare. PGT was a joint venture between consumer goods company Proctor and Gamble and the pharmaceutical company Teva. Proctor and Gamble is one of the biggest fast-moving consumer goods (FMCG) companies in the world. Pantene, Gillette, Tide, Pampers and Oral-B are just a few of their mega brands. Teva is a global pharmaceutical company based in Israel. It operates in 60 countries and was one of the largest generic drug manufacturers in the world. These two companies joined forces in November 2011 to become PGT and were valued at a whopping $130 billion. They were keen to do a joint venture with us to distribute our products in 30 countries across the Americas, Europe and Asia. As appealing as this sounded, my first response was to say, 'thanks but no thanks,' as I feared their objective was to swallow us up and buy us out. They had tried to meet with us for many months, but I had always dismissed them as being too big for us to partner with. In time, we thought they may become the right organisation to sell to, but we weren't ready yet. Ulrich, being the persistent professional that he was, insisted we meet with them this one time to hear them out.

Upon further investigation, we discovered PGT was a subsidiary of the larger parent group and was therefore small enough to stay focused on being high growth and entrepreneurial, yet still have access to the vast infrastructure of the parent corporations. PGT's remit was to find brands in the consumer health sector that they could license or buy and distribute. This sounded more like a company with whom we could do business.

PGT recognised, as we did, that there was a global opportunity in the consumer mass market for premium natural health products and that Swisse could fill that gap. Our due diligence revealed that PGT had spent hundreds of millions trying to launch a vitamin range like ours over ten successive occasions and had failed each time for a variety of reasons, one of those reasons being that they could not reach the economies of scale when purchasing raw materials, which made their cost to manufacture too high. They saw our go-to-market method as the most likely method of success across multiple markets. Knowing that a company of this size couldn't achieve their goal without our help reinforced how powerful our brand, and the systems and processes that supported it, really were. I was pleased to learn this. Having our manufacturing and operations process validated by a $130 billion company was a great boost to our confidence.

We needed the PGT deal too, but for different reasons. We predicted that once we consistently ranked as Australia's number one natural health brand, our growth would tap out. Our plans to launch into China had evaporated, so our plan B was to expand into the United States instead. We'd need to keep trying to independently raise money to support our US launch, while simultaneously working towards doing a PGT deal that would see us launch in countries such as the UK, Holland, Italy and other countries we'd never get around to launching in ourselves.

An early offer

Prior to us launching into the United States, Archer, one of Australia's largest private equity firms offered to buy us for $150 million, which would value us at $500 million. The shareholders would get $50 million and $100 million would stay in the business. The deal came with conditions. They wanted us to abandon our plans to expand into Skincare, Superfoods and Sports Nutrition, and overseas, and just focus on being the number one natural health supplement business in Australia. They saw all the challenges we were about to face and didn't think we were up for dealing with them. In many ways they were right, but we never shied away from a challenge, and we weren't about to start now. We declined to proceed with the deal. Michael and Stephen could have taken this offer, but they believed in our overarching strategy, and I appreciated their vote of confidence to keep doing what we were doing, as it gave us free rein to get on with expanding our global footprint and creating a more valuable business.

CHAPTER 22

THE (BAD) AMERICAN DREAM

Our first goal in 2012 was to find a distributor who could sell our products to the people of America. KKR, a private equity firm that was interested in acquiring us, had some good contacts in the United States, and, wanting to demonstrate in advance what a great partner they could be to us, smoothed the way for us to present to a host of America's top retailers at an upcoming convention in Miami.

Our team back in Australia worked like crazy behind the scenes to come up with a promotional ad package that would excite and incentivise these retailers to stock us. The retailers needed to know we had the operational capability to service this huge market and could fund a national advertising campaign to support the launch of a new brand into this intensely competitive market.

To prove our credentials, we compiled a highlights reel of all the international reality show formats we had been involved with in Australia: *The Voice, Dancing with the Stars, MasterChef,* the Tour de France, the Australian Open, and of course, the ultimate reality show, the Olympics, which had really put us on the world map.

We needed a global ambassador to complete the picture and tie all the promotional elements together. This ambassador would need to represent everything our brand was – premium, proven and aspirational. They would need to be healthy, authentic, above reproach and have an impeccable track record. Mitch Catlin made a short list of desirable ambassadors and came up with Nicole Kidman, Cate Blanchett and Hugh Jackman. We were delighted when Nicole demonstrated an interest as we thought she'd be perfect for this role. The good news was she already used natural health products and loved our story. The bad news was her fee. Her agent advised it would cost us many millions to secure her services. This would be a stretch. Our board was already nervous about the American expansion, and this would be by far the biggest ambassador fee we had ever outlaid. The Australian business faced some serious headwinds in that we were racking up large amounts of debt to pay for the Australian advertising campaigns, plus we were already committed to spending tens of millions to fund the expansion into the United States.

But we *really* wanted Nicole. We knew she would be perfect, not just for the American campaign, but for the rest of the global expansion that was bound to come. From even the most cursory conversations with retailers, we could tell her involvement was going to create a massive frisson of excitement for everyone involved in the campaign. Everyone was intrigued by Nicole and we knew she'd lend that star power to our products and promotions too. She was an international superstar and the marketing campaign featuring her could be used in a host of different countries. We were a local Aussie company but we always thought global, right from the start, and this was our chance to take things up a notch. Choosing the right global ambassador was critical to the success of our international campaign. PGT also thought she was the perfect fit. We had one shot to get this right. The stakes were the highest they had ever been. We needed Nicole and nothing was going to get in our way of bringing her on board.

How to negotiate with a Hollywood agent

At this point, we had collaborated extensively with a variety of agents who represented Australia's leading actors and athletes, and we believed we had a good handle on how to negotiate with an agent. How wrong we were. Nothing prepared us for dealing with Hollywood agents. These agents were next level. Just when we thought we'd nailed the deal, agreed on the terms and had the pen poised, they'd pull the rug out from under us to extract more concessions. For example, little did I know but when you hire elite stars such as Nicole as brand ambassadors, you have to hire their entire entourage too. They demanded we use their TV commercial director, writer, producer, stylist, hairdresser, make-up artist, camera operator, editor, and everyone else they wanted to give a job to; and everyone, of course, charged top-tier fees.

We understood the intent. They wanted to protect their star client and ensure that the end result was world class. (It was also a case of rewarding, or 'tipping', all those who had helped them get to where they were. That's how the American movie star system worked and we'd soon learn their retail universe was similar.) We didn't really have a choice as to whether we used these suppliers or not. If we didn't, the deal wouldn't get done. Nicole cost us (a lot) more than we anticipated, but we were thrilled to get her. It was a coup. We weren't prepared to sign on the dotted line until we'd tested the concept with our American, European, Australian and Asian retailers, and now that we had Nicole's agreement in principle, we could pitch to the retailers with confidence.

Nicole was as excited about the deal as we were. I don't know if Australians are quite aware of what a superstar Nicole is in the United States, but she is Hollywood royalty. She is an intensely patriotic Aussie and relished the opportunity to introduce Americans to our laid-back lifestyle and iconic brand. She also, I think, wanted to re-establish, remind and, to some degree, reinvent her brand in Australia, and this was the perfect vehicle for her to do so.

Now that we had the world's number one movie superstar on board, we were fully invested in the American launch. The next question was, how do we shape the flywheel for the American market? As always, we thought big. Why not get Ellen DeGeneres, then America's number one daytime television superstar, to be our other celebrity ambassador? But wait, there's more. Let's get Ellen to interview Nicole on her top-rating TV show! Why stop there? Let's bring Ellen, her crew and the 400 people in her studio audience to Australia for an all-expenses paid trip! All courtesy of Swisse! This was going to be the most epic promotion we had ever staged.

A marathon deal

Hammering out the PGT deal memo took longer than expected. My old boss and CEO at Village, George Livery, had come to work with us as our Commercial Director, and was charged with leading this negotiation. In my mind we had no better a person to negotiate the outcome, but PGT were impossible to negotiate with. We flew literally to the other side of the world to their head office in Geneva to sign off on the deal. When we got there, the deal memo we had all agreed to was different to the deal on the table. We didn't sign. We then flew to Singapore a week later to do the same and it happened again. It reached boiling point when they arrived in Melbourne to complete the deal and they reneged on the agreed terms *again*. We even blocked them from entering the office until they could demonstrate they were operating in good faith and would agree to the terms of the deal we had negotiated.

They reneged on promises, withdrew concessions made, and constantly changed the goalposts, even after everything had been formally agreed and documented. Their negotiators were authorised to deploy almost any tactic to better the deal for them, so nothing was off the table in achieving it. We were forced to play their game. George played the bad cop, Ulrich was the good guy. Adem would bring out the sledgehammer and I'd nudge the conversation back on track with their CEO and smooth the waters. It was a marathon.

Pitching to the American retailers

With the in-principle agreement to have Nicole and Ellen as our brand ambassadors in place, we were ready to proceed with our pitch sessions with American retailers. We weren't prepared to lock in the deal for these celebrity contracts unless the American retailers placed a significant pre-order and committed to a full retail promotional support package, just as our Australian retailers did.

We attended the retailer conference in Miami where all the major retailers would be in attendance. We flew in, checked into the hotel, found the function room, cleared out the furniture and set up our marketing collateral. The retailers filed in, one by one, to hear our

15-minute presentation. We'd been rehearsing the pitch for weeks and knew it backwards. We were all pretty tired from the jet lag but our second wind had kicked in and we were energetic, dynamic and bright-eyed. We felt we had the deal of a lifetime and that they'd be as excited as we were. But these stone-eyed, cold-hearted buyers worked for the biggest retailers on the planet; they'd been there, done that and seen everything. They were tough nuts to crack and were obsessed with seeing a point of difference. Once they heard we had Nicole and Ellen, they perked up considerably.

The biggest meeting of the day was with Walgreens, the largest retail pharmacy chain in the United States. By this time, we had been presenting for hours and were a well-oiled machine with a unique offer so we were not surprised when they confirmed they'd take our range. We were beyond excited. We had one of the most iconic drugstore brands in the country as our partner. They had 7000 stores across the United States and sold everything from Halloween costumes to home decor to hairspray. By way of comparison, Australia has just 5000 pharmacies *in total*. Over the coming weeks we also secured CVS and Rite Aid and a range of other distributors, which meant we would now be stocked in over 30 000 stores around the United States.

We pre-sold over $15 million in stock to these retailers, which paid for Nicole's and Ellen's contracts, so now we could confidently go back to their Hollywood agents and ink the deal. We never left anything like this to chance. Our process was always to get enough sell-in to validate our campaigns before they began, and to ensure we had the sell-through plan in place. We were set. This was the beginning of the Swisse global expansion.

When the best laid plan(ogram)s go astray

We met with the buying teams from Walgreens, CVS and Rite Aid and briefed them on the promotional campaign, the celebrity ambassadors and the complex flywheel that had become our unique intellectual property. We worked out what levels and range of stock they would need, how it would be funded, the time frames and how it would all work. One of the key reasons we specifically chose those retailers was because they all had one thing that was very important to us: a central planogram. A what? I'll explain.

Smaller retailers like mum-and-dad pharmacies generally let the sales reps come into their store and stock the shelves, set up the posters, construct the end caps and do what they want. The bigger operators such as Walgreens (and Aussie retailers such as Coles and Chemist Warehouse) have what's known as a central planogram. It's a document that clearly states what product goes where, what shelf space those products will get, what shelf it will go on, how it will be displayed and many other variables. Every store manager has a copy of this planogram and is duty bound to adhere to it. Shelf space and positioning are critical factors to retail success and this document ensures everyone plays by the rules – because not everyone plays by the rules, as I was to discover.

In addition to a team of sales reps, most companies like Swisse have in-house professional merchandisers whose job it is to call on these large retailers to 'tidy up' the shelf, restock the products to ensure the shelf looks full, and to check that the pricing is correct. Importantly, they also ensure that no other merchandiser from a competitive brand has snuck in, shifted the products around, removed the price tag or damaged the product to make them unsellable. Yes, these things do happen in merchandising land.

Knowing we did not have the budget to pay for our own merchandising team to call on the 30 000 stores across the United States to 'tidy up' the shelf, we only chose retailers who had a central planogram. This, at least in theory, would guarantee that our products would be displayed properly, get restocked and have premium positioning placement on the shelf. We paid for this service with an off-invoice discount and in return, the retailer promised us that their team would adhere to the planogram and that our products would be in good hands. That's what they promised us. What they delivered was something else entirely.

CHAPTER 23

WHERE'S OUR STOCK?

The US campaign launched in the last few months of 2012. It went brilliantly. The TV advertisements went to air, Nicole appeared on *Ellen*, the point-of-sale went up, the catalogues got delivered, the cross-promotions took place and the editorial mentions skyrocketed. Our flywheel was in full motion. The retailers were excited and so were we. We couldn't wait to see the sales results come in off the back of this mega promotional drive.

I pulled into the parking lot at a Walgreens in Chicago on day one of the campaign. The first thing I saw was our awesome point-of-sale posters of Nicole and Ellen, clearly displayed at the entrance. I then walked up and down the aisle, scanning the shelves, looking for the Swisse stock. It wasn't where it should have been. I moved to the next aisle, thinking maybe they'd stocked it on the wrong shelf. I walked up and down all the beauty and personal care aisles, scrutinising every display to see if our stock had been mis-merchandised, but to my growing distress, other than a few bottles tucked away in a corner on the bottom shelf, there were no Swisse products to be seen at all! This meant that while we were spending millions on TV commercials, and print advertisements, and social media, and our global ambassador was spruiking our wares on America's highest-rating daytime talk show, and thousands of customers were walking into 30 000 drug stores around America to buy it, *our products were not even on the shelf.* Where were the products? They were sitting on a dusty shelf in a third-party distribution centre somewhere in the middle of America!

But wait, there's more.

When the stock did eventually arrive in-store, the Walgreens team dropped the ball *again.* We assumed that because we had a central planogram in place, their internal team of merchandisers would ensure it was honoured and our product would be stocked in the premium positions we had agreed upon. But it wasn't, and they weren't. The Walgreens system was a colossal failure. The centrally planned planogram merchandising system that would supposedly guarantee us a premium position on the shelf just didn't materialise. Now we had the stock in-store, but no-one could find it.

Trust but check

A well-executed planogram was crucial to Swisse's success. The primary objective of a planogram is to create a strong brand 'block' that catches the eye and draws the consumer in. We were assured that Walgreens would follow our agreed planogram, but they didn't. We were spending millions on our advertising to drive customers in-store. When the customers got to the store, our stock was nowhere to be found. Our error? We trusted Walgreens to follow the planogram. We didn't have enough boots on the ground to call in on the stores and check. The lesson learned? Trust but check.

There was more challenging news.

In the event that the stock we shipped to the United States did not sell for some reason, we had a contingency plan in place that would ensure the stock could be repatriated to Australia and sold there instead. (We were always prepared for the worst-case scenario should the stock not sell.) Sure, we'd be out of pocket for millions for the advertising and the cost of the ambassadors, but we'd at least have the $15 million in stock up our sleeve to sell back in Australia. But there was a fly in the ointment for this plan too. I subsequently discovered that the stock we had manufactured in the United States was formulated *differently* to the stock we sold in Australia. This was not meant to happen. There was *one* state in the USA that wasn't legally able to sell one of the ingredients in the formulations, so instead of changing it up for that *one* state, the contract manufacturers changed the formulation for *all* the states. Our contingency plan to bring the products back to Australia was no longer an option as those formulations were not able to be sold in Australia. This was not ideal, to say the least. Now we'd have to revert to the worst-case on top of the worst-case scenario. But we never let these setbacks deter us from our mission. Our positivity was relentless. Whatever challenges came our way, we were committed to finding a way to solve them. Failure was never an option.

Zero margin

Back in Australia, things were not going well either. The margin pressure exerted by the grocers was squeezing our profits. These grocers had initially enjoyed a 30 per cent profit margin, similar to what the pharmacies had, but over time they increased it to 40 per cent, then 50 per cent, eventually leaving us with zero profit. (The irony was we had worked so hard to get into the grocers. Now we couldn't wait to get out!) To make matters worse, the grocers held us responsible for theft (or 'shrinkage', as they call it), even though it occurred on their premises and was out of our control. I'd usually be all over all these matters but I just couldn't be everywhere. Our executive team was beyond stretched as well, as we were growing way too fast to keep up with all the activity.

On the upside, consumer demand back in Australia was flying high, our cost of manufacturing was reducing, we'd started shifting customers from the expensive grocery channel to the margin-friendly pharmacy channel, and had made significant cost reductions across the business. In addition, the PGT deal (including $10 million in royalty payments, which gave them the licensing rights to sell our products) was about to come in and would provide validation to the banks that our operations were on track, and give us some breathing space with our board while we tried to deal with the credit crunch that we could see coming on the horizon.

The cost of growth

By this point, we had more than 300 team members in Australia. Over 100 of them had been with us for less than 12 months, which meant we were inducting at scale. Growing so quickly brought cash flow issues, understaffing, and operational inefficiencies. It became harder to maintain the quality of our products and services, something we couldn't afford to compromise. Decision making became rushed, which increased the risk of costly mistakes. Our team did not follow the customer account management systems we had set up, and it affected our margin, our marketing campaigns and slowed down new product development.

We had always kept an eagle eye on every cost line, knowing how critical this was and how quickly and easily it could all go wrong. I'd always personally ensured every element of the plan was perfectly executed. But I hadn't mapped the system properly so it was left to interpretation, and when I was away and not able to guide the process, things went awry.

Growing 50 per cent year-on-year

Throughout my entire time at Swisse, it felt as if we were in constant start-up mode. We grew 50 per cent every year, year on year — in revenue, team members, new products being launched — which meant that the business we were managing and building every year was new and different and required a different mindset from the year before. It was like launching a new business from scratch every year.

On the brink of bankruptcy

As if that wasn't enough, we faced cultural and organisational challenges. Preserving our core values while scaling up proved to be quite a task. Maintaining our culture had been straightforward when we had a smaller team. However, maintaining the culture when we had 300 employees required us to have some robust systems in place.

The true test of our culture came when things got tough. Fatigue and stress started to erode the little courtesies and gestures that were part of our culture. Despite having robust cultural and communication plans in place, we had lost our way. I was not across the detail with the product formulation mix-up either. If I had thoroughly read the contract and understood the labelling requirements, I would have noticed the issue and realised it could have been easily resolved with a simple adjustment to the label on the bottle.

I was stretched way too thin to be an effective leader. I was out of the office for three out of every four weeks, (still) negotiating the PGT deal, managing the US business, running the Australian business, crisscrossing the globe flying from Geneva, to Chicago, and then back to Melbourne to meet with all the stakeholders and trying to be back in Australia to sync in with Helen's fifth IVF schedule.

To cap things off, the debt collectors were closing in, threatening to stop supply of all our goods, and we were in danger of breaching our banking covenants. If that happened, the banks would stop our credit, we'd be unable to pay our team and our suppliers and we'd be put into administration.

This was the cost of growth everybody talked about. We'd been through it in the past with the GFC and again when we oversold stock into Coles. We knew this challenge was coming too and had plans in place to ward this off, but the cash flow crunch moved too quickly and so here we were again — on the brink of bankruptcy.

I couldn't ignore the undeniable truth that this array of challenges we were dealing with was under my remit. I took full responsibility for everything that was happening, and the debacle that was the United States. Michael and Stephen would have been well within their rights to sack me. People had been sacked for a lot less. The fate of the company, of our people's livelihoods, the history and heritage of this iconic brand, the fortune of the two men who had put their faith in me, and my own personal wealth, were all at risk because of me.

We had made the calculated decision to enter the US market and we had failed. People often asked us why we took the risk. The answer was simple. When you become Australia's number one natural health brand, you don't have any further avenues for growth. Going to the United States, whilst in Australia expanding into adjacent categories like Sports Nutrition, Skincare and Superfoods, seemed like the best way to achieve that growth.

Despite all challenges (and this may come as a surprise), I never once wavered in my belief that we would ultimately succeed. We were on a knife's edge but I knew we could ride out this tough patch. My intuition shone brightly, no doubt honed by the thousands of hours that I put into building the Village business, and now this business. This experience gave me the confidence to trust that we were on the correct path, and that this setback was merely a stepping stone toward even greater success.

PART III

CHAPTER 24

EXITING AMERICA

The American experience was a disaster. I knew within a week of trading that our strategy was not right. We hadn't followed the most important part of the flywheel: the sell-through. We had also repeated the mistake we had previously made with our skincare range by launching the advertising before the product had been on the shelf for at least three months. It was heart-wrenching. All that work. We needed to stop the haemorrhaging of cash that the American experience was costing us, or we would break our banking covenants and the company would be wound up. However, we had already paid Nicole and Ellen up front and were financially obligated to continue with the rest of the campaign.

I am not proud of how I dealt with the fact that our American launch was dead in the water before it had even started. The memory is still vivid. My team and I were leaving our Chicago office in our rental car to go to the airport and make our way home. We were beyond exhausted. We'd worked tirelessly for seven days a week for months on end to make the American launch work. In that moment, the litany of failures hit me like a freight train. Every mistake, misstep, and oversight came crashing down on me. I could not contain my frustration any longer. I turned around to face my team and unleashed my anger. I told them how angry I was at myself, and at them, for how we had veered off course; for how we had disregarded our established systems and neglected our carefully crafted culture plan; for how we had overlooked major details in our haste to get things done; for how we hadn't communicated frequently, accurately, or quickly enough to cover off the thousands of decisions being made every week.

After I had vented my spleen, I slumped in my seat, red faced and out of breath. I had really lost it like never before. This was not the way I had envisioned myself behaving during a crisis. I had displayed a moment of raw emotion fuelled by exhaustion and disappointment. It was not my finest moment. We had all made mistakes, but ultimately, as the leader, I needed to accept the blame and take full accountability. I had been entrusted with complete authority to manage this business according to my judgement, and instead of steering it to success, I had driven it straight into a wall. Now, it was imperative for me to rise to the occasion and do what I had always done — let my actions do the talking and demonstrate to everyone that I could turn this situation around. We believed, as always, that there was a solution to any challenge. This was just a particularly large one to resolve.

There is always a solution

You will face many obstacles in business and things won't always go to plan. When it happens, get creative. Don't give up, or throw in the towel. There is always a solution. If Plan A fails, turn to plans B, C, D and E. Make sure everyone in your team is focused on creating successful outcomes and reward those who offer possible solutions.

The cost of growth

When you build a business, important decisions need to be made early on:

- What is the goal of the organisation?

- How will success be measured?

- What are we prepared to sacrifice to get it?

In most sectors (other than tech, where success is typically measured via the number of downloads, users or revenue), profit is the yardstick of success. In our case, profit wasn't, and couldn't be, our measure of success. For us, growth took precedence over everything. We reinvested every dollar back into the business to fuel its expansion. Revenue flowed in, only to swiftly flow back out again. We were on an aggressive mission to grow the category in Australia and the business worldwide. But the expansion into the United States, the tens of millions invested in stock, and the squeeze on margins in the Australian grocery sector had cost us dearly. In addition, we had also been paying Stephen and Michael over $200 000 each in salaries per year, and over $50 000 per month to the three of us in dividends. The business had also loaned me money so I could pay back the debt that had enabled me to buy into the business. As a result of all this, we were now $30 million in debt and had zero profit. To exacerbate matters further, our longstanding financial partner, HSBC, predicted that the expenditures stemming from the US venture would propel us to be $70 million in debt. Their loss of confidence in our strategic direction led to a demand for the return of their funds, which meant we'd need to refinance the business.

All in all, just another day at the office!

As bizarre as this might sound, that $30 million (with a path to $70 million in debt) and zero profit did not faze me. Growth came at a cost, and carrying debt in a high-growth business was not unusual for a business on this trajectory. I knew we needed to focus on our core business to get back on track; that the investments we were making in the business were sound; and that eventually the profits would flow. Besides, it was not in my nature to give up, look backwards or cry over spilt milk. I was totally committed to reaching our goal of building a billion-dollar business. Yes, our first foray into international expansion had failed, but we had learned some lessons that we could apply to the next attempt, and we had a plan for how to extract ourselves from this credit crunch we were experiencing. (Everyone fails at some point but the real test of character is if you have the humility to learn from it.)

If push came to shove, our plan was to stop the $50 million we were spending on marketing and use it to pay down the $70 million debt. The continued growth of our core brand, evidenced by the fact we had over $250 million in sales in Australia (a substantial increase on the $181 million from the year before), gave us the confidence to know we could sustain our revenue while the savings in marketing would go straight to the bottom line. We'd been advertising so consistently and methodically for so many years, and had imprinted our brand so deeply into the consciousness of health-conscious Australians, that we knew our loyal customers would continue to buy Swisse whether we advertised or not. A hiatus of 12 months would not affect sales in the long-term. Our 68 per cent customer retention rate would make sure of that.

The turnaround begins

We struggled on for 12 more long months to make the United States work. We were obligated to fulfil our retail obligations and move through as much US stock as possible so we had to persist. We tried various other price-driven strategies and some PR, but without significant funds to reinvest in the flywheel, we knew success would be futile. After a lot of effort, we had to pull the plug on the United States. The experience was bruising for all of us on so many levels: physically, mentally and financially. We had lost the trust of the founders, the banks, our consultants, and even some of my own team questioned whether I was the right person to take the business forward. They were all worried that we wouldn't be able to control our cost base, maintain our revenue and pay back the debt.

Two of our core values at Swisse were Health and Happiness. At this point in my journey, I had neither. I knew deep in my heart that I had what it took to bring this business to its fullest expression, but it was clear we needed to do things differently. I needed to bring our team and stakeholders along the journey with me more effectively, and let them know how we were going to go about it. Like my father, I excelled at simplifying complex concepts and strategies, however, I occasionally struggled to effectively communicate the underlying intricacies to others, especially when transforming these complex ideas into what I saw as straightforward plans. It was not enough that I knew I could do it. I had to inspire others to believe we could do it too. I needed to let them know that while the business was heading in the right direction, we were under significant cost pressures and that we had to tighten our belts. I had been a growth CEO. I now needed to be a turnaround CEO. It was time to flick the switch and turn this ship around. It was time to pay down the debt and focus on profit.

Get a mentor

During the height of this stress, Helen and I travelled to Guatemala for a brief holiday. We stayed in a hotel by a lake and the owner of the property invited us to drinks one night. He was a fascinating man with a big backstory and he delighted in telling it. He mentioned that he was a member of a worldwide mentoring group called Young Presidents Organisation (YPO), and that it had been very helpful to him. When I got back to Australia, I was asked to help out on a product launch for a friend and he also mentioned he was a member of YPO. I thought the universe was trying to tell me something, so I joined. My group consisted of around seven CEOs, all of whom were entrepreneurs or owners of non-competing businesses. We met monthly in an environment of strict confidentiality, and one of our peers took on the role of chairperson. Essentially, it functioned as our very own personalised advisory board. This robust source of support evolved into a valuable touchstone for maintaining my sanity during this challenging time and proved to be an invaluable asset throughout my entire career.

CHAPTER 25

CIRCLES OF INFLUENCE

During this stressful time I always came back to the mantra that had served me so well: 'control the controllables'. It's all anyone can do. To stress about events, people and circumstances over which we have no control is a waste of time and energy.

Controlling the controllables at work

After much collaboration and consultation with the team, we gathered our collective energies and got to work to create a swathe of new strategies that would set us on a new path. We:

- *improved our communications*: Using new and improved communications channels, we dialled up the frequency and depth of our company updates and meetings. We used these meetings to honestly share with the team where things were at, what had gone wrong, and what we had done to demonstrate that we'd learned from our experiences. Our regular 360-degree feedback sessions, where everyone got to give feedback about everyone, led by Cath and Steph Brown, our Performance Manager, were confronting, but exceptionally useful. They helped us optimise our communication and gave us the tools we needed to become a better-connected team.

- *reviewed our labelling*: When we carefully examined the $15 million worth of unsold stock sitting in those US warehouses, we discovered that with some small changes to the product label, we could easily repackage the stock up and re-sell it back in Australia. What we couldn't sell, we could give away as bonus stock to incentivise our retailers to buy more, or offer as 'value packs' to drive sales of our core products and market ancillary lines.

- *renegotiated our contracts*: We went back to Nicole's agent to extract more concessions. We had nothing to lose. We asked for more appearances at events, more interviews with leading magazines and more involvement in the PGT promotions when we launched into the new territories. (Nicole went above and beyond to help us out and could not have been more gracious.)

- *signed off on a distribution deal*: We finally got PGT to sign the deal. It was only 15 months after we started negotiations, but better late than never. The much-needed $10 million advance on royalties came too late to save our American dream, but it did give our creditors and bankers confidence. That said, we managed to hold up launching the United States for long enough to convince PGT to do the deal, as they were worried that if we succeeded in the United States we would be able to do the deal without their support. There were a few upsides to this deal. We had just secured one of the largest licensing deals ever done with an Australian consumer product range, which meant we could now launch into 30 countries over the next five years, increase our global footprint and use our unique flywheel to sell our product to the rest of the developed world. PGT also agreed that when we launched into new territories, they would pay a portion of Nicole's fees.

- *reviewed our systems*: The systems we used back in Australia worked very nicely for a market of 23 million people, but to think we could just transplant those same systems into a country of 316 million and hope they would work was a stretch.

We didn't know nearly enough about how all the US systems worked. We thought we did, but we underestimated the difficulty and assumed too much. The equity firm that valued us at $500 million had predicted that our capital base was underprepared and PGT had advised us that we'd need to invest $70 million to launch into a market like the United States. They were both right.

- *documented our processes*: PGT found us appealing due to the robust sales and marketing process we had meticulously developed. Our documented flywheel had become a valuable intellectual property asset. Consequently, they approached our team to assist in training their country teams on the art of implementing the flywheel model to launch our products into new territories worldwide. Helen and her talented offsider Clare McKeown took on the task of fully documenting this, and, after many months of hard work and collaboration with the wider team, delivered a 210-page manual for PGT that summed up all our processes. The new territories now had a single source of truth for every process, principle, policy and procedure within Swisse, from how to write to advertisement, train a retailer and engage a celebrity, to crop a photo, launch a product or position a logo. It was a step-by-step, practical guide to all things Swisse.

- *committed to our cultural, communication and business plans*: Instrumental to our overall turnaround success was our commitment to ensuring our culture, communications and business plans were followed and reviewed quarterly. Our overarching goal was to keep things simple. For example, our corporate strategy was distilled into a two-page document. Page one outlined the strategy and the key performance indicators (KPIs); page two documented the actionable steps required to achieve those KPIs. The document was amended for each business unit to make it more relevant, which ensured each team member in that unit understood their specific role in the overall strategy and what was required of them for success.

- *found a great retail partner*: We knew one week into the US launch that the campaign would fail. Accepting that this was our reality, I took the bit between my teeth to focus on opportunities within our core territory and approached our largest retailer and closest partner, Chemist Warehouse. We put together an exclusive advertising and marketing package featuring an Ellen DeGeneres promotion that focused on her Australian tour. We struck an epic deal with the CEO of Chemist Warehouse that would see them commit to a stock-buying plan and a promotional sell-through that would move $60 million worth of stock over three months. The PR buzz created around Ellen's Australian tour was extraordinary and dwarfed everything we had done in the past. This was the epitome of the flywheel in full flight.

In this most challenging of times, our Chemist Warehouse deal was testament to the fact that our partnership with them was always based on win-win. Yes, the deal was commercially sound, and they wouldn't have gone ahead if it wasn't, but it was gratifying to know that the alliance we had nurtured and strengthened over many years had proved to be our pillar of strength when we needed it most. We had driven ridiculous category growth, and inspired our competitors to work harder to match our focus on delivering growth and margin to our retailers.

From this period onward we clearly became Australia's number one natural health brand on a consistent, week-by-week basis, and the deal won me back the respect of all and sundry in the Swisse world.

Controlling the controllables at home

I had set in motion a series of plans to control the controllables in my working life. I now had to focus on controlling the controllables in my personal life. It's relatively easy to be in control of your mind and emotions when things are going well; it's when things go badly that we are truly tested. This is when we need to double down on the things that bring us equanimity.

I needed to reach a peak mental and physical state and focus on my circle of influence to be best prepared for what was ahead. To achieve this, I:

- *stopped drinking for long periods of time.* I wasn't a heavy drinker, but what with all the stress, the travelling and the corporate entertaining, by the end of the week I'd drink a little too much to prevent my mind from racing. The alcohol made me tired and dulled my senses, and, at this critical juncture of the company, I needed to be at the top of my game at all times, including the weekend.

- *used exercise to generate connection.* I walked 4 kilometres each morning with Helen and our fur baby Floella, the most adorable sausage dog you could find. (I particularly love this breed as their little legs don't get in the way when you want to give them a hug and you can get some serious heart-to-heart hugs happening.) On one of our regular walks around the Yarra River, Floella met Buddy, another little sausage dog, and after a bit of 'sausage' action between the two them, Floella got pregnant and gave birth to a litter of four mini-sausages. (At least someone in the household was fertile!)

- *stepped up my gym regime.* I had let the gym slide as I was travelling so much but it was time to reset so I started working out with my buddies at the office gym. This was great for my mindset, but it was also a great way to connect with my colleagues too. I had been away a lot and I truly believed that a team that played together stayed together.

- *changed my eating habits.* Long-haul travel, airline food, late nights and living out of hotels had not been conducive to healthy eating. Helen was a brilliant cook, so we took turns cooking and found relaxation and romance in each other's company by creating beautiful meals together.

- *started meditating again.* I had dabbled in mindfulness over the years, but as life got busier, and the methods I had been taught didn't stick, I had to find a new approach. Helen was keen to learn too, so as an anniversary gift to each other, we asked Jonni Pollard, a Vedic meditation teacher, to teach us meditation. We both emerged from this four-day home retreat with a suite of new empowering practices that would set us up for the next stage of the Swisse journey.

Meditation: get the edge

There's a reason why elite sportspeople, actors, musicians and businesspeople meditate. It's not just a soft and fluffy relaxation tool; it's a mind training tool. As leaders, we need to be stoic, strong and to make the best decisions for the situation at hand. Meditation helps us prepare to enter every room, no matter what has just happened, or is about to happen, and bring our most honourable self to the team. Helen and I got so much from our training with Jonni that we invited him to run meditation workshops for the entire team. Many resisted what Jonni offered but went along with the practice and ultimately benefited greatly from the experience. (To this day, I still get thanked by many past team members for introducing them to this ancient form of stress relief and am told it has consistently helped them get through some challenging times in their lives.)

All of this was an attempt to help me focus on controlling the controllables. But it did not alter the fact that we were still facing some serious headwinds as to how we were going to turn the company around and make a profit.

CHAPTER 26

THE SALE PROCESS BEGINS

To stay ahead of the financial requirements of the business we needed to raise $70 million from an outside source. Our preferred method to do this was with debt. This would give us the space we needed to complete the turnaround and sell the business at the right time. We were now the consistent number one natural health brand in Australia, and I always had the view that if we were to sell the business, the price should at least resemble Blackmore's value. (They were listed on the Australian Stock Exchange for $500 million and we'd been offered this sum before by the private equity firm, so that was what I thought we should be valued at.) Surely the American failure hadn't cost us that much in equity value? (At the time, it felt like I was the only one in the world who thought we were still worth at least that.) Now that Stephen and Michael could see a finish line in selling the business, both were keen to start a sales process. I was not so sure, but I was ready to go along with their vision. It wouldn't be easy. To achieve this sort of valuation, we'd need time for the turnaround to permeate through the rest of the business. We'd been carrying so much stock for the United States, it would take at least 12 months for the full effect of our cost of goods efficiencies to flow through, and the same could be said about our other cost management initiatives. The turnaround would work. It would just take time.

Nonetheless, we still needed to increase our debt facility to $70 million as the cash flow situation was getting worse. Suppliers were threatening to call in the debt collectors again and we were shuffling funds from one part of the business to another to buy us some more time. We were constantly chasing our tail, searching for growth, getting it, and then struggling to pay for the next wave of growth that was beckoning on the horizon.

I reached out to Clarence da Gama Pinto, an old acquaintance and mentor from the Melbourne Business School for some advice. I alluded to our financial situation, and he suggested I meet his son, Michael, a finance expert. This was fortuitous as we had promoted Adem, our existing CFO, to the role of COO, so he could focus on reducing our cost of goods, which meant we now needed a strong numbers person to replace him. After some negotiation, Michael da Gama Pinto (we'll call him Michael D.) came on board as a medium-term solution to ready us for the sale process, and to get us out of this credit crunch. We were excited to have him bring his formidable expertise and experience to the table. As soon as he came on board, he took control of the numbers, advised us what we needed to do and determined how much funding we would need to buy us time and get us through this cash flow issue. He also worked out what our options were for debt providers, and initiated a competitive banking process to raise the debt. In the meantime, we skilfully worked through managing the balancing game: cash in and out, timings on payments and regularly communicating with all the suppliers. It was really hard work as the pressure was on, but Michael D. was up for it and he did a brilliant job of getting us through this difficult time and setting us up for sale.

When should you take on investment?

If I knew then what I know now, we could have made things easier for ourselves by raising capital earlier. We could have had the shareholders invest more cash into the business, brought on an investment partner, or deferred dividend payments earlier on. We did talk about option one, but unfortunately the shareholders didn't have the capability to put money back in the business. It seemed we had been poorly advised on dividend payments by our board's financial advisor and we'd not found the right person or entity to inject capital into the business. If I was more confident, I would have pushed harder to raise more capital earlier, but I was just trying to keep up with everything that was going on around me and I was overly bullish on our value. Don't wait for a credit crunch to raise capital.

Doubt grows

As often happens when a new recruit joins a team, they cast a critical eye over the current system and the incumbent team. In this case, Michael D.'s critical eye landed on me, and he started to doubt that I had what it took to take this business to market. He questioned my abilities, my choices and my strategies. I questioned why I had hired him. I already had everyone breathing down my neck. I didn't need this new guy doing it too. Michael D. had worked in advisory roles in private equity and accounting firms but had never worked in a senior position in the day-to-day running of a business. Operating a business was a different beast. That said, feedback is always a gift and one should always see it as an opportunity to improve. Clearly, I needed to improve.

He recommended we run a competitive process to find an investment bank to fund our debt, prepare us for sale and help find us a buyer. This was his strong suit and he did a stellar job of it. Every banker we interviewed left the room feeling like a rock star, convinced that our business could not thrive without their involvement. Simultaneously, he skilfully conveyed that we had other alternatives available, compelling them to offer us competitive pricing in order to secure the bid.

By July 2013, we had narrowed the short list down to J.P. Morgan and Goldman Sachs. After the bid closed, Michael D. called me and said, 'I have good news and bad news. The good news is J.P. Morgan and Goldman are both willing to give us $70 million so we can get on with the business and keep growing.'

'What's the bad news?' I asked.

'The bad news is that J.P. Morgan will only provide the debt if Stephen says he is prepared to fire you,' he said.

Gulp. That was not the news I wanted to hear but if that was what we needed to do to save the business, I would go along with it.

To make sure we got the best deal from Goldman we needed to be able to tell them that we had another party offering a debt facility. I needed to call Stephen and get him to play ball with J.P. Morgan and say that he was prepared to fire me if it was deemed necessary. I felt nauseated at the prospect, but I had no option. (I could handle anything the business threw at me, but I found these kinds of political power plays very stressful.)

As part of J.P. Morgan's due diligence process, I met the person they had pegged for my job. I couldn't believe how incompetent he seemed. I recall he spent the entire meeting waxing lyrical about how talented he was, how qualified he was to do my role, how great the sale process would be with him leading it as our chairman, and what a great 'support' he would be to me (which was code for him firing me and being CEO). He didn't ask questions or seem to know anything about my role, the industry we were in, or what we were trying to accomplish. His apparent lack of acuity about the business he was earmarked to run worried me. If this ineffectual individual got my job he'd run the company into the ground and the value of our shares with it.

J.P. Morgan knew that if I was gone, they would be free to run the company as they saw fit. Their due diligence was deliberately light as they knew that with the revenues we were amassing, and the savings to come from the upcoming cost-focused turnaround, we would deliver a healthy profit, pay down their debt with interest, and also provide warrants on the business that would earn them a very handsome profit on any sale over $100 million, which, in this scenario, we were easily worth.

Thankfully Goldman Sachs provided the best terms, and they wanted me to run the business, but their terms didn't get sharper until we were able to squarely tell them we had another bank that would do the deal at 'better terms'. (We didn't tell them that getting those 'better terms' meant I would lose my job.) This $70 million investment was Goldman's largest in the Asia–Pacific region, so it was a big deal for them. (It was a big deal for me too, as it meant I would get to keep my job.)

Goldman Sachs' due diligence was thorough. They were immediately more interested in learning about the fundamentals of the business. They took the time to do what was needed to prepare the business for sale, were genuinely keen to know what drove the business, and bought into the vision of where we were headed. They also understood that we just needed time. Finally! A team that could see the wisdom of our strategy. We could finally follow through on the turnaround process that was in progress.

We learned a lot from watching Goldman Sachs in action, and in particular Adam Gregory, the head banker assigned to our business. Their mantra, invented by Gus Levy, the founder of Goldman Sachs, was 'greedy-long', which was a banker's way of saying, 'Do the right thing by the client in the short-term, and in the long-term, the client will look after you.' Adam clearly subscribed to this maxim also. (We had knocked them back a few years earlier when they had pitched for another piece of work and they had the humility to pitch again without rancour, which we found impressive.) Adam and his team took the time to really dig deep to find out who we were, what we did and where we were going. The most important thing we did with Goldman was to treat them the way we treated everyone: as partners. We genuinely respected them and we would do all we could to show this with our actions. Their culture was very similar to ours, and this laid the foundation for forging a very successful business partnership. Their deal, however, also came with a condition – one that would influence the rest of my journey with Swisse and bring our team, and me, close to breaking point.

Don't wait too long to take on investors

You may be able to finance your company without investors. That's nice, but rare. Even if you can self-finance, you may want to consider taking on 'smart money': investors that add strategic value and de-risk your operation. There are lots of ways to raise money, and lots of people who may give it to you. Here's what you need to get started on your capital-raising journey:

The documents:

- business plan
- culture/values plan
- communications plan
- financial plan
- investment memo

The questions you'll be asked:

- How much investment do you need?
- What is your company valued at? How was it valued?
- How do you plan to raise money?
  - ☐ debt
  - ☐ equity
  - ☐ safe notes
  - ☐ convertible notes
  - ☐ common stock
- Who will you raise it from and why? Your options are:
  - ☐ angel round
  - ☐ series seed
  - ☐ venture capital, family offices, private equity, banks

What does your cap(ital) table look like? Who owns shares in your company? Not sure what a cap table is? Below is a sample. It summarises who has a shareholding in your company.

#	Shareholders	Common shares	Per cent (non-diluted)	Per cent (diluted)
1	Shareholder 1	21 500	75.12 per cent	72.07 per cent
2	Shareholder 2	1500	5.24 per cent	5.03 per cent
3	Shareholder 3	983	3.43 per cent	3.30 per cent
4	Shareholder 4	983	3.43 per cent	3.30 per cent
5	Shareholder 5	756	2.64 per cent	2.53 per cent
6	Shareholder 6	605	2.11 per cent	2.03 per cent

Capital raising is not easy for non-financial people but it's super critical you get your head around the detail or you will not be able to source the capital you need to enable the business to reach its full potential.

CHAPTER 27

BACK ON THE ROAD

As December 2013 approached, the business still faced significant challenges and struggled to improve its performance. We'd closed the door on the American expansion. The grocers had squeezed our margin to zero, so we needed to migrate our grocery customer base back to pharmacies. We could now do this as we had the sales data and we were able to prove to the pharmacies that if we were given the same shelf space as Blackmores, we could achieve the same sales as them. That said, the marketing dollars we invested to help us achieve this outcome were costing us a fortune, and our cost reductions in the supply chain weren't happening fast enough. We were also under a lot of pressure to pay down the debt by cutting even more expenditure. This was tricky to achieve, as we needed to balance the cuts with the need to grow. To make matters worse, the board had turned even further against me. Our back was up against the wall. Oh, and Helen was now up to her sixth IVF cycle.

I did a deep dive into the data to see if it would reveal any insights of value that would help us find a new source of revenue or growth and noticed an interesting anomaly. The sales results showed a trend that indicated pockets of stores in certain areas were doing ten times the sales of stores in other areas. This was intriguing. What was going on? Why did these stores outperform the others?

I shared these insights with Matt Holmes, our National Field Sales Manager as he had mentioned to me a few times that he had also seen some unusual spikes in sales in certain areas around Australia. I needed to get out of the office, reconnect with my intuition and find a way to capitalise on this potential opportunity for growth. So, I did what I always do when under duress. I went on the road and did a national tour with Matt to find out more about what was actually happening at the coalface and reconnect with what our customers and our retailers needed from us.

An unexpected opportunity

A stopover in Adelaide proved to be a game changer. We were in a Terry White pharmacy in Rundle Mall, a block away from the university. We noticed a group of Chinese students at the checkout purchasing boxes and boxes of Swisse products and stuffing it all into big suitcases. It was odd to see them buying our product in such huge volumes. I asked the pharmacy assistant, 'What's going on there?'

She said, 'This happens all the time. The Chinese students buy as much Swisse product as they can get their hands on, package it up and send it back home as gifts for family and friends. Apparently, giving the gift of health is a huge thing in China.' This trend was exactly what Matt had been talking about. If this purchase behaviour was happening in Adelaide, maybe it was happening elsewhere? Could we harness and leverage this trend to our advantage? Was this the niche market that would give us the growth we so desperately needed?

We spent the rest of the tour trying to validate our hypotheses by looking for spikes in sales in Chinese-dominated suburbs. Our instincts were correct. After some extended travel across the country and a deep dive into the sales data, we discovered that this was not just a one-off spike in sales in Adelaide, or a few isolated suburbs. This spike was happening in suburbs all over the country. Box Hill in Victoria. Chatswood in NSW. Robertson in Queensland. This was a trend, a big one, and, judging from our sales results, it was getting bigger.

We did some further research into the Chinese diaspora in Australia and the numbers were startling. One million Chinese nationals had migrated to Australia over the past five years; over one million Chinese tourists travelled to Australia each year; and over 400 000 Chinese students enrolled in an Australian educational institution that year.

This was it! We had just found our next major source of growth: China. We had cracked an export market, except we would not have to do the exporting. These students buying products in Australia and shipping them back home would do it for us. The Chinese market in Australia was our rocket ship: it would make up for the losses we had made in the United States, help us pay back the debt and sustain the growth we needed. We'd hoped to partner with a Chinese-based distributor to enter the China market, but based on the sales we were seeing here in Australia, we could start in Australia and do it ourselves without a partner. We didn't need to go to China to expand into China; the Chinese market was already here. We promptly dedicated a sales and marketing team to manage this opportunity and thus, in January 2014, Project Gold was born.

The power of diversity

Pursuing the Chinese market within Australia was a game-changing exercise in unlocking the potential of diversity. When you embrace insights from a wide range of individuals, both within your workforce and among the general population, you tap into a wealth of perspectives and experiences. This welcoming of diversity not only deepens your understanding of the market but also fuels creativity, fosters inclusivity, and equips you to address the ever-evolving needs of a fragmented customer base. By welcoming diversity, you not only expand your horizons but also position your company for sustained success in an increasingly interconnected world.

Project Gold begins

We called this new venture 'Project Gold' because gold is a colour held in great reverence by the Chinese community, and to us internally, it represented winning and fed smoothly into our earlier Olympic campaign. Project Gold aligned perfectly with the rise of daigou shopping, a form of cross-border e-commerce where personal shoppers in one country purchase products on behalf of customers in another country. (The term 'daigou' is a Chinese word: 'dai' means to act on behalf of or represent, and 'gou' means to buy.) The daigou phenomenon began in 2008 when China was rocked by a baby formula contamination scandal that left over 300 000 infants sick and six dead. Consumer confidence in Chinese-made products never fully recovered and parents, worried that they would not be able to feed their babies, turned to family and friends in Australia, and around the world, to buy baby food on their behalf and ship it back to China.

This crisis sparked the rise of the personal shopper, and, as China's burgeoning middle class grew, so too did the appetite for internationally sourced 'clean and green' products. With the explosion of Chinese students in Australia needing to pay for rent, study and accommodation, they turned to daigou shopping as a source of part-time work. The rise of marketplace platforms such as Taobao, Tmall, JD.com, and VIP further enabled the daigous to quickly re-sell the products online, which meant they could expand their services beyond friends and family, and receive orders from anyone in China. As a result, the daigou business exploded from a handful of students with shopping baskets into a multibillion-dollar economic backchannel that integrated retail, marketing and logistics services across the country. Daigou shopping is common practice now, but it was new back then and we were one of the first to stumble upon this practice and harness it to our advantage.

Courting the daigou

We engaged Michael Howard, as our director of sales, to create a strategy to maximise this daigou opportunity. Michael had been a brand manager at Christian Dior and was now the General Manager of Tissot, a $20-million-dollar high-end watch company that was part of the larger Swatch Group. Michael had zero experience with vitamins, but he had deep experience selling luxury watches and jewellery into the Asian market. He was also a great leader, a fantastic people manager, and a strong marketer who had a deep commitment to customer service and understood that sales were driven by advertising. This appointment perfectly aligned with our strategic approach of recruiting talented individuals from diverse sectors, and utilising their vast knowledge and expertise to drive the success of Swisse.

We also hired another person for this role to hedge our bets. This candidate looked great on paper. Despite eight interviews and my instinct shouting out 'don't hire her' on all eight occasions, we hired her. (Sometimes we let our logic override our instinct. This rarely leads to a good outcome.) Unsurprisingly, she didn't work out and caused a lot of headaches along the way. There are always two sides to every story and my side of the story was that she undermined Helen's work and disparaged me and our culture at any opportunity. However, to me, it seemed she had her voice in the right ears and swayed them sufficiently to have Helen fired. It was an extraordinary situation. Helen (and I) were devastated at this unfair turn of events. Helen, stoic as always, packed up her office, left without revealing the true nature of why she was leaving so as to not cause any further upset to the rest of the team, and never breathed a word of what happened to anyone. She knew it could only cause more friction. She was, and still is, so selfless. Her inherently spiritual approach to life enabled her to see this grossly unfair situation as a source of personal development: a 'gift from the universe' that would open different doors and provide opportunities to explore new horizons.

My relationship with Stephen from here on suffered. This was never about Helen and her work. It was about me and Stephen and the fact that he had lost all trust in me and my judgement. I had created this mess and I needed to get us out it.

Start people on probation

We can be dazzled by charm and a great resume but these assets may not reflect the applicant's true ability or nature. Give people at least three months for their true self to show up and then make a judgement based on that. There is no way you can get to know someone in a couple of one-hour interviews and a few psychological tests.

Michael H. (we had a few Michaels!) was now our director of sales and marketing and perfectly positioned to manage our flywheel. His first goal was to meet with the pharmacy retailers in these Chinese-dominated suburbs to create deeper relationships and think about how we could maximise the Project Gold strategy. Most of these retailers spoke Mandarin as their first language, so when we offered to train their teams and provide them with point-of-sale material in their native language, they jumped at the opportunity. They were hard-working small business owners with a keen hunger to succeed and were eager to see how our unique flywheel could help them sell more Swisse products. These strategies included offering hyper-niche and exclusive sales promotions that targeted cultural events such as Chinese New Year, Golden Week, Singles Day, and significant date days such as 7/7, 8/8, and 11/11.

We invited them to the Melbourne Cup, Wimbledon, the Formula One Grand Prix and all our other VIP celebrity 'meet-and-greet' events. They loved every minute of it, and it gave us that all-important time we needed to foster relationships, which was very important in Chinese culture. The retailers took up all the opportunities we offered them, and the daigous, who bought their products from these pharmacies promoted our products at every turn, regularly posting positive reviews and five-star recommendations on all the global marketplace platforms for the world to see.

The Nicole factor kicks in

The effort we invested in establishing Nicole Kidman's connection to Swisse proved to be invaluable. China's leading online influencers were already familiar with Nicole through her brand partnerships with Chanel, Jimmy Choo and Omega. Her association with fashion, style and luxury resonated with them, so when they saw her endorsing Swisse, they became curious about our products. After trying Swisse themselves and experiencing its positive effects, they enthusiastically recommended us to their millions of followers. When these influencers saw that our Olympic athlete ambassadors also took Swisse, it gave them even further confidence to recommend us. Subsequently, these reviews caught the attention of the sports and nutrition community, and they started buying our products too. This in turn persuaded other online high-profile sports influencers to try our products, which amplified our reach even more.

Unbeknownst to us, the Chinese government were committed to helping its citizens access the burgeoning world of global shopping marketplaces and had set up lucrative 'duty-free' tax incentives to encourage them to get active on these new platforms. This tax incentive made our products much cheaper to buy and gave the daigous a higher profit margin. For example, if you bought a Swisse product from a traditional brick-and-mortar retailer in China, the product attracted a 40 per cent tax. If you bought the same product from one of these authorised marketplaces, the tax was just 10 per cent or even less.

The popularity of the daigou shopping phenomenon spread rapidly throughout China and had a huge impact on our other non-Chinese pharmacies in Australia. They could see that the daigous' demand for product was increasing, so they allocated Swisse more shelf space in prominent locations and eagerly collaborated with us on promotions. They also benefited from the exclusive training and business development opportunities we offered them.

Train your retailers

It's hard getting a retailer to attend a training event offsite, so take the training to them. We hosted in-store training events at breakfast or lunchtime for our pharmacy buyers and made it a fun, light-hearted and enjoyable session. Each attendee received a free meal, refreshments, a Swisse gift bag, a range of product samples and educational booklets. They left the event feeling good about Swisse and far more equipped to recommend us.

All this activity generated an extraordinary burst of sales momentum for our retailers, and bolstered our brand presence in both Australia *and* China. Within a year, we had over 100 000 online resellers, each buying and selling our product and using it as the basis for their side hustle. We didn't know who was buying our product, who they were selling it to, or for how much, but they were buying it and lots of it, and that was music to our ears. Finally, things were turning around. It was a slow burn, but it was happening.

Board games

Meanwhile, Goldman Sachs was hard at work refinancing us and getting to know our operation. We were impressed with the way they went about their business and relieved that they understood our strategy. They could see that it was just a matter of time before the raft of cost-cutting and profit-generating strategies would start to show up on the bottom line. They were aware of Project Gold but they hadn't yet got their heads around the potential scale of the opportunity, and were not factoring it into their projections. They were not convinced it was a sustainable trend. It didn't matter to us. We knew Project Gold was going to be big; we followed our instincts and got to work on fine-tuning this much-needed new source of revenue. While Project Gold was stabilising our financial position, our board felt this traction was just a temporary blip on the radar — that it was an unreliable, unsustainable source of revenue and could not be counted on to be a reputable, repeatable sales channel. They understood our strategy, but they were still cautious as to whether I had the ability to lead the company into this next phase.

As a condition of the $70 million loan, Goldman Sachs had installed one of their team on our board as an 'observer' to oversee their investment (and us). David Gribble was duly appointed and we welcomed his oversight. The Goldman Sachs crew were smart operators and we were happy to be observed. They also requested that we appoint an independent person, chosen by both parties, to join the board. They provided us with an extensive list of potential candidates, from which we selected three names for further consideration. After meeting with each of them, Trevor O'Hoy emerged as the standout candidate due to his experience as the former CEO of Carlton and United Breweries (CUB), a firm whose experiences closely aligned with our current circumstances.

I had met Trevor years ago through the Ricky Ponting Foundation, and thought he had all the qualities that would serve us well in the future. In fact, I'd extended an invitation for him to join our board at that time, but Stephen and Michael deemed it unnecessary. Nevertheless, our existing rapport and established relationship played a significant role in our decision-making process, as strong relationships were always key.

Despite encountering distinct challenges during his tenure at CUB — much like our experiences at Swisse — we believed Trevor's expertise would prove invaluable. CUB, like us, had operated within the Australian market, and leadership experience like his, which spanned all strategic aspects of an organisation, was hard to find. This was particularly relevant considering that most Australian businesses of our size primarily focused on domestic operations or subsidiaries of international conglomerates while Trevor had navigated the complexities of a multinational enterprise across diverse categories. Furthermore, his first-hand familiarity and struggles with managing the overarching CUB brand marketing strategy, contending with overseas expansion, and taking on too much debt was exactly the kind of specialised experience we required. Trevor and I connected well, and I was confident he'd give me the help I needed to align the team with our strategic vision.

I believed that Trevor would back our strategy and provide us with some boardroom support. His primary expertise was being a 'turnaround' CFO, and we needed all the help we could get to continue our turnaround. I also knew his appointment would buy me time to finish the turnaround — and, time being what we needed, I recommended we engage him.

Our board at the time consisted of Michael, Stephen, Gary Graco (Stephen's personal accountant), myself, the newly appointed David Gribble, and now Trevor, who arrived in December 2013, just as the turnaround began to gain traction. Trevor took on the role of Executive Chairman a year later and quickly gained the ear, and trust, of Stephen. The board's tolerance for our performance was showing signs of wear. They felt the strategy that we had initiated was taking too long to deliver a result and they had lost trust in us. The board had my measure to some degree. I felt Stephen, in particular, knew I could invest prodigious amounts of energy to achieve a goal, and his tactic for motivating me had morphed into what felt like goading, criticising and challenging me every step of the way, which subsequently turned me into the board's whipping boy. I also felt that the board knew I responded well to inordinate challenges and that conceding defeat was not in my nature, and I felt they played on this to pile on the pressure. It didn't feel fair, but I surmised that Stephen's attacks on me weren't personal and he was doing what he could under stressful circumstances. I knew he had the best interests of the business at heart, and besides, I had broad shoulders and could handle it.

Cutting costs

The $70 million cash injection provided by Goldman Sachs took the pressure off. Project Gold was in progress, our cost cutting and supply chain optimisation program was in full swing, and we could pay our suppliers. Adem was managing this complex supply chain project and we were well down the path of eliminating several layers in the chain that would cut costs, increase profits and improve the quality of our product.

We were already pushing everyone in the team to reach some ambitious targets, but it felt like Trevor was pushing us harder and harder to make more cuts — cuts that I thought would affect the momentum we were building — and this was when my frustration crept in. Ironically, I had understood that the key reason Trevor wanted to join Swisse was because of our culture. But when it came to cost-cutting, the cultural initiatives that made us special were the first things to be cut.

From my perspective, his approach to cost cutting was to make people redundant, or slash their wages, or to reward them with money if they performed and take the money away if they didn't. Yes, using money as a lever to motivate people can work, but it's a blunt tool with a limited capacity to change people's behaviour on a long-term basis. I thought that sustaining a culture was a lot more complicated than that.

Our key goal in cost recovery was to focus on our two biggest costs — the costs of goods and our trading terms/retail co-operative marketing spend, but in my view, Trevor only focused on reducing the marketing spend and moving people on and cutting perks. On their own, these were never going to deliver us the savings we needed and could stifle the renewed consumer growth we were seeing. Yes, we needed to cut costs, but to my mind he was squeezing a lemon that had no juice left to give. Trevor and I clashed on this badly and from here on, I felt our relationship deteriorated. I could see that the turnaround was working, and that China was about to kick in, but it appeared that Trevor saw things differently.

How to cut costs

Lowering our costs of goods was one of our highest priorities. To achieve this, we would:

- commit to larger volumes
- cut out the middlemen
- shorten our payment terms to 60 days end of month.

Renegotiating our trading terms and our retail co-operative marketing spend was our other priority. To achieve this, we would:

- shift customers from grocery to pharmacies
- offer less discounts to support co-operative marketing spends
- use bonus stock to offset our cost of discounts

When he saw that the business had shifted into a new gear, he seemed to panic for some reason, and I recall he suggested we smooth our earnings profile at $70 million as he felt the market 'wouldn't believe our growth story' if we were to sell the business with this growth trajectory. The EBITDA at that time was at around $30 million, so $70 million did not seem like an unreasonable goal to others unfamiliar with the business, but I knew $70 million was a fraction of what the business was capable of doing, and that it was about to go a lot higher than that very soon. In any event, I believed that if we in some way constrained the momentum the business had, we'd be in danger of losing the opportunity to sell the business at the highest possible price. Surely everyone in the company was invested in selling the company for the highest price possible?

Around this time, the question of whether I should be fired arose once more. The Bain consultants had done some fantastic work for us in proofing up our trading terms position and confirming our cost of goods reduction strategies. It was my feeling that they supported the quest to have me fired. I was really disappointed about this as I had been fully supportive of Bain whenever anyone had questioned their value. Thankfully Goldman strongly recommended they keep me on. They understood the business and knew what was best for it. I was saved, at least for the time being. I resolved to do what I had always done when under pressure. Take the feedback on board, work harder, prove them wrong, and let my actions do the talking.

Welcome a different viewpoint

We worked with many big consultancies during this challenging time. These firms are often not welcomed by executives as they fear their performances will be scrutinised. We had a different perspective. We welcomed them and their input. We didn't always agree with their recommendations but by listening and challenging each other, we generally found a path forward that delivered a much better result.

CHAPTER 28

HOW AND WHY WE SUCCEEDED IN CHINA

Expanding into international markets is always a challenging endeavour, and entering the uniquely complex Chinese market presented even greater complications. The disparities in language, culture, customs and values created a series of formidable hurdles we had to overcome. We needed to change the way we worked quickly. Fortunately, our team were always up for a challenge.

I can also say quite proudly that the seeds of our China strategy were planted many moons earlier when Michael, Stephen and I would meet for breakfast, and plot and plan and dream about what this business could be. We always thought global, even back then, when we had no reason to believe that any of our dreams or plans would come true. What we did have was a deep passion to make something amazing and a commitment to launch it onto the world stage.

If you want to expand into China, you can take a leaf out of our flywheel playbook to help you do it. Of course, we were at a certain time and location that enabled us to leverage the winds of technological change. Those opportunities will be different for you today, just as the technology available today is different, but here is how we used the flywheel to do it.

How we used the flywheel to launch into China

We used our marketing flywheel to launch into China with great success. This case study documents the eight-step process we followed to achieve that success. Key to this was targeting the local Chinese community, tourists and mainland Chinese via the daigous, retailers and Power Sellers to increase our brand recognition and drive sales. This is a detailed breakdown of how the campaign ran, what we did to reach our target audience, and who we partnered with to make it a success. It looks simple here but it was a massive logistical exercise to bring together so many moving pieces.

What is a Power Seller?

'Power Sellers' are experienced and reputable sellers who are active in online marketplaces such as Tmall and JD.com, which are like massive online Westfield shopping centres, where the e-tailers pay rent to 'lease' their online store. Achieving Power Seller status is often based on criteria such as sales volume, feedback ratings, and adherence to platform policies. They were critical to our success.

1. Connect Swisse with large-scale TV and/or events

We targeted large-scale events and high-rating television programs that resonated with the Chinese community (local and in China). This drove brand awareness and sales. These events included:

- Spring Racing carnival (featuring Nicole Kidman in 2012)
- *The Voice, MasterChef* and *My Kitchen Rules*
- The Celebrate Life ball
- Robbie Williams Swisse VIP Concert
- Ricky Martin Swisse VIP Concert
- Chinese International Film Festival.

We engaged global celebrities like Ricky Martin to perform for our VIP clients.

2. Source partnership associations and sponsorships

We used sponsorships and partnerships that were directly related to events and TV programs. To target our Project Gold customers, we partnered with a range of organisations including the:

■ Australian Olympic Committee

■ Victorian Racing Committee

■ Australian Grand Prix Corporation

■ Hawthorn Football Club

■ Australian Football League.

These sponsorships/partnerships provided us with significant benefits, such as:

■ category exclusivity

■ legitimacy

■ intellectual property

■ content

■ in-program integration.

We also welcomed our Project Gold customers and Power Sellers to the Swisse Marquee during the Melbourne Cup Spring Racing carnival. The Chinese-inspired Marquee provided a platform to drive business and relationships while celebrating its partnership with the Chinese community.

Network Seven conducted interviews with our ambassadors during the events, which generated valuable content integration opportunities.

3. Engage ambassadors that connect with our media events

Our core values of Premium, Proven and Aspirational messages were communicated through Swisse's relationship with Nicole Kidman and other celebrities such as Karen Martini, Ashley Hart and Singapore Ambassador Rebecca Lim. Nicole in particular represented luxury brands including Chanel, Omega and Jimmy Choo, which were all strong brands in China.

4. Launch multi-platform 360-degree advertising campaigns

We invested heavily in targeting the Chinese community via national media, including:

- 31 TV commercials

- 119 billboards

- 33 large format outdoor billboards

- 307 transport shelters

- 37 shopalites in key Chinese centres

- 6800 TV commercials in Chinese Cinemas

- 68 retailer catalogues

- 260 social media posts.

(This breakdown in media was *just* for the Spring Racing carnival only. We invested a lot more in the Project Gold campaign over the year.)

5. Guarantee an exclusive retailer commitment

It was critical the retailer bought enough stock in advance to cover our media commitments. Retailer promotions were a key component of our flywheel model and every campaign linked back to a retailer promotion and in-store activation to drive sales.

This created opportunities for purchase and blocked out competitors via a visual/sensual offensive to ensure Swisse was always top of mind.

Retailer promotions were often associated with a 'money can't buy' Swisse offer or experience, and heavily supported by retail point-of-sale and off-location displays, all designed to reduce the risk of consumers purchasing competitor products or shopping exclusively on price.

6. Amplify our events, sponsorships, partnerships and ambassador associations

We used the flywheel model to leverage the TV show/event ambassador relationships and sponsorships to increase exposure and generate free PR. Our digital team worked with PR agencies, editors, journalists and bloggers to push our messages of Health and Happiness. They used TV, print, digital and the social media channels (Instagram, Facebook and Twitter).

In addition, our Power Sellers and the Chinese community used Weibo and WeChat to drive strong brand awareness and create positive consumer sentiment. (The 2012 Melbourne Cup generated over 2000 media reports and articles featuring Swisse.)

7. Provide high-quality, impactful point-of-sale materials

We used eye-catching images and props to drive consumer engagement and awareness at the point-of-sale. These included off-location displays, such as gondola ends, to highlight promotions and key selling products on promotion.

In addition, we provided Project Gold retailers and partners with Mandarin-specific brochures, which highlighted key brand messages and top-selling products.

Swisse had a range of premium customised retail solutions targeted to Project Gold customers, which lifted the brand's visibility and products' shop-ability in-store to ensure maximum sales and brand presence at the point-of-sale.

8. Appear within the in-store catalogues

The final piece in the flywheel was the use of retail catalogues (print and online) to drive consumer awareness of promoted products and 'money can't buy' opportunities.

CHAPTER 29

CULTURE WILL PREVAIL

During these challenging times of the turnaround, culture became more important than ever. We had learned our lessons from the American experience, and as a result had worked hard to enhance our processes through our executive meetings and off-site strategic retreats, and regularly reviewed our systems and culture via the business planning sessions. We needed a team that were absolutely committed to getting us through this extraordinarily challenging time, and our focus on the three plans that Cath and her offsider, Steph, had initiated – the cultural, communications and business plans – were at the heart of that. Everyone was up for the challenge. Jonni, our meditation coach, talked to the importance of us all choosing to be elite at what we did; that these next few years of the business's journey was our 'grand final', and that we needed to give our absolute all to be successful. We had just a few years to make our goals a reality and if we could sustain our energy and focus, we could achieve it. This is antithetical to what most meditation coaches teach but we found it inspiring to discover that meditation could be used as a tool for accomplishment as well as relaxation. Jonni was pivotal in supporting our executive team's mental health throughout this very stressful period. We constantly reinforced our mission of 'make people healthier and happier'. It was also important to us at this time that we continued to give back to the team and community as we had always done and not let these boardroom tussles take us off track. So long as we held on to our values, we would prevail. We were a purpose-led company and, while profits were important, we knew that the numbers would not materialise, and that our cost-cutting programs would wear thin, if we did not abide by our values.

Make your meetings exciting

Make your internal meetings worth attending. Have fun, smile, pre-circulate the agenda 24 hours in advance so everyone can prepare. Provide a sit-down dinner, have the CEO deliver a motivational speech, get an interesting person on stage to entertain or provide skills training, or ask a customer to talk about your product. And if you're meeting with retailers, don't forget to attach an exciting sales opportunity to generate a return on investment.

The Celebrate Life Foundation ball

We deeply appreciated the unwavering loyalty of our community, and we seized every opportunity to offer a range of enjoyable, inclusive and vibrant activities to express our gratitude. These created the much-needed purpose around what we did. At the heart of the Swisse community program was the Celebrate Life Foundation, which aimed to inspire wellness among individuals and the community as a whole. Through this foundation, we aspired to 'bend the trend' of rising rates of preventable diseases by educating people about the significance of proper nutrition, mindfulness and physical activity.

We hosted the Celebrate Life Foundation ball during the turnaround, which was one of the busiest and most stressful times in Swisse history. The board, Trevor and even our bank weighed in and said, 'Why are you doing this? Is this the best use of our time and money right now?' but we believed it was the right thing to do and it sent a signal to everyone that our commitment to our culture, community and people came before profit. We asked our people to dig deep and deliver for the brand, so how could we as a company not do the same for those facing adversity? Michael Saba was one of the few who endorsed our support of these charity endeavours at this difficult time, and was an advocate of giving back no matter what was happening in the business. He told me of an earlier time when he and Stephen could barely afford to pay for a chair and computer for the office, yet donated regular sizeable sums to the Royal Children's Hospital. 'Giving is the reason we do what we do,' he said. 'You just have to give.'

Our team members were putting in extra hours, staying back late to bring to life these extraordinary events, not because they were obligated to, but because they genuinely wanted to contribute. This meant that the boundaries between work and home were blurred, but it also meant that they felt valued, needed, and were driven by a greater purpose. When things settled down, we always gave the team the time back so they could rejuvenate and rebalance.

The ball, attended by some of the country's biggest celebrities, including Nicole Kidman and Keith Urban, Ricky Ponting, Natalie Bassingthwaighte, and Jessica Mauboy, raised an impressive $1 million for our foundation. We were so proud of our team and the way they went about organising and delivering this incredible event, particularly when they were all under significant pressure at the office to deliver on the turnaround. The team were more motivated because the event created a 'feel good' promotion of our brand, gave us a break from talking about the turnaround and gave us more purpose in why we were doing what we did.

Keith often accompanied Nicole to her events; they were the ultimate power couple

What is community?

Community is such an anodyne word and can be bandied around without real thought about what it really means. To us, community was not some faceless, anonymous group of people. Our community was made up of our team, retailers, suppliers, agencies, and the thousands upon thousands of people who bought our products every day. We were part of that community and we always lived up to our values, even when it was difficult, inconvenient or costly to do so. It gave us purpose, a reason to 'be' beyond just being profit focused, and enhanced our culture. Our team was genuinely inspired by this work.

The Colour Run

We sponsored dozens of other community events during this time. One of our biggest was the Colour Run, a vibrant event that encouraged people to embrace an active and healthy lifestyle. One of the founders of Noisy Beast discovered this event when he was visiting the United States, and we were all struck by the sheer joy it created and thought it would work well in Australia.

The event celebrated health, happiness and individuality, which aligned perfectly with our values. Of course, at the end of every run, everyone received a Swisse goodie bag and paraphernalia and we soon became the talk of the town, earned huge media coverage and the Colour Run became a signature Swisse event. We took the existing, well-worn idea of a traditional fun run, added a twist, made it new and different and the community responded.

Thanks to our partnership with The Colour Run, Swisse introduced a fundraising model that successfully raised over $900 000 for local Australian charities. Moreover, we extended financial support to various other nonprofit organisations, including the Murdoch Institute, Monash Children's Hospital, National Institute of Integrative Medicine, Osteoporosis Australia, Second Bite and the Australian College of Midwives.

Nature – our most important partner

We raised more than $10 million for various charity organisations by running events like the Colour Run and Celebrate Life Ball. We loved that we could enhance our culture by giving back to our community and our partners who supported us. In 2007, before it was cool for corporates to associate themselves with environmental causes, we actively worked towards offsetting carbon emissions, and were proud to see our initiative gain entry into the Australian Government's National Carbon Offset Standard (NCOS) program.

This achievement reflected our belief that there was an integral link between healthy people and a healthy environment. We believed that a leader in health and wellness should take an active role in protecting and preserving our natural environment. It made sense, was great for our brand perception, and it felt right, but, beyond that, it was part of our job and the right thing to do.

Cutting the cost of goods

With Project Gold in progress, I could now dedicate my attention to executing a range of intricate turnaround strategies to make the business more profitable. I had demonstrated that I could be a 'growth' CEO, but I still had to prove to the board I could be a 'turnaround' CEO. This would require a very different mindset and suite of skills, but I was confident I could do what was required. This cost-cutting process had begun back in 2012 with optimising the supply chain, but it was a task that would take many years to come to fruition. Our cost of goods was much higher than our competitors because we sourced high-quality ingredients from trusted sources, and because we packed more active ingredients into each tablet to create therapeutic dosages. 'Cutting the cost of goods' sounded so simple in theory, yet it was ridiculously complicated to implement.

Our focus on creating growth had generated substantial revenue, so we knew that there would be plenty of opportunities to make a better product and create efficiencies. There were multiple players in our supply chain and we knew we could eliminate a layer or four to sharpen up the bottom line, while retaining our commitment to quality. This was not a quick or easy win. It required detailed planning, tough negotiations, and an arduous travel schedule. We were up for the task. The challenges we faced with product labelling in the United States served as a valuable learning experience, and provided us with profound insights into the manufacturing process. As a result, we gleaned some valuable ideas on how to effectively lower our costs.

Adem was full steam ahead on reducing our cost of goods, which was our biggest cost. I said, 'We need to reduce it by 30 per cent.'

He sighed and said, 'That target sounds a bit aggressive.'

It was, but I knew he could do it. We had a plan to achieve it too. Firstly, we'd change our payment terms. Our policy had been to buy from our contract manufacturers and ask for really long payment terms, which would take the pressure off our cash flow. We put a stop to that, did a reset and said, 'We're going to pay you on time, so give us your best price.'

Our second strategy was a lot more complicated. We'd aim to:

- own our formulations
- perform our own (very costly) stability trials
- hire a team of purpose-driven people to lead the process
- put our supply chain to a global tender
- cut out the raw material middle-men
- buy direct from the raw material producers.

We said, 'Rather than you purchase all the raw ingredients and formulate the products for us, we will directly source the raw materials from a range of suppliers and deliver them to you. Your task will be to just formulate the products to our specifications (which is called 'toll manufacturing') and send them to our distribution hub in Sydney.' To ask a contract manufacturer to toll manufacture you must own your intellectual property and this takes years to develop (something that we had well underway). It was a massive shift in the way we did business but we were dedicated to reducing the cost of goods, and if we were committed to maintaining our high quality and therapeutic dosage, this was one of the only ways we could do it.

Protect your intellectual property

It may not seem important now but when it comes time to sell your business, the buyer will want proof that you own your intellectual property. Do you have the correct paperwork that proves you own your logo, your company name, your formulations, your domain name and other assets? Don't wait for the sale documents to be on the table before you get your paperwork in order.

At the time, we were one of the biggest buyers of nutrition raw materials in the world, so going direct to the raw material suppliers was no small task. But by doing so, we took several layers out of the supply chain, optimised our operations, delivered a cost reduction of 30 per cent and, most importantly, ended up with a better-quality product. This was all due to Adem and his colleagues, especially Federica Nicolao, our Head of Sourcing and Procurement (another Village person), and Rachel Di Leva, Head of Regulatory and Scientific Affairs – both outstanding women who were instrumental in harnessing this complex jigsaw and bringing the job to completion.

Sometimes you need to be irrational

Adem worked exceptionally hard during this time. He was constantly travelling to long-haul locations such as China, India, Romania, Germany and the United States. My relentless goal to cut costs by 30 per cent did test our relationship at the time, but as a leader I occasionally had to be a little irrational to get an irrational result. Adem, as always, was up for the challenge and did a magnificent job finding wonderful suppliers who could provide us with the world-class ingredients we needed. His focus meant our turnaround was coming like an H&H

(Health and Happiness) steam train to save the day; it would just take years to get to its destination. This was not a fast process.

Knowing how hard you can push is a great art form: you have to know exactly how far you can go before you lose people. That said, you need to constantly stress test this, and be very quick to admit when you may have gone too far. That was why culture was so key: if the environment was right, people would be more motivated to exceed their own expectations and would give more, and do more, than they ever thought possible.

The delicate art of nagging

I owe a debt to my mother for inspiring this management quality in me. She was the queen of nagging and, while at times it made my teenage life tough, it did instil in me the belief that nagging people, and getting permission from people to nag them, was one of the most potent ways to get people to do things.

Backed by science

We'd already had our battles with the Therapeutic Goods Administration, Australia's regulatory body, so imagine the level of oversight and detail needed to deal with all these other worldwide regulatory bodies. We had always made it a top priority to use ingredients that were backed by scientific research and traditional evidence. Now that we were responsible for sourcing our own ingredients, we had to double down on this. Governance was a huge factor in our ability to satisfy these regulatory bodies and source our own ingredients. There were numerous reasons why our governance system was so strong. We had hired a team of in-house scientists years earlier so that they could manage the formulation process, provide scientific and academic validation to our claims, help us document the intellectual property to our formulations, and be quick to produce any patent, clinical study or peer-reviewed paper on demand should it be required by an authority.

Why governance matters

Governance is just a fancy word for 'Are you doing things right? Are you following the rules?' We made a lot of mistakes with our American launch because we weren't across the product labelling regulations, but we learned from that and incorporated those lessons into our new governance procedures. Buyers will pay less for your business if they think your systems will leave them open to investigation or scrutiny. If you want to sell your business, take care of governance now.

This commitment to governance enabled us to set the standard for what a leader in the sector should aim to achieve. We set the benchmark (or BM, you may recall) for the industry, so we took pride in setting the bar for what high-quality really meant. Safety was always our overriding preoccupation and we welcomed the scrutiny that these governing bodies offered.

Investing in the future

In 2012, $800 million of funding was going to universities each year for drug research, compared to natural medicine research, which only received about $800 000. Just over 12 per cent of all consumer health dollars was being spent on natural health, so wouldn't you think government should match this with 12 per cent of research dollars invested in natural medicine research activity? Instead it was 1 per cent, and, unlike drug medicine, natural medicines attract the goods and services tax. Incredible.

Despite the lack of support and interest from the government and other medical and health institutions, we were determined to contribute to the body of evidence and make a real impact. We were all about pushing the boundaries of knowledge, so we invested tens of millions in research and development. We set up the Swisse Scientific Advisory Panel, a group of esteemed experts specialising in integrative medicine, who were able to provide valuable insights during the formulation process. We also collaborated with La Trobe University and Swinburne University to establish the Complementary Medicine Evidence Centre.

This groundbreaking centre conducted comprehensive reviews of essential Swisse products, which ensured an updated evidence base. We'd not only review our ingredients, we'd also do research on the other principles of nutrition, mindfulness and movement. Rachel led this work and uncovered some startling results. For example, we did a double-blind clinical study on the effects of doing two 20-minute sessions of meditation per day, and found that after 60 days of practice those who committed to meditation showed significantly enhanced Emotional Intelligence. Importantly, all the research we did on our products was on ingredients that were not patented and this research was available to all in the industry who used those ingredients in their product. In other words, everyone could benefit from our research. We wanted to push the industry forward; we wanted everyone to win.

CHAPTER 30

A PR CHALLENGE

When I took on the operations role at Swisse back in 2005, my dad warned me that the TGA regulation and bureaucracy would be challenging. He was right. It was a lesson in being aware that a PR disaster could land on your doorstep at any time, and when you least expect it, or deserve it.

Our PR challenge started when we received a fax from the TGA questioning (again) our famous tagline: 'Tired? Stressed? You'll feel better on Swisse.' We wrote back, confirming that our tagline had been signed off by the TGA seven years earlier. (On that occasion, a competitor had complained that our tagline was a marketing claim and not a scientific claim. They won. We appealed and we won. Case closed.) We attached the ruling we had received from the Federal Health Minister, sent it to the TGA and waited.

This fresh (anonymous) complaint was brought before a committee made up of professionals, consumers and industry reps whose job was to come together and decide on whether a complaint should stand or not. They advised us that the complaint would be upheld and we'd have to drop the tagline.

A few days prior to getting the ruling from the TGA, I got a call from a journalist from *The Daily Telegraph*. She said, 'We've been contacted by someone from the TGA who's advised us that you've lost your case, and that the complaint will be upheld and you'll need to drop your tagline.' I told the journalist we'd been down this track before, and had won every single time, and that it was a beat-up probably instigated by sceptics of natural medicine with little actual knowledge of how nutrition works.

The journalist didn't seem interested in hearing my point of view; likely she'd already written her story and had the clever headline ready to go. 'The story will go live tonight,' she said. My stomach clenched. Now I really was tired and stressed. I constantly refreshed my phone waiting for the story to drop. On the stroke of midnight, the story appeared on *The Daily Telegraph* website with the headline, 'Tired? Stressed? You won't feel better on Swisse.'

I couldn't sleep for worrying about the damage this would do to the business. Sure enough, it ran in the hard-copy newspaper on page three the next day. It was a big story. By mid-morning, there were over 300 comments on the story. Many were supporters but the naysayers seemed to all say the same thing, which made us think it was a setup. It felt so unfair. We'd done nothing wrong. I called my team together for a crisis meeting to work out how we were going to manage this. We advised our team, partners and ambassadors to let them know this damaging article was in the public domain, and that we would fight it. Rachel and Michelle Aitkin were particularly outstanding in ensuring we were ahead of the curve during this very stressful time.

The media attack took a nasty turn when *The Daily Telegraph* ran another story a few days later with the headline, 'The celebrity-loving CEO and his father', accompanied by a goofy photo of me jumping in the air. The other man pictured in the shot wasn't even my father. (It was Stephen Ring.) The irony was the photo they used was the same photo they had used to depict me, in an article about me a few months earlier where I talked openly and frequently about how my dad had worked on research for Swisse products.

Worst of all, the story intimated that we didn't disclose the fact my dad worked on research for our products, and that he had tweaked the results of clinical trials to skew the results to benefit Swisse. To accuse a medical professional of fraud is a serious matter. We all know that when a public figure is dragged through a trial by media the truth is often the first casualty. The damage was done the minute the story went to air. The journalist didn't seem to bother to check that there were at least seven other authors attached to all the research trials Dad was involved in, and that the research was conducted by independent, credible organisations in which Dad had no involvement. He did consult on the design of the study, on dosages, and made suggestions around what blood markers and behaviours to test for, based on his knowledge of nutrition. As a preeminent scholar and professor with over 300 peer-reviewed articles to his name, he was the right and appropriate person to comment.

It seemed to me that if they'd conducted a skerrick of research, they would have seen the same information on our website and in the public domain. We had made a point of publishing all our formulations and the science that backed up our claims on our website and had done so for many years. This was our valuable IP and we put it out there for the world (and our competitors) to see, all of whom could use it to formulate their own products and leverage our hard-won knowledge. We gave up our considerable competitive advantage to prove that we had nothing to hide and to demonstrate that we, as the market leaders, were committed to furthering the sector in this most tangible of ways. (The media also failed to acknowledge the many millions we had invested in medical research to help document the link between natural medicine and better health outcomes.)

I was so outraged on behalf of my father, I flew to the newspaper's headquarters in Sydney and requested a meeting with the journalist, editor and managing director. I got short shrift. It seemed like they couldn't have cared less that their stories were inaccurate. They had their clicks already. I made it very clear that I thought their reporting was gutless, and that to attack an innocent person and destroy a reputation built up over 50 years was galling.

To counter these attacks, we engaged Swinburne University and Queensland University to conduct a full independent review of our advertising claims. They did so and their research was made available to the public on our website and to the court during our trial. The court found overwhelmingly in our favour and furthermore admitted that we had not been subject to fair process and the matter was sent back to the TGA panel for further review. Unfortunately, the TGA eventually ruled against us, and we were prevented from using the tagline going forward.

This whole shabby episode reinforced my existing belief that we needed to invest in the science behind the formulations, provide the data needed to rebut ridiculous claims and keep doing the hard yards to ensure that our claims were backed up by science, clinical evidence and robust trials.

Our consumers stayed loyal and sales did not miss a beat. I don't think they even noticed the brouhaha that had erupted. They knew they felt better on Swisse and no beat-up story was going to convince them otherwise. Unlike many of the world's largest pharmaceutical companies, who have been fined upwards of billions of dollars, we've never been subject to any fines or charges whatsoever. We never took risks with our claims and this emboldened us to keep doing what we had always done, which was make great products. (From then on, we'd change the tagline for each campaign. We used every challenge as a learning experience.) Our products had an industry-leading 68 per cent retention rate, the highest-quality ingredients, and the best scientific advisory team in the country. Transparency was the name of the game and we were up for it.

How to handle negative PR

These PR experiences taught us that no matter how hard you work to do the right thing, there are always some who will try to bring your good name into disrepute. If you find yourself in the middle of a PR crisis, act immediately. Don't think it will go away. It will need to be addressed, and quickly. We always acted with integrity, took the high moral ground and never resorted to cheap tricks to land a blow. Our customers knew what we stood for and our sales were not affected, even when we were front page news. When you break new ground and threaten the status quo, you will be attacked by those whose position you threaten. That comes with being the market leader.

When *The Checkout* checked out

Another PR challenge we had to contend with during the very stressful turnaround phase and the American exit came from an unlikely source – the ABC. I've always enjoyed the irreverence and madcap mania of The Chaser boys. I appreciated the way they pushed the creative envelope in coming up with new TV formats and went where others dared not go. But they took it too far when their new program, *The Checkout*, a consumer affairs show that aired on the ABC in 2013, took aim at one of our products, and, in particular, my father.

We had a weight management product called Appetite Suppressant. These source ingredients had been used for hundreds of years in India to reduce hunger. The formulations had succeeded in trials so we released a product with the claim that the ingredient had been traditionally used as an appetite suppressant. Prior to launching, we confirmed with the TGA that we had approval to use the claim on the label. A few months after we released the product, the TGA said that our claims were being audited, and that we could no longer call it an 'appetite suppressant' because appetite took into account thirst as well as hunger. They said we could relist the product and relabel it as 'hunger control'. Some opponents of alternative medicine had a field day with this, telling the media we had our product deregistered, when in reality it was only so that the label could be rejigged and updated.

When I watched the *The Checkout* skit, I felt that it implied that my dad had doctored the trials around a weight loss product to get a clinically proven outcome. Dad had nothing to do with the appetite control product or supporting clinical trials. It might as well have painted him as some harebrained tribal witch doctor. It was horrendous, wildly inaccurate and deeply damaging to his reputation. Even worse, they didn't bother to contact my father, myself or anyone at Swisse for our side of the story – something every reputable journalist is supposed to do. My father sued the ABC for defamation and ended up settling. He never wanted a cash outcome, just a statement from the producers and the ABC that they'd made an error. Interestingly he told me that when he met them face to face they made a big fuss about how sorry they were. Yet when it came to the settlement, they refused to apologise but instead made a statement of regret around the incorrect content. I guess if you admit you regret something then it's as close as you would go to giving an apology.

Business is a full-contact game and every executive team needs to have a thick skin to absorb the slings and arrows of inquiry and governance. But for the public broadcaster to run a deeply damaging personal attack on an innocent person – a respected professor of surgery, who has given his all to help people fight chronic disease – was beyond the pale. By all means, go after a brand but don't play the man, especially one who has done nothing wrong. Prior to this episode airing, the ABC show *Australian Story* had planned to feature Dad as a guest to celebrate his life story and his contribution to integrative medicine. When *The Checkout* episode aired, that invitation was quietly withdrawn. A few months later the ABC ran the same *Checkout* episode again, unchanged, despite the statement of regret. We let it go. Unbelievable.

In my experience, I have found that these kinds of attacks on natural medicines often have the result, by design or otherwise, of protecting pharmaceutical companies. Pharmaceutical companies themselves take this approach by lobbying for more regulation of natural medicines (which they see as a competing product), and by ring-fencing their grant dollars to make sure their research and associated findings are not threatened. I felt like my dad and I had been pawns in a global chess game that worked to protect that space, maintain the status quo and shut down natural medicine as a serious component of people's health regime.

This bruising affair taught us many things, but the key take-out was that for us to take on Big Pharma, or to even make a dent in the public conversation that natural and integrative medicine was a viable pathway to good health, we needed to have hard data to prove our claims.

Years later, Dad was rightfully recognised when he was awarded an AO, the first person to receive it for services to integrative medicine. I cried with joy and belief to see that finally, this most decent of men was receiving the recognition he deserved.

CHAPTER 31

LOSING PATIENCE ....

By January 2014, the turnaround had not progressed as quickly as we would have hoped. Everyone was losing patience with me. Goldman Sachs's perspective was, 'We've given you the $70 million to get yourself out of the hole; we've given you time and support and haven't interfered, so why haven't we seen the results of the turnaround?' They were worried about losing their $70 million investment and wanted third-party assurance that we knew what we were doing. To verify that our turnaround was on course, they sent one of their heavy hitters from Hong Kong to interview me. I needed to convince this man that the results were coming, and soon, or I would be out of a job. I knew the hockey stick of massive return was coming up but no-one else was as confident as me; but then no-one was as close to the business as me. This man also interviewed Michael and Stephen, who both supported me, but once again, my leadership abilities were called into question, and every time this happened, it eroded my all-important reputation capital. You only get so many chances to prove your worth as a CEO.

At this time, the board seriously considered selling and some were willing to walk regardless of the price and asked key advisers what would be a price to get a quick sale. While no adviser prepared a written valuation the board formed a view that an appropriate figure would be $100 million; $70 million would go toward the debt, and the remaining $30 million would go to shareholders. This was more than surprising to me. Just 18 months earlier we had offers valuing us at $500 million, and I knew we were in a much better position now than we were then.

I don't believe that Goldman Sachs ever intended that valuation to be taken seriously, as they were never going to buy the company and it was never, to my knowledge, communicated in writing or was ever considered to be a true and accurate representation of the company's value, but the mere airing of it would have costly ramifications. By now, it felt like Stephen and Michael had had enough, and were ready to walk with their profits.

I could go bankrupt

At this point, there were still only three shareholders. Stephen had 70 per cent, and Michael and I each had 15 per cent. I was the only one who had debt against their shares. During the turnaround phase and the credit crunch, we had stopped paying dividends many months ago. Despite having always met my targets, I had never been paid a bonus, and all dividends had gone toward personal debt reduction. (Thankfully it was agreed that as the dividends had been turned off, the company would continue paying the interest on the loan.) The only challenge was that I would have to pay interest twice: once against the loan the company was giving me to pay down the debt, and on the second set of interest against the bank loan I had taken out. I was now paying *double* interest on the millions of dollars and the debt had ballooned to over $14 million. Do the math. If the deal went ahead at a valuation of $30 million, my 15 per cent shareholding would be worth $4.5 million, leaving me with a debt of $9.5 million. That caravan on the foreshore of Byron Bay was fast becoming a reality.

You could say I was pretty stressed at this time. Controlling the controllables, meditating, exercise, good communication and disciplined habits at home and at work enabled me to get through without showing signs of weakness or doubt. I pleaded with the board to hold the line, stay strong and have faith that the turnaround was coming.

I think we all could see the turnaround coming: Goldman, Bain, Michael and our executive team.

Still, nine months later, concerns were aired that the business was going to run out of money unless we sold some of our shares. I knew that we were never going to run out of money as the turnaround was well on its way now and we had reduced costs right across the business without affecting sales, but I was supportive of this strategy if it meant the executive team would be rewarded for their hard work and efforts in implementing the turnaround. Trevor bought a stack of those shares based on this bargain-basement valuation. At the same time, the six members of the executive team all bought their own tranche of shares at the same valuation. I used my entire superannuation to buy in also. Why wouldn't I? It was the cheapest valuation of the business I had seen. It was also a way to stem the dilution of shares I was suffering. It was pretty galling though to watch everyone buy into the business at the low valuation set 9 months earlier, which was now 1 times EBIDTA, when I had bought in at a 15-times multiple years earlier. I supported the executive team's incentivisation, even though four of the six members of the executive team had only started with the company in 2013 or 2014 and had been on the board for a year or two. However, I believed that they were as deserving as we were; they were part of the essential team that would deliver the turnaround and what was beyond. There was also a bonus plan that meant that after I had diluted my shares, I became fourth in terms of pay package when compared to the executive team. These transactions were challenging for me, but I always found solace in the fact that the executives being rewarded played an integral role in our success.

While these boardroom machinations were very distracting and stressful, I couldn't let them deter me from our core mission.

Finally, the turnaround kicks in

And then, finally, after all the heartache and headaches, the accusations and recriminations, the presentations and ruminations, the turnaround started to deliver the profits. The focus on culture, the transition back from grocery into pharmacy, the explosion in demand created by Project Gold, the optimisation of the supply chain and the flywheel, the tightening of all costs across every aspect of the business — all this had led to a phenomenal explosion in sales, and a corresponding profit. The business didn't just take off, it soared! Revenue went from $187 million in 2014 to $364 million (nearly double the year before), and profit in the same period went from $5.5 million to $116 million, an increase of over 2100 per cent. The board thought it was bonkers, but we knew that this would happen. The demand was overwhelming, and it kept on coming. It was like a tap had been turned on and it just kept on flowing. The only barrier to growth was our ability to supply the product!

Bain had earlier suggested it would take us three years to pay back the debt, but we were now on track to easily pay down the $70 million debt in just nine months. We had become China's number one natural health brand in the online market (and were still Australia's number one natural health brand), and the growth trajectory for the future was out of the park. (Ironically, Trevor was *still* concerned about our growth. There was no chance of it stalling. Nothing could stop us now.)

We had more gas in the tank to grow. We knew that any sales process would take months, and that the business had the momentum to sustain any sale process. This was the perfect time to put a business on the market. It was time to get a deal done.

CHAPTER 32

FOR SALE!

The sale process started in March 2015. We gathered the executive team, allocated them roles and got to work. Goldman Sachs looked at the results that were coming in and estimated the value of the business to be around $700 million – a far cry from the $30 million (after debt) that had been touted three or four months earlier. It seemed, however, that Trevor still wanted to smooth our growth profile out to $70 million and have it progress at a slower rate than what the business was actually doing. I did not agree with this approach. The next day Adem told me that Trevor and Michael D. had approached him to step into my role! Adem, ever loyal, declined and said that if that were to happen, the entire executive team would walk.

Pitching the business

We split the team into groups to manage the various aspects of the sale process. Michael D. and I were responsible for managing the prospective bidders, and George was responsible for legals and led the 'deal team', which was a cluster of people from marketing, sales and legal tasked with keeping the data up-to-date with new due diligence developments. Goldman Sachs was responsible for generating interest from qualified bidders. To ensure the business wasn't distracted, only the deal team and the executive team knew of the sale process.

We did a pre-deal roadshow before the sale process began to get a feel for demand. We pitched the business quite broadly as we felt that our buyer could exist beyond Australia. To ensure all potential buyers moved quickly, and to create competitive tension, we revisited the large international and local private equity firms we already had relationships with, along with a number of new organisations. It was all about creating the best conditions to find the right partner and the highest price.

We then put out an Information Memorandum (IM) containing an indicative profit forecast. As soon as we released it, we had to upgrade the forecast because our numbers were going through the roof. (The value of the company was increasing so quickly with every passing day that we had to issue three profit forecasts over six months to keep up, which was highly unusual.) It went from $85 million to $116 million and then it kicked up dramatically when we received the outer forecast of $240 million for 2016, which was a crazy number but that's what the business was trending towards predicted! (The massive momentum in the business would ensure a competitive process that would deliver a price that was what we always believed we were worth; at least what I believed it was worth.)

Where once we had hoped PGT would *not* buy us out, we now hoped they'd be our most ardent suitor. But they, like many, were spooked by our China growth and were not willing to invest in a business heavily reliant on Chinese demand for its value.

Some aspects of our China business model were of concern because of pricing. With over 100 000 resellers offering our product at various price points, every retailer wanted the best price. Factors such as overstocking or fear of regulatory changes led retailers to seek lower prices and ask for additional margin from us to stay competitive. This often triggered a cycle of declining margins and profits. Fortunately, we had a wide range of product lines, which mitigated the risk, and if the pricing pressure became too intense for a specific product, we'd shift our focus to another product in our range. (This dynamic strategy, developed through years of experience, allowed us to effectively adapt and respond to monthly market pressures.)

The China business model spooks some buyers

Despite our phenomenal success in China, the shareholders, our banks, some potential buyers and even some of our team were worried about this rather unorthodox business model. We appreciated their apprehension. Conducting business in China, regardless of the approach, was risky. China was unique: the regulations, taxes, sales methods and distribution channels we used were all volatile and subject to constant changes. Moreover, the cultural, legal, and cross-border differences between China and Australia posed additional challenges. However, we had done our due diligence and felt comfortable with the model. We applied our 'what's the worst that can happen' test and figured we could live with whatever consequences came our way.

The other buyers didn't seem to care. They wanted in. Whereas you'd normally get one or two bidders for a business, we had 40. It was a dream scenario. The buyers flew in from the four corners of the world to meet with us, and we crisscrossed the globe to go and see them. It was relentless.

As we approached the final stages of the sale process, it was crucial to determine who would remain with the company after the sale, and who would go. The potential new owners expressed a desire to meet the management team before the bidding closed to evaluate who they would be partnering with in the future. Consequently, it was important for this management team to be present at these meetings to ensure a smooth transition and showcase their capabilities to the prospective buyers.

It was my intention to work for two years to complete the handover.

From the discussions, I believed that Adem, Michael H., Ulrich, Michael D. and Trevor all intended to stay on also. (I was hoping Trevor would say no, but what the heck. We could find a way to work together.)

The 40 bidders had now been whittled down to four. One was a private equity group that had expressly wanted the current management team to stay on as senior executives. Michael D., Trevor and I hosted a dinner with the private equity group where they asked, 'Who here is going to stay on with the management team?' Before I could open my mouth to say 'I am', Michael D. and Trevor both said, 'We're not.' What? Wow. That was news to me. It felt like it came out of nowhere.

But that's nothing compared to what happened the next day.

We had another day of meetings with late-stage bidders before they made their decision. Prior to the meetings, Adam Gregory took us all aside to align our strategy. This was the final stretch. There was no room for error. Just as we got up to speak, some of the board members accused me of jeopardising the whole deal by telling the private equity group that I would be leaving as soon as the sale was completed. I stood there, mouth agape, like a goldfish. I was so shocked I couldn't even speak. Nothing could have been further from the truth! I had explicitly said I was staying on for another full two years, and had informed Adam and the team of this months earlier.

Fortunately, Adam weighed in, defended me and set the record straight.

We were now down to three bidders. We were about to sign with Biostime, one of the largest Chinese-owned baby formula brands in the world (who we'd met in China years earlier), when one of the other bidders, a Chinese state-owned bidder, offered us $300 million more than Biostime. Adam went back to Biostime and they increased their price even more, which would make Swisse more valuable than Biostime, the company that was buying us! (We also had the largest Chinese private equity group in the mix as a backstop if negotiations failed.)

Going through the roof

My instinct to hold off on the sale for as long as possible was vindicated. As we got down to final negotiations, our revenue forecasts had soared to $500 million revenue, and EDBITA to $116 million. This remarkable growth placed us in an incredibly strong position to negotiate a favourable deal. This was validated when Biostime, despite all the last-minute challenges, agreed to acquire Swisse for a staggering $1.67 billion.

Biostime's bank made the deal conditional in an attempt to retain management's intellectual property and further safeguard the debt they'd provide to Biostime. This meant that the executive team would need to leave 30 per cent equity in the business and Stephen and Michael 10 per cent. Trevor was able to negotiate leaving only 20 per cent.

Adam, his team, the Swisse deal team and the lawyers stayed up all night preparing the contracts. The next day, we all arrived at our lawyer's office to sign off on the deal. Just as we were about to enter the conference room to sign the papers, Adam came out into the foyer, ashen faced, took me aside and whispered, 'Rad, we have a problem.'

'What is it?' I asked.

'They want to add one more condition.'

'What's this one?' I asked.

'It's about you,' he said, pointing at me.

'Me? What do they want?'

'They must like you,' he said.

'Why's that?'

'They want to add a clause that locks you into working for them for the next 14 months.'

I was perplexed. I had already told them I would stay on.

'I'm fine with that. I said as much in the meeting. It's in the contract. But just out of interest, what happens if I don't?'

'They'll sue you for $150 million,' said Adam.

Wow. I wasn't expecting that. I was kind of flattered that they wanted me to stay, but what a litigious way to go about it. What bothered me the most, given our history, was that I might need to work with Trevor for another 14 months. I insisted there would be no deal unless we agreed that Trevor couldn't represent us on the Biostime board, and Stephen signed the agreement there and then.

With those conditions all taken care of, we signed the paperwork, exchanged contracts, and we were done. Swisse had been sold. The baby birthed by Stephen, Michael and I had grown up, flexed its wings and flown the coop. It was a bittersweet moment.

Did I feel like celebrating? Not really. While I was deeply grateful that this stressful saga had come to a close, and we had, against all odds, achieved an astonishing outcome that surpassed all expectations, including my own, the overwhelming feeling was relief.

I rang Helen to let her know the deal had been done, and she asked me how I wanted to celebrate. I said, 'Please cook me up a bowl of your amazing chicken soup and pour me a nice glass of red.' I was done. I just wanted to go home.

How to conduct a corporate turnaround and set a business up for sale

You don't just flick the switch from a growth focus to a profit focus and expect the profit to correct itself in the next day. We had spent years refining our processes, developing our systems, building our culture and being transparent with the team about our position, so when the results came, it *appeared to be* a rapid turnaround. But it wasn't just one factor that made the difference; it was the marketing iterations we put in place, the sell-in and sell-through strategies with the retailers, and the sophisticated tactics we used to manage every cost in the business. It was a range of factors that cumulatively created the difference, but the most important was communication. This is how we got everyone to do their bit to get on board for the mission; it was this team effort that made Swisse a success.

If you'd like a masterclass in how to turn a company around and set it up for sale, here's our 'recipe for success'. Our turnaround was successful because of our:

- *alignment with our core values.* Our values (Principles, Passion, People and Profit) drove our culture and unified our efforts towards achieving our vision.

- *well-defined plans.* Our Business, Culture and Communications plans guided our strategic decisions and the team's actions and the plans were consistently and expertly executed.

- *focus on company culture.* Our people loved coming to work and strove to set a benchmark in all they did. Our culture plan was as important as our business plan.

- *transparent communication practices.* On-the-run coaching and feedback, and regular team updates ensured everyone knew their role and responsibility in delivering on their stated goals.

- *desire to be everyone's number one partner.* We always gave before we asked, worked hard to be everyone's number one partner and ensured everyone won.

- *global mindset from the start.* We thought big even when we were small, invested in our brand assets and focused on creating a worldwide impact.

- *dedication to a disruptive 'push stock' and 'pull stock' strategy.* Our marketing and advertising flywheel program gave our retailers confidence in our process and their commitment to pre-purchase de-risked our campaigns.

- *commitment to new product development.* This program enabled us to launch new and innovative products, and enhance the profitability of our shelf space.

- *creation of intellectual property.* This enabled us to own and protect our formulations when we expanded into PGT's territories. More importantly, we were able to tender our manufacturing out, which reduced the cost by 30 per cent and enhanced the quality of the product.

- *strength in governance and regulatory management.* This ensured we were always compliant, could support our claims with scientific evidence and ran to the highest standards of operational excellence.

(continued)

- *commitment to profitability.* Our marketing was inextricably linked to sales, and every step in the marketing process was optimised to lead to a profitable sale.

- *commitment to cost reduction.* We optimised our supply chain operations, eliminated unnecessary layers in the process, sourced the highest quality products in the most efficient way and delivered a superior product.

- *superior financial management.* We built deep relationships with our banks, kept them updated and informed at all times and were transparent with our goals and challenges.

- *creation of the Project Gold program.* We nurtured our Chinese-Australian retail partners and consumers, created customised programs to support them and dedicated resources to building this sector.

PART IV

CHAPTER 33

IT'S NOT OVER

What many people may not know was that Biostime bought 83 per cent of Swisse for $1.67 billion, with the remaining 17 per cent of the company to be sold three years later. At which point Swisse would be independently valued and the shareholders would vote on whether they would accept the valuation of the business to close out the sale.

This was why it was so important that the executive team stayed on, as we knew that we could assist with the transition, train the new Biostime team, and protect and grow the value of the remaining 17 per cent left in the business for the benefit of everyone. If the value of the company fell, so did our fortunes. Our executive team had 30 per cent of our total remaining shares locked up in Swisse, and amongst this group, I was now a near majority shareholder, just short of Stephen.

I was still CEO of Swisse but clearly Fei Lou, the group's CEO, had his own vision for steering the company. This was fair enough; it was his company now. We worked hard to support them in every area, particularly culture and sales/marketing, as these were two of our key superpowers that elevated us above all the competitors and made us unique. (We chose Biostime over the others because they, like us, recognised the power of their team to deliver on the vision. They also went on to become an employer of choice and win multiple awards for their outstanding culture.) We always placed our retailer relationships at the forefront of our operational strategy and worked hand-in-glove to deliver them a win-win result. In contrast, Biostime leaned heavily on pricing strategies and field sales retail management as their primary tools of influence.

The cultural differences were interesting too. We were no strangers to hard work, and our work ethic, compared to most Australian companies, was unparalleled. But the Biostime work rate was next level. It wasn't unusual for their team to work from 9 am to 11pm every day. Work was life. Life was work. Their version of 'giving back to community' was very different also. Turning up to work, doing the job, paying taxes to the government, and providing work for others was considered 'community service'.

When you merge two companies, it's natural for differences like these to surface. We needed to find a middle ground so that we could maintain the value of the business without stepping on the toes of the new team. Telling them that 'this is how it should be done' was not the way forward.

Due to some regulatory uncertainty in China, the business was not flying as high as it had been in the first six months after the sale process, but it was still doing well, with a run rate of $230–250 million EBITDA. If the business continued to grow at this rate, Fei would not be able to afford to buy us out over the next two-and-a-half years. In addition, after a few months of working in the Biostime office, it became clear that having two staunchly independent entrepreneurs at the helm would be challenging. Our backgrounds, culture and East-meets-West viewpoints were just too far apart to find consensus, so we agreed to get a deal done as soon as possible that would suit all parties. This would give Fei total control over the company without needing to keep the minority shareholders happy; he could fast-track the integration of Biostime with Swisse, and the executive team could get on with doing what was right for the broader group, rather than what was right for Swisse. Adem took on the role of Managing Director of Swisse, and I stepped down from the day-to-day-running. While I was still CEO in official terms, I agreed not to go into the office, similar to what Michael agreed to all those years ago when I took over.

Biostime still needed funding to pay for the remaining 17 per cent so they engaged Goldman Sachs to manage that, and the deal was done in 30 days. The talented Adam Gregory negotiated on behalf of the Swisse minority shareholders to be bought out at a 30 per cent increase on value per share: a figure that valued Swisse at $2.1 billion; with $629 million in revenue and profit of $228 million. The timing of the deal fell right on the time I was contracted to stay for, with the threat of being sued for $150 million if I had walked no longer an issue. Adem had been under a lot of pressure to hold the line in terms of trying to do the right thing by the business. We would both step down officially (and unofficially) at the end of 2016, when the minority buyout was completed and the deal was done.

'Greedy-long' pays off

Goldman Sachs played the long game and it paid off. On top of getting their $70 million back, Goldman Sachs was paid just under $100 million in interest, options issued with the debt, and merger and acquisition fees. In addition, they also funded the debt that Biostime used to buy us out, and, at the time of writing, they still manage Biostime's financial affairs. 'Greedy-long' certainly paid off for Adam and the Goldman Sachs team. They did a mighty job for everyone.

Everyone did well out of the sale. Michael, Stephen and I became financially free. Our executive team had cash and share portfolios worth tens of millions. Biostime's share price went from $13 HK to $60 HK when news of the sale hit the media.

Saying goodbye

My departure from dear Swisse was low key. We'd employed another 150 people in the last 12 months, most of whom I didn't know. I'd spent the best part of the last year working out of the office and in the China office, so I was disconnected somewhat from the Australian operations. I'd done a few quarterly updates so they knew who I was, but the company was different to the one we had built. It was a global company in every sense and the decisions were now made from China by a group of people who had a different vision for what Swisse would be.

People still ask me even now if I have any regrets about selling: about not being CEO of Swisse, or if I miss the place. I can say, hand on my heart, that the time was very right for us to sell and for me to move on. Swisse had grown so big and its culture so central to its success that it would look after itself and continue to thrive like it has. As Michael and I would always say to each other, 'the organisation is far bigger than any one individual'. Swisse had outgrown me and I was off on the next exciting adventure.

Can you make your own luck?

People often ask us if our success was due to luck, hard work, serendipity or a combination of all three. I think it's the latter. But I think you can make your own luck — you just need to give yourself every chance to take advantage of it. Uncovering the China market and tapping into its demand for our products was the result of various events, actions, conversations and unexpected encounters. For example:

- If I hadn't been on the road and witnessed Chinese students enthusiastically buying Swisse products and shipping them back home, would we have thought of creating point-of-sale materials in Mandarin for our Chinese-owned pharmacies?

- If we hadn't taken a global approach from the beginning and boldly partnered with Hollywood superstars and organisations such as the Australian Olympic team, would we have been successful in China?

- If we hadn't noticed micro-influencers on Taobao endorsing our international marketing assets, which inspired others to try our products, would we have discovered over 100 000 Chinese influencers willing to sell our products?

Luck can come from random occurrences, but you increase your chances by actively engaging with the world and making things happen.

The Datsun upgraded

I'm often asked, 'What was the first thing you bought after you left the business?' Reader, I bought a car: a Ferrari FF. (I hadn't hit 50 yet so you couldn't call this a mid-life crisis purchase.) For as long as I can remember, I vowed that when I could afford it, this would be the first thing I would buy. My first car was a Datsun Stanza. I had come a long way. My dad loved cars and he had bought a 365 four-seater Ferrari in 1976, the year I was born, and subsequently passed on his passion for cars to me. I am not hugely acquisitive and have never sought solace in material items, but I can't deny it was thrilling to pick up the keys to this exquisite machine. I had waited 40 years for this moment and now it was here. I started the engine, turned up the stereo and took it for a joyride down the freeway. In that moment, I was living the dream and I thoroughly enjoyed every second of it. Of course, hedonic adaption soon sets in and the thrill of the new eventually wears off, but I have to say that I have never stopped loving that car. It still gives me a buzz to take it out for a spin. This treat was a reward to myself for the years of hard work I had put in. It didn't define me, or make me feel successful. For me, success was always about making the world a better place.

People also asked, 'Surely this financial windfall got rid of all your problems, right?' It does to some extent, in that I never have to worry about money again. I can now live life 'upgraded', as I call it. So what did I have to worry about? I worried about the weight of what would come next, about what I would do with it all, about the legacy I would leave; about who and what we would support, and how we could give back. I also worried about how to stop ourselves from losing it all! It's in my DNA to build businesses, and taking a risk is part of that. We are investing heavily in a huge range of businesses right now and few, if any, of them, are cash positive. I could lose it all again. Life has taught me that nothing is ever assured.

The price of success

I adjusted to the surreal fact that I had achieved a large chunk of what I'd set out to achieve: I had the freedom to do what I wanted, when I wanted and with whom I wanted. But for every action, there is a reaction. Some call it the price of success. The preceding 20 years and the roller-coaster life I had been living took its toll. When the craziness stopped, I developed a condition called Acute Stress Disorder, a mental health issue that usually occurs months after experiencing a traumatic event, but can also show up many years after the stressful event occurs. For me, the effects showed up three to four years after I left Swisse.

It often kicks in when the adrenals have settled and the body feels safe because that's when the trauma sets in. The symptoms manifested in a range of ways. I relived past events in my mind and played out the worst-case scenarios on a continuous loop. I was quick to lose my temper and the smallest things would set me off; I had trouble sleeping and concentrating, and was easily irritated. I got dizzy if I had to get up and speak to a group of people or deal with a stressful situation. I even ended up in the back of an ambulance suffering what I thought was a heart attack. Looking back, it was just a very intense panic attack. It was incredibly distressing and debilitating.

I sought help and was fortunate to have a good team of people around me who understood and offered assistance. Helen, my rock, was there at every turn. Jonni, my meditation teacher, was invaluable. He said, 'What we resist, persists. Don't fight it. Sit with the uncomfortable feelings and memories; let them in, accept them, and then you can process them.' With their help, lots of exercise, meditation, sleep and good food, I was able to get back to my normal, positive self and enjoy my life again.

CHAPTER 34

LIGHTING UP THE WORLD

Just before we sold Swisse, many of the wise mentors at Young Presidents Organisation, my mentorship group, told me to make sure I had a new job or project lined up and ready to go after the sale so that I wouldn't be transitioning from a full-time frenetic schedule to doing nothing. It was good advice. I have had many colleagues, bound by non-compete clauses, go from a hundred to zero and find themselves cut out of the industry they knew and loved for years. I was only 40 years old too. I had plenty more to do.

Just before finishing up at Swisse, Helen and I founded the Lightfolk Foundation, an organisation that aims to inspire conscious living. It's a response to the stressful disconnected existence of so many of us today. In deference to Lightfolk we named our investment and ventures firm Light Warrior, a for-profit entity that uses capitalism for good. (When Helen first told me she loved me, she called me her 'light warrior'. It was such a cool name we decided it was a fitting moniker for our new company.) Our goal was that the 'warriors' would provide for the 'folk', with both entities driven to bring light to the world.

I feel passionate about this topic. Four out of five Australians work in private enterprise, so life would be a lot better for everyone if the leaders of these businesses committed to making their workplace exceptional places to be. Business needs to lead the way in making our society better, and creating a great culture is the foundation for a successful business. We proved that at Swisse. If people felt great about going to work, we'd have a much happier society. Governments and enterprise should aspire to provide the best society for their people to live in, and to use capitalism for good.

Light Warrior is dedicated to finding and supporting businesses that share our philosophy: businesses that consciously contribute to society and the environment. This philosophy has propelled some of our best-known companies to great success, and we're now proud to be a leader of purpose-driven investment in the Australian market.

Our focus is to generate strong investment returns by investing in high-growth companies, and partner with those who have an ambitious commitment to creating shared value. Our approach goes beyond capital investment. We leverage our expertise and global network for accelerated growth, profitability and positive impact. We actively invest in affordable and disability housing, renewable energy, land regeneration, education, health and wellbeing. Culture is at the forefront of every business in which we invest.

We have a majority shareholding in Conscious Investment Management and Wanderlust, and a shareholder interest in a range of other companies including Strat, Anthem, Commune, myDNA, Jamieson Coote Bonds, Hydralyte Global, Exponential Age, Adventus, and Our Crowd. Our portfolio network has over 650 team members.

What we look for in our partners before we invest

People often ask me what we look for when we invest in a company. In short, we look for companies that have:

- a proven founder and talented team
- a positive culture that is purpose driven
- a highly scalable business model within a growth sector
- a proven point-of-difference from competitors

- an executable business model complemented by strong financials and a robust capital plan

- the opportunity for significant equity ownership

- the ability to utilise Light Warrior Group's expertise and network to fast-track growth and returns.

When I left Swisse, I asked Adam Gregory to join me as CEO and Chief Investment Officer at Light Warrior and he accepted. We then handpicked elite individuals from revered institutional banking organisations such as Goldman Sachs, Macquarie, and UBS to join Light Warrior. At the interview, they'd get this quizzical look on their face, as if to ask, 'Is that what it's *really* called?' They'd then smile, ask for some time to think about it, and then come back and say, 'I'm in. How could I not be?' The name itself puts a smile on everyone's face, and makes us all feel instantly lighter, which is exactly what we are about. It also sets the tone for our expectation of anyone in the group to truly bring light to the world.

Adam and I are in the prime of our lives and at the peak of our powers; we are driven to make an impact on society for the better. We didn't want to be just another family office. We wanted to create a purpose-driven investment and ventures firm, and we're doing that. It will take at least a decade to create a movement that has the capacity to make significant changes, and it wouldn't have felt worthwhile if the task was easy. I have plenty of battle scars, failures and a keen awareness of the gaps in my ability, and am also fully aware that these don't need to hold me back from achieving my full potential.

The first $10 million is the hardest

We quickly learned that investing in ventures in the early years is hard, and without a doubt, the first $10 million revenue is the hardest. Once we have that core product, or the heartbeat, or 'drum beat', as I call it, things get a bit easier; not easy, but easier. We fully expect to see a few of our investments fail. Some will muddle along, but if we get it right, we will have two or three that make up for any losses, and then some. We take a seven- to ten-year vision on all our investments before expecting any kind of return on investment. Great things take time.

Buy a going concern

The first sale is the hardest. That's why I recommend you buy a going concern or a business that has gone bust. The hard yards have been done – the set-up, the brand building, the momentum, the database. If you're building a billion-dollar business, the first $10 million will be the hardest, but stick with it. Yes, that may sound like a lot of money to most, and it is, but once you reach that critical mass, it gets easier.

How to pitch for investment

I often get asked to invest in a business. I received 150 pitches last year and I invested in four. I also get asked for tips on how people can pitch more effectively to people like me. While my perspective is subjective, I can share the key aspects I prioritise in a pitch. We ask these seven questions when evaluating potential investment opportunities:

1. Who are you?

2. Can I add value?

3. Have you done an apprenticeship?

4. What's the worst-case scenario?

5. Can you take on feedback?

6. Does it have momentum?

7. What's the return?

1. WHO ARE YOU?

I need to know who I'm getting into business with. The consequences of a business partnership can be for life. It's like a marriage, but harder, because you probably don't have the love and commitment (and, let's face it, the attraction) that you have when you choose your life partner. But the legal and emotional connections are every bit as real as those you have in a marriage.

It's important to realise that before you do a deal, *everyone* is on their best behaviour; *everyone* is behaving really politely, which is nice, but we need to be able to move to a point where we can have those hard conversations upfront. I'll often push people on some issues to see how flexible they are, but to also see how strong they are in protecting what they see as the core values of what will make their business successful. I don't like being indirect, but I have to 'game out' what the relationship will be like in good times as well as the tough times.

Sam Gance, one of the founders of Chemist Warehouse, said to me years ago when I bought shares in Swisse, 'How's your relationship with your business partners?' I said, 'Oh fantastic.' He said, 'That's great, because it's the hard times that will really define what your partners are like.' He was so right. At Swisse it was how we all behaved in the hard times that made it the success it was. My goal ever since has been to discover how the people we are about to partner with deal with hard times *before* we go into business with them. I also spend a lot of time with the person and get to know them to see if I really like them. Time is our most precious commodity. I want to spend it with people that I love being around, who challenge me and who are driven to bring light to the world.

Fast forward to the tough times

Many bankers, consultants and partners who want to do business with you will always be on their best behaviour *before* the deal gets done — always ready and willing to be of help and assistance. When the deal gets done, however, is when their true nature shines through. Our goal when working with all our partners was to try and fast-track the relationship, have those tough conversations quickly and then establish whether we could work together.

(*continued*)

2. CAN I ADD VALUE?

This is a big one. I am currently on over a dozen boards. Some have a commercial focus; most are community oriented. I choose to be on these boards because I can add value to what they're doing. However, I've previously sat on boards where I knew my input was not being valued. Maybe it was because my ideas were not good enough, or they were good enough, but they were just being ignored. I resigned from those boards because I needed to be able to add something to the organisation. If I can't, there's not much point me being there.

I apply the same mindset to investing. Why would I be a good partner for you? What value can I offer? You could go to anyone, so why have you come to me specifically? You need to make me feel that I am essential to your business success, and make me feel that I have something unique to offer that others can't. If you can define that clearly and detail how my involvement will super-charge your business, I will be much more receptive to your pitch.

(It's the same with business buyers. When we sold Swisse to Biostime, we needed to make them feel that they were the very best buyers for our business, and that, above all others, we wanted to work with them. Our pitch to Biostime was authentic; for Swisse to reach its full potential, we needed a company like Biostime to help us achieve it.)

3. HAVE YOU DONE AN APPRENTICESHIP?

The first thing I look for in a partner is business experience, a business education or a combination of both. Have the founders done their 'apprenticeship' somewhere? Have they sweated out their idea and seen some early success? I don't want to run the business, so when I see areas of concern that the owner isn't addressing, it makes me think, 'Right, I am now going to have to get involved in running this, and I don't want to do that.' I want the business owner to be sufficiently competent to run the business, to take care of the issues and to get on with the day-to-day minutiae.

4. WHAT'S THE WORST-CASE SCENARIO?

You need to acknowledge with your potential investors that the journey may not be rosy all the time. When I see pitch decks that promise hockey stick returns, or say that 'the world is their market', it means they haven't thought through the worst-case scenarios. You need to create a full business plan and stress test the assumptions to find out what the best- and worst-case scenarios are. (The worst-case scenario needs to be palatable because you'll probably end up there.)

We have some pretty full-on conversations before we've even started, but that's what we have to do. The harder it is to get investment money from someone, the better, because it means they've asked the tough questions and challenged you. Your business model needs to be robust. Some get freaked out by the intensity of the questions we ask and say 'Hey, this is too hard. I'll go and find money from an easier source than this', but we want to predict the future scenarios that might occur *before* they actually happen. Some call this process a 'pre-mortem', whereby we canvass everything that could go wrong and then plot out a response to it, so that if, or when, it does happen, we are prepared for it. You can't avoid surprises, but when they do arise, you can be less surprised in how you react to them. You especially need to address the tough questions you don't want your investors to ask. They'll definitely be thinking about them, and it's best you address those questions before they do.

5. CAN YOU TAKE ON FEEDBACK?

I give as much feedback as I can to those who pitch to me. I want them to succeed, even if I don't invest in them. I ask them to take the feedback with an open heart, and think about how they're going to make their business better as a result of it. I also tell them that just because I've declined the opportunity the first time, it doesn't mean that they can't come back and try for a second time. In fact, I welcome this. I encourage them to keep in touch, to tell me what they're up to, to demonstrate how they've pivoted and what results they're getting. I want them to take me on the journey they're on. I love seeing young leaders having a go and putting their heart and soul into something.

(continued)

When the CEO of Anthem pitched to us for the first time, we turned him down. He went away, thought about the feedback, applied it, kept in touch and a couple of months later came back, re-pitched and we invested in the business.

6. DOES IT HAVE MOMENTUM?

I am not the right person to invest in an absolute start-up. I've founded eight businesses — we had three successful exits and the other five are thriving. When we invested in them, each already had a solid revenue opportunity, a core business and a customer database. In other words, before I get involved, I need my investments to have a 'drum beat'. I'm very selective and I won't just start up a whole lot of random companies. They need to be able to reinvent the social impact or wellness sector somehow, and support the other businesses in which we invest. It takes a minimum of ten years to build up a successful company and I'll be on this journey with you for those ten years too, so the business has to really grab me by the scruff of the neck and make me think, 'This is exciting!' I need to see your passion too. We'll be doing this together and I want to have fun, so rather than just pitching, think about how you can connect with me and build a relationship.

7. WHAT'S THE RETURN?

I've put this point last because seeking a return is last on my list. People are always shocked that I don't automatically ask about the return on investment or about how quickly I'll get my money back. Your idea needs to have a high likelihood of success financially, but for us, it also needs to have a great purpose behind it. It must move the dial on making the community better in some way. Is it wellness? Is it helping us love ourselves more? Is it helping solve a massive community issue, such as helping people with disabilities get access to good housing? Workplace culture must also be a core value and something that excites you. The numbers and ROI are important but we have to start with what the business *does*, its purpose, and how will it help the community, because that's what we *do*. We are a purpose-led investment fund.

Have a plan

Many start-up gurus often say, 'Don't bother about writing a business plan. The market moves so fast it will be redundant before you get the chance to implement it.' I don't agree. You must have a business plan. I won't invest in anything that doesn't. (And you must review the plan every three months to make sure it is alive and evolves with your business.) Here's the basics of what your business plan should include:

- executive summary
- culture/values plan
- financial projections
- communication plan
- industry overview
- market analysis and competition
- sales and marketing plan
- ownership and management plan
- operating plan.

What we invest in

Central to all Light Warrior Group investment decisions is its shared value ethos: that business growth is only sustainable in the long-term if it benefits all stakeholders, and that business has a responsibility to make positive contributions to society as a whole. Our group mission is to:

- seek profit in a responsible and purposeful way
- actively give back to our community
- empower and develop our people to achieve their potential.

Coupled with this is our commitment to advancing reconciliation with our First Nations people via our Reconciliation Action Plan. This is based around the core pillars of relationships, respect and the desire to provide opportunities that offer tangible and substantive benefits such as increasing economic equity and supporting self-determination.

Wanderlust

After I left Swisse, Helen and I put all our energies and focus into our IVF quest. We knew Los Angeles was the most innovative city in the world for wellness and health so we spent the next 12 months flying back and forth to undergo more rounds of IVF. While we were there, we spent a lot of time at Erewhon Market, a high-end organic and wholefoods store frequented by all the Hollywood celebrities. It stocks all the latest and greatest innovations in health. The liquid herbal extracts caught my attention. This is a new category in the wellness sector. These extracts are created by extracting the active compounds from medicinal plants using alcohol or glycerine as solvents. They are highly potent, contain a greater concentration of beneficial plant compounds, are commonly used in herbal medicine for their quick absorption and dosing flexibility, and are frequently used by naturopaths, Chinese medicine practitioners and even mainstream medical doctors.

I was looking to build a company within the health and wellness sector, and do something new and innovative. I didn't want to do what Swisse had done, so when I saw these liquid extractions, and could see an opportunity to make them far more potent than most tablets, I got excited. They would be 100 per cent plant-based, with no synthesised ingredients and no fillers; and, being liquid-based, the ingredients would be more bio-available. There was nothing like it in the Australian market and our range would be far purer than any product globally. My passion had always been nutrition and wellness. This was my opportunity to express that passion through launching a new range of plant-active, naturally derived herbal-led supplements and wholefoods.

As mentioned, it's much easier to launch a business that is already a going concern. Trying to launch Evidin, ProvenSlim and countless other brands all those years ago taught us how hard it was to launch an unknown product from a standing start. Wanderlust met that brief of already having a drum beat. It was founded in 2009 in the United States and became quickly known for staging a series of the world's biggest yoga festivals. The brand already had over 1 million Facebook followers, an excellent Google rank, a high profile, a wellness heritage and an audience that already loved the festival experience, which in turn, created a positive affinity for the brand. However, despite the owners investing around $70 million in the brand, the onset of COVID-19 and the general challenge of making an events business profitable got the better of the organisation. I subsequently bought the company, and used the events as the foundational marketing tool to promote the plant-based supplements. We relaunched it with a mission to share the ayurvedic principles of yoga, meditation and nutrition with the world and bring together a community of like-minded people who were keen to explore the ancient wisdom that could help people deal with today's challenges.

In an evolution to our Swisse ambassadorial program, we engaged prominent people to front our campaigns. The difference now was that the celebrities we partnered with were not just ambassadors, but activists: high-profile people who lived and breathed our purpose and were living embodiments of our products. As the media market had changed, the flywheel needed to change to reflect the changing media landscape, and excite our consumers in new and exciting ways. TV was still a big factor in our activation campaigns, and we invested heavily in staging our high-end 'True North' events that represented who we are and what we believed in.

MEDITATION, MUSIC AND MOVEMENT

Similar to how Robert Kirby blended a bar, restaurant and cinema to create Gold Class cinema, these events artfully combined the elements of a rejuvenating yoga class with music, inspiring speakers and the transformative experience of a holistic retreat, all wrapped up in the carefree spirit of a great day out. Our 'True North' events featured a range of heart-led, health-focused individuals including Michael Franti, Xavier Rudd, social commentator Sarah Wilson, Australian of the Year and AFL Brownlow medallist Adam Goodes, former child soldier turned international rap star and all-round force for good, Emmanuel Jai, and leading yoga and meditation teachers such as Tahl Rinsky and Simone Buchanan, and many others.

We love these big event activations. They worked well for us at Swisse but we could only invite a limited number of retailers and guests to the Grand Prix or the Melbourne Cup Bird Cage. Our new event format enables us to invite everyone and the tickets we sell pay for the activation! Our success will be gauged against a 'triple bottom line' — people, planet and profit — which underscores our holistic commitment to creating a meaningful impact.

Wanderlust is flying. We have an awesome events calendar, over 70 different products, $20 million in revenue and are ranged in over 2000 retailers. I am confident the sum of the above will be the best purpose-driven ride I have been a part of yet.

Conscious Investment Management (CIM)

Founded by Light Warrior in 2019, Conscious Investment Management is a global impact investment manager with a vision to unlock the power of mainstream investment markets to fund assets that create positive social and environmental impact. All investments stem from CIM's collaboration with our expert Impact Partners to better understand people and society's needs. Then, using our finance experience and capital, we structure, design and invest in assets that genuinely create a better and more sustainable future.

Currently CIM is working to address some of our largest global challenges including environment and climate, health and education, and sustainable development. Since 2021, we have invested over $350 million into social housing, disability housing, social impact bonds, land regeneration and renewables projects.

Strat

Strat Agency is Australia's largest independent creative agency, offering production, media buying and digital media to a range of clients including Chemist Warehouse, The Good Guys, L'Oreal, RSEA, Pedders, The Shaver Shop, Wanderlust, and ironically Swisse *and* Blackmores!

Anthem

Anthem is an events-based marketing agency that provides integrated strategy, creative and advertising services. Through our partnership model, we work with our clients to ensure they cut through the competitive noise, not just to get noticed and recognised, but to find and grow their audiences through emotional storytelling. Strat and Anthem are strategic adjacencies for us as they play nicely into our Wanderlust business and we engage them on a regular basis to assist us with our events.

Giving back

For us, corporate social responsibility means more than giving back financially. We look to our charity partners for opportunities to engage first-hand with the people and causes they care about and represent. We have donated over $10 million to a range of organisations including the National Institute of Integrative Medicine, La Trobe University, Children's Ground and Igniting Change to name a few. I spend around 50 per cent of my time on our for-profit work and the other half on our not-for-profit work, with the goal being to fuse the purpose of our community work with the profit potential of our commercial work. I love figuring out ways in which both can work together to solve society's greatest challenges. When the forces of capitalism and democracy unite with purpose-led, heart-centred work, society flourishes.

Igniting Change

To this end, we support Igniting Change, founded by Jane Tewson, a (deliberately) tiny charity that's passionate about sparking positive change for people doing it tough in our communities. Guided by people experiencing injustice and inequality, Igniting Change brings people and resources together in creative ways to inspire action. As the chairman of the organisation, I help generate awareness and support for their events including their powerful 'Meet the People, Feel the Issues' session and many other ventures. Jane and Igniting Change help us curate first-hand experiences to walk alongside people who are leading the change to fight unfashionable issues such as homelessness, drug addiction, racism and poverty.

Matthew Tominc is the CIO of Igniting Change. He came to Light Warrior after working with Adam at Goldman Sachs. Aside from being a first-class individual he has studied human rights law and has always dreamt of creating an impact fund. He really shone when the Light Warrior team experienced a visit to a Children's Ground event in Alice Springs to visit our First Nations elders. I loved seeing him in the red dirt around a campfire while learning to make damper and saying to a group of locals that it was not much different to making pizza growing up, referencing his Italian heritage. Our aim with the fund was to be at the forefront of this new wave of conscious capitalism and provide like-minded investors with access to our experience in impact investing.

We need to talk about George

George Calombaris is one of Australia's most talented chefs. He's also one of my closest friends. I loved his food, ethos and positivity and thought he was one of the most creative individuals I had ever met. We partnered with him in his MAdE Establishment business, which spanned 15 restaurants, including the Jimmy Grants casual Greek eatery. Prior to Light Warrior joining the business George only owned 10 per cent of MAdE. When he invested with us, his shareholding increased to 30 per cent. The prior shareholders would only deal with George upon the transition, which restricted and constrained our ability to conduct our due diligence.

In April 2017, three months after we bought out George's other investors, we hired Troy McDonagh, a professional CEO, to run the business. One month into Troy's tenure, he found that there was a fundamental lack of systems and processes across the entire business due to a lack of central leadership. Of most concern were some anomalies in the payroll systems. This had been identified less than a year earlier, reported to the Fair Work Commission, and the business was given a year to remedy it. When we arrived, we immediately called in KPMG to assess whether or not the business had delivered on that undertaking to the Fair Work Commission. It quickly became clear that it had not.

Once we understood the enormity of the issue, we immediately self-reported to the Fair Work Ombudsman and moved with haste to ensure all staff were paid and classified correctly. MAdE back-paid a total of $7.83 million in wages and superannuation to 515 current and former employees, and $16 371.49 to nine employees of Jimmy Grants. To put this in perspective the average worker earned around \$65 000 per year and the underpayments were on average 3 per cent per year per person, which equated to an underpayment of around \$2000 per person per year, or \$39 per week over the six years in question.

It would take until July 2019 before the Fair Work Commission would close out their investigation, but when the story hit the media, it was insinuated that we hadn't remedied the back payments – that it was the Fair Work Commission that had forced us to make the back payments, and that we hadn't self-reported. None of this was true. George was as shocked as we all were by the accounting anomalies, but what this demonstrated was that the award pay rates were (and still are) far too complicated for even the most sophisticated, publicly listed companies to navigate. The Award's executive summary alone was 40 pages and there were 60 different hourly rates to run a restaurant.

Of course, this payroll issue should never have happened, and George knew he was a public figure and needed to be held accountable, but it did happen, and when we discovered the anomalies, he (and we) did everything in our powers to rectify it. George was subsequently painted by the union as a villain and a 'wage thief', and most of the media ran with that story, without bothering to check the facts. We met with the union and asked them to back away from the false campaign. They refused, as they saw it as a way for them to promote themselves as the 'protector of the sector' and drive membership, and, as far as they were concerned, they were winning. We reminded them that this wasn't just about George, but about the 600 people that worked at the MAdE Establishment. Their response was that they didn't care as none of those workers were union members.

If the facts had been reported correctly it would have been a non-story, as it was (and still is) for many other businesses and government organisations who had done exactly the same thing. This issue was endemic to most restaurants in this country and also other sectors. Woolworths, BHP, Wesfarmers, the University of Melbourne, government social services, the ABC, and many others all faced similar issues, yet few, if any, of those leaders had their reputations dragged through the mud as George did. I can't account for why George became the lightning rod for this situation, but the politicians and the media who couldn't wait to denigrate George in such a publicly malicious fashion should reflect on their actions.

It was a topic of national debate for over two weeks, and the fact most of it was based on many mistruths was shocking. George paid a high price for his mistake. Under the weight of negative press, we made the devastating decision to close the business and 600 people lost their jobs. COVID-19 and the lack of both local and international visitors didn't help. George also lost his house, media contracts and speaking engagements and was verbally abused at public events. His mental health suffered terribly. But he is a resilient man, and now, years later, his new restaurants are performing well, his team as always love working with him and patrons enjoy what he is doing. He deserves future success.

What's in a name?

What do Alannah Hill, Peter Alexander and Marcus Blackmore all have in common? They all used their personal names to build their corporate brands, and when the venture capitalists got involved, they all lost the right to use their own name. Try not to be the face of your brand. It's okay at the beginning to help you get traction but once you've got some momentum, spread the risk and bring in other names and faces. You will change over the years and the needs of the company will change too. If naming your company after yourself was a good idea, then Apple would be called Jobs, Virgin would be called Branson and Canva would be called Perkins.

What did we learn from this? It reinforced that we must stick to our values and that values-based business decisions drive business success. If we had chosen not to disclose the payroll issues; if we had not paid back the staff immediately and not tried to shed light on why it happened and not worked hard to prevent it from happening again, Light Warrior wouldn't be Light Warrior. One thing I have learned from business is that the hard road is the most rewarding road. We lost $20 million on this investment. It was an expensive lesson, but one of the most valuable in my business journey to date.

CHAPTER 35

THE WORLD'S GREATEST SOCIAL ENTREPRENEURS

One should never only judge business success by profits, but also the relationships and opportunities that come with it. In early 2016, Ryan Trainor, the founder of Adventus, introduced me to Jane Tewson. Jane was the powerhouse co-founder of Comic Relief in the UK, co-founder of Red Nose Day and many other initiatives. She was also the founding trustee of Richard Branson's philanthropic vehicle, Virgin Unite. Over time I'd learn that Jane was one of the world's greatest social entrepreneurs. (If she had focused her mind to the world of business, she'd be one of the world's most successful entrepreneurs.) Thankfully her measure of being rich is about giving back to society and enhancing it for all. Jane and I met in a café to talk and for her to ostensibly assess if I was an appropriate person to join her on a trip to meet Richard on Necker Island. We got on brilliantly. At the end of the meeting, she asked whether I'd like to come to Necker. I said, 'Of course, I'd love to.'

Richard's spectacular home on Necker Island is used to host events featuring the world's greatest change makers. When you arrive, you are transported to this magical paradise where you get to witness an amazing group of world-class presenters talk about how they are moving the dial on doing something great for society. You are then provided with the support needed to launch real action and apply what you have learned back in your day-to-day life. Each trip generates millions of dollars in support and electrifies other business identities to lead with more purpose.

Honey, I bought an island

When I failed to properly read an email from Richard Branson, I unwittingly became the owner of an island. It all started when I received an email from Richard. He and Brett Godfrey, the co-founder of Virgin Blue Airlines, owned an island called Makepeace Island, just off the coast of Noosa in north Queensland. Richard emailed me to let me know he and Brett owned it and that if I was interested, I could share the island with a couple of other families. I thought this was a great idea. I've always loved getting away, and the thought of spending time on an island with Richard, Brett and a few other families sounded like a grand idea. If I'd read the email more closely, I would have realised I wasn't just saying yes to a visit to the island, I was saying yes to actually buying a share of the island! But I am a man of my word and after doing some due diligence, realised it would be a great investment. We settled a few months later and it enabled me to spend many special times with Richard on the island.

What many do not know about Richard Branson is that Virgin was one of the earliest proponents of consciously creating a positive workplace culture. In alignment with that, he has donated hundreds of millions to not-for-profits to help make the world a better place. He was one of the first to support Jane 40 years ago, which propelled her to raise billions more. He is truly one of the world's greatest social entrepreneurs. (I've discovered the best time to get him is early in the morning when his mind isn't so distracted with the hundreds of projects he is involved in. I still haven't beaten him at tennis. Yet.)

The B Team—playing for the world

Our current economic model is broken. It did not break itself, and it will not repair itself. Those of us in the private sector know that there is a better way of doing business. Capitalism and democracy are under fire around the world, and as business leaders we need to do more to show that capitalism can be a force for good — that it's capable of focusing on people as well as profits. That's why our majority-owned businesses are certified as B Team organisations. These are businesses that meet the highest standards of verified social and environmental performance, public transparency, and legal accountability to balance profit and purpose. We envisage a world where businesses strive to better the world, the lives of the people living in it, and the natural environment on which our quality of life depends. Today there are over 4200 Certified B Teams around the globe.

Through collaboration between business and civil society leaders, B Team aims to cultivate an ethical and purpose-centred corporate sector and demonstrate that bold leadership can steer businesses towards positive impact. The B Team Australasia is focused on shaping progressive principles for the evolving labour landscape, achieving net-zero emissions by 2050, and uniting members to inspire a transformative approach to work that empowers individuals and communities worldwide.

Our founding members, and their respective roles at that time, were:

- **Sir Richard Branson**, Co-Founder, The B Team, Founder, Virgin Group

- **Sharan Burrow**, Vice-Chair, The B Team, General Secretary, International Trade Union Confederation

- **David Gonski**, Co-Chair, The B Team Australasia, Chairman, Australia and New Zealand Banking Group Ltd (ANZ Bank); Chancellor, University of New South Wales

- **Lynette Mayne**, Co-Chair, The B Team Australasia, Director, Chief Executive Women

- **Peter Allen**, CEO and Executive Director, Scentre Group

- **Michael Cameron**, CEO and Managing Director, Suncorp Group

- **Andrew Liveris**, Former Chairman and CEO, Dow Chemical and B Team Leader

- **Geoff Lloyd**, CEO of MLC

- **Susan Lloyd Hurwitz**, CEO and Managing Director, Mirvac

- **Sam Mostyn**, President, Australian Council for International Development

- **Radek Sali**, Chairman and Founder, Light Warrior Group

- **Ann Sherry**, Executive Chairman, Carnival Australia

- **Catherine Tanna**, Managing Director, EnergyAustralia.

Led by the indefatigable Lynette Mayne, The B Team formed the Climate Leaders Coalition. (The members of this group comprise leading companies that represent a quarter of Australia's total emissions.) Our remit wasn't to influence government; it was to get on with it. BHP, one of our members, and one of the world's largest emitters of carbon, had just set the goal of net zero emissions by 2050 and hailed the net zero opportunity as the greatest its business would face over the coming decades.

The forum is a safe zone in which we can share challenges and information in our quest to solve similar carbon issues. I represent 'the entrepreneur' in the group and lead the Carbon Investment Scheme (CIS), an investment fund that provides financial returns and delivers measurable carbon investment schemes. I'm out of my league in comparison to the size and scope of the businesses these CEOs represent, but I see my presence as the 'bridge' to making the CIS relevant to all businesses, with the goal being to encourage the government to incentivise organisations to take part in the initiative. After dedicating nearly three years to a project, I'm thrilled to announce that we have successfully progressed to the plotting of the pilot stage. Great things really do take time.

CONCLUSION: OUR OWN LIGHT WARRIOR

Family shaped me; school formalised my base of friends and introduced me to life outside of the Sali family bubble; and university was more than just an adult education, it took me out of my comfort zone and challenged me to become a better person. Village Roadshow was the best apprenticeship I could have ever asked for, and Swisse showed me what it was like to be a key player in one of the biggest private company transactions in Australian history.

Life is a journey and series of experiences and if you had the good fortune that I did — loving parents, a first-class education (even if I did squander it!), outstanding health and mental wellbeing (other than my brush with Acute Stress Disorder after the sale of Swisse), loyal friends, the good luck to grow up in a country such as Australia, and the opportunity to build a successful business that delivered a spectacular result — then it is our responsibility to give back and to give people who did not have that luck the ability to increase their health and happiness. I must also express deep gratitude for all the challenging people, events and situations along the way that forced me to step up and dig deep to find the courage, grace and persistence to manage those scenarios. I found the kernel of wisdom in each of them, which I can now pass on to others to help them with their journey.

Now it's Light Warrior's time, and I will use all my learnings to make the world a better place. It is one thing to sell to a foreign company and cash in. It is what you do next that defines you. I have a responsibility to use the great privilege and power of wealth to move the dial, give back and contribute to the significant betterment of society. Four out of five people work in private enterprise. It's our job as business owners to provide them with a workplace and culture that contributes to their wellbeing. I have always wanted to leave the place better than when I arrived.

I have an even better reason to do so now. On 26 September, 2018, when I was 42 and Helen was 45, on our ninth IVF attempt after ten years of trying, we welcomed a beautiful little girl called Elodie into the world and she has become the light and love of our lives. The wait was worth it. She is our little Light Warrior.

ACKNOWLEDGEMENTS

This book is dedicated to my cherished daughter, Elodie. Your presence has been the guiding light that fuelled my unwavering commitment to the creation and completion of this book. Its pages reveal a glimpse into the world of your parents before your existence—a legacy for you to explore and discover.

First, I want to acknowledge the weaving of creation and the higher force that presented me with an abundance of good fortune; that surrounded me with the best parents a child could hope for, and for my brother and sister, for being there for me and being so supportive throughout the years.

Helen. Thank you. You are my wife, best friend, and partner in everything. You inspire me daily to become a better person. You are my muse and inspiration.

To my extended families on both sides; thank you for providing me with a joyful childhood and many fond memories. I am who I am because of you.

To my close friends, some of whom are mentioned in this book and to those who are not, thank you for making life such a joy.

I'd also like to thank those who gave me a hard time or made my life challenging — you made me step up, improve, and inspired me to become a better leader.

I am not a natural writer. It took me eight years, countless drafts, 160 000 words and a lot of irrelevant venting to bring this book to life. I am grateful to Hatchette publishers who first contracted me to write the book and then fired me. Without you, I'd never have written this book. Thank you to those who read and edited the raw manuscript — Helen, Catherine Moolenschot, Martin Flanagan, Adam Gregory and Ulrich Irgens.

Thank goodness for Bernadette Schwerdt. You saved this project, rewrote the entire book with me, found us the perfect publisher in Wiley and here we are with a book that is everything I'd hoped it would be.

Thank you to the team at Wiley for bringing this book to the world.

A huge thanks to people I worked with at Swisse who helped me create conscious workplaces and launch bold community initiatives. Every one of you played an instrumental role in achieving what we did.

To our suppliers, ambassadors, and retailer partners — without you the Swisse adventure would never have happened. A huge thank you to Michael Saba and Stephen Ring, two of the most amazing business mentors I have ever had. I am incredibly indebted to you for your belief, love and support. Thank you for constantly challenging me to be my best.

A huge thank you to the team at Village Roadshow. You gave me the best apprenticeship one could ask for and taught me what entrepreneurship was all about.

Thank you to my team at Light Warrior, and the organisations in which we are invested. Your ongoing and unwavering belief in our purpose and passion enables us to practice what we preach in this book.

Thank you to Jane Tewson for your inspiration; not only for the work that you do, but for defining how powerful and rewarding giving back can be. Finally, thank you to Richard Branson for your inspiration in demonstrating how someone who has been given so much in the world can then do so much to give back.

Printed and bound by CPI Group (UK) Ltd, Croydon, CR0 4YY

28/03/2024

14476950-0001